BUILDING A PRO·BLACK WORLD

CYNDI SUAREZ AND THE STAFF AT NPQ

BUILDING A
PRO·BLACK
WORLD

MOVING BEYOND DE&I WORK
AND CREATING SPACES FOR
BLACK PEOPLE TO THRIVE

WILEY

Published by John Wiley & Sons, Inc., Hoboken, New Jersey.
Published simultaneously in Canada.

For general information on our other products and services or for technical support, please contact our Customer Care Department within the United States at (800) 762-2974, outside the United States at (317) 572-3993 or fax (317) 572-4002.

Wiley also publishes its books in a variety of electronic formats. Some content that appears in print may not be available in electronic formats. For more information about Wiley products, visit our web site at **www.wiley.com**.

Library of Congress Cataloging-in-Publication Data is Available:

ISBN 9781394196906 (cloth)
ISBN 9781394196890 (ePub)
ISBN 9781394196876 (ePDF)

Cover design: Paul McCarthy
Cover art: © Devyn Taylor
SKY10048754_060223

Contents

BUILDING A PRO·BLACK WORLD

Enacting Pro-Black Leadership: A Better World Is Possible

Going Pro-Black

Cyndi Suarez

At the end of 2021, *NPQ* convened an advisory committee on racial justice and asked the question, What is the edge of current racial justice work? The group converged on "building pro-Black organizations."

I had several experiences at the same time that reflected a deep schism in racial justice work, depending on where one is situated. The crux of this schism is the line that divides nonprofit organizations and philanthropic ones.

One experience: while participating on a panel on media covering philanthropy, I was asked to speak on the recent controversy in a large philanthropy network. I was unaware of the controversy, but when a fellow panelist eagerly weighed in, I learned that it was that conservative philanthropists feel the philanthropic sector is too radical, which made them feel there was no room for them. On hearing this, I shared that I did have a perspective on this. It perfectly illustrates the lack of alignment of which I'd been speaking earlier between the field and the funders: that no one I knew was accusing philanthropy of being radical—in fact, quite the opposite; it is being held accountable for not living up to its touted values; and, finally, that we needed to consider what, in fact, is the purpose of philanthropy. This caused quite a stir and excitement in the audience, some of whom emailed me later to tell me what "a breath of fresh air" it had been to hear me speak what they know to be the truth. Though it also made me wonder: why are so many in philanthropy sitting on their truth? What are we waiting for?

Another experience: a large philanthropic network sought to partner with *NPQ* to work with its leading-edge funders, who are all interested in advancing racial justice. These funders hope to inspire the field with their leadership on the issue. Their main interest in partnering was in connecting with leaders of color in the field. It just so happens that *NPQ* has been investing in highlighting the voices of leaders of color, as they are woefully underrepresented in the sector. But the network had one caveat: that we change our language and work to not focus on leaders of color. But we are. What's wrong with saying that?

A third and final example: a big funder approached me about working with its staff on race and power. One of its key values is being bold. Yet, while the focus of the funder is to advance grassroots movements, the staff members are reluctant to "give up power" and there is a "scarcity mindset." In fact, it is not yet in conversation with grassroots movements. As one of *NPQ*'s staff members recently said in a meeting, "Are we ever going to move past symbolic solidarity?"

We're moving beyond DEI (bodies at the table), racial equity (measuring POC against white people), and perhaps even racial justice (the righting of racial wrongs) to an actual focus on what Black people need to thrive (building pro-Black).

These parallel realities exist right now. But there is a gap between the leaders of color and radical white conspirators at the edge—and the funders who claim to be.

It's high time we focus squarely on the goal and stop talking around it. Like most consequential change, it's going to require new language. Not everyone will be comfortable with that, but if you want to be at the edge or bold, step up to the future waiting to emerge.

Defining *Pro-Black*

Cyndi Suarez

There is a shift afoot in the field, from critiquing white supremacist culture and calling out anti-Blackness to designing for pro-Blackness. So, we followed up with some of the writers who lent their expertise to this edition and also interviewed Shanelle Matthews, the communications director for the Movement for Black Lives in order to go more deeply into defining what we mean by pro-Blackness. We asked them the following questions:

What does pro-Black mean?
What are the characteristics of a pro-Black organization?
What would a pro-Black sector sound, look, taste, and feel like?

The conversations that ensued can be found in full in Spring 2022 issue of *NPQ*. What follows are some of the main takeaways from those interviews.

What Does *Pro-Black* Mean?

The key characteristic of pro-Blackness is that it deals with power. In fact, *pro-Black* means not only directly dealing with power but also building power for Black people. As such, it is perceived as a bold or daring statement that often triggers discomfort in white people.

Dax-Devlon Ross, writer and equity and impact strategist, shares his reaction to being invited to be part of a conversation on being pro-Black:

> *It made me think of Black Power and discomfort. It also made me feel a certain level of challenge. I thought, Oh, they want to go there with this! And it literally sent a sensory experience through my body. And I thought, Okay, let's go; let's actually explore this and try to forget about all the people who might be offended, or who*

might say, "Oh, but what do you mean, and who are you leaving out?"... Let's just name and center this right here as pro-Black.

Liz Derias, codirector at CompassPoint, a nonprofit leadership development practice that has been focusing on pro-Black approaches for the past few years, says,

> To be pro-Black *is to build pro-Black power. And when we talk about building power at CompassPoint, we define it as building our capacity to influence or shape the outcome of our circumstances.*

Shanelle Matthews, communications director for the Movement for Black Lives, says,

> *For me, the root of this conversation is power. So, that's being able to exist as a Black person in this country without the gaze of whiteness or having to pretend to be somebody that one is not, in terms of one's self, one's identity, and one's self-determination in one's everyday life.*

Building pro-Black power requires an understanding of what power means for Black people. Derias says,

> *Building Black power, building pro-Black organizations, and building a pro-Black movement requires us to take a look back at the ways that power has existed for us in our communities before systems of oppression in an effort to bring it into the current context—not only to challenge the systems of oppression but also to carry forward what has been intrinsic to our communities.*

Matthews agrees:

> *At the root of what I think pro-Blackness is about is advancing policies, practices, and cultural norms that allow Black communities to be self-determined and for us to govern ourselves. To have enough economic, social, and political power to decide how, when, and where to have families. To determine where to live. To have the choices and the options to make decisions, just like everybody else—about schools, education, jobs, and quality of life.*
>
> *There's also an element [about] governance. What does it mean to be able to determine how our cities exist? We are often cornered into particular places inside cities that don't give us very many options in terms of grocery stores . . . and other essential needs.*

There is a point of tension about whether pro-Blackness takes anything away from other racialized groups. For Ross, his expected negative reaction from white people is one that demonstrates a misperception of what pro-Black actually means. He says,

> *It's not just a place where Black folks can thrive and be. It's a place where* all *folks can thrive and be. Because in my understanding, and how I have referenced and thought about history, whenever Blackness is centered, everybody wins.*

However, Isabelle Moses, chief of staff at Faith in Action, has a different take:

> *I guess it depends on what people value, what they perceive as giving up versus not giving up. So, if people value having the top job, and if that's a zero-sum thing—where the only way you can express leadership or power is by being the top of whatever the food chain is, or the apex predator, so to speak—then yeah, you might feel like you're giving up something. But if you can reframe what it means to be powerful, then I think we have a chance.*

***

> *So, it just depends on how people think about what the trade-offs are. And I think if we can collectively reframe the trade-offs, then we get closer to creating more conditions for more people to thrive—which, in my opinion, is way more rewarding than having the most money that I could possibly have for myself.*

For Matthews, there isn't a misperception about what pro-Black means in terms of power. In fact, that is exactly where things fall apart. She observes that being pro–Black Lives Matter does not mean one is pro-Black. The "racial reckoning" of the last few years has led many to publicly voice their commitment to the Black Lives Matter social movement. But class interests often clash with these commitments. She says,

> *For all the people who bought the books, who had one-off conversations, who marched in the streets, who maybe replaced one white board member with a Black board member—well, I don't want to diminish people's commitments . . . but those actions are insufficient. The question we have to ask ourselves is, What are we willing to give up in order to be pro-Black?*

Moses concludes:

Pro-Blackness isn't a zero-sum game. It shouldn't be seen as anti anything else. I think right now there's this kind of binary orientation. But I think we need to understand pro-Blackness as a way of saying pro-everybody—and by that I don't mean the equivalent of "all lives matter"! What I do mean is that if you're pro-Black, you are actually pro-everybody, because you can't be pro-everybody if you're not pro-Black.

Pro-Black also means Black people being able to be authentic. Kad Smith, an organizational development consultant, asks, "What would it look like to truly honor the experiences of Black folks, with no asterisk? As in, no conditions attached to the question of what kind of Blackness is palatable and what kind isn't." Quoting from a CompassPoint-led cohort member, Smith continues: "Pro-Blackness just looks like being comfortable in my skin."

Matthews echoes this:

People often support a particular type of Blackness. So, folks are comfortable with people going out and protesting, but if things get what they feel is unwieldy, or people start to uprise in a way that is uncomfortable to them—so, folks bashing in police cars, because police have killed their family and they don't particularly care about that piece of property over the dead bodies of Black people, or the movement's demand shifting from accountability to defunding the police—then we often see people's allegiances to the movement fade.

For Moses, the path to pro-Black is a very personal one of becoming grounded in Black culture, as both identity and community.

I live in Detroit, Michigan. I've been here for about four and a half years. And one of the reasons I moved here was to be grounded more in Black culture. I grew up in a supersocialized, white context in San Francisco, going to private schools. Then I lived in Washington, DC, for a long time. And I wanted to have a more rooted experience in Black communities. And Detroit, I felt, was a place where I could have that experience of being somewhere that really values and centers Black culture as just everyday life. I felt like I hadn't had that experience before. . . . So, that sense of rootedness in Black community is something that I have been longing for.

She continues,

I've learned that it takes more than just having Black skin. What I've learned, at least for myself, is that because of the era that I grew up in—the colorblind era, the 80s and early 90s, when folks were embracing this kind of assimilation mantra—I needed to reclaim my identity as a Black person. Because the frame that you're asked to assimilate into is obviously a white normative frame.

Basically, to be pro-Black is to not have to adhere to the white-dominant status quo.

What Are the Characteristics of a Pro-Black Organization?

Themes are emerging for those building pro-Black organizations. At its most basic, it means being able to talk about issues affecting Black people. Smith shares,

We're met with a certain level of resistance when we speak about Black-specific issues. So, that is anti-Blackness rearing its head in a very petulant and kind of gross way when Black folks talk about things that are particular to Black people and are met with resistance. A lot of what was coming up in articulating the pro-Black organization is the eradication of that dynamic. So, I can speak to what it means to be a Black person even if I'm the only one. Or even if I'm one of four. I'm not going to be met with, "Wait, wait, wait. We're not anti-Black. We're not racist." We're going to say, "Oh, let's go further there. Let's understand what's coming up for you." I feel like that would be in lockstep with other movements toward progress.

This is very tied to another characteristic of a pro-Black organization: Black people being able to step into power without punishment. Smith explains, "A couple of folks from the [CompassPoint] cohort mentioned safety. Safety from discrimination, from undeserved consequences, from systems of oppression."

Being disadvantaged by existing organizational policies is also punitive. Derias shares,

When I came in [to CompassPoint], I observed that the majority of people who worked at the organization were women, and all the Black women at the organization were mothers. . . . We

took a look at what it is that Black mothers value. They value the health of their children. They value time with their children. They value psychological safety for themselves and not to have to be here and worry about their children. . . . And the organization didn't offer 100% dependent coverage. So we had mothers, and sometimes single Black mothers, working at CompassPoint and then working at other jobs just to provide healthcare for their children.

So, in an attempt to build a pro-Black organization, we decided to flip that policy on its head. We wanted to figure out how to prioritize putting money into supporting our staff [members], which at the core would mean supporting Black mothers. This year we passed a policy of 100% dependent coverage for all our parents. Centering Black women wound up expanding the center, because now all of our staff [members] . . . can get care for their children. . . . When we center Black people, we challenge the punitive nature of organizations.

Isabelle Moses agrees.

We operate at Faith in Action under the belief that if you take care of Black people, specifically Black women, everyone in the organization will be taken care of—because the needs of Black women in particular are often so overlooked. And Black women are expected to be the providers, the caretakers, the folks who do things without actually ever being asked, and a lot of that labor goes unseen, unrecognized, unappreciated. And if you start to pay attention to all of the things that Black women do to make an organization successful, and then you provide resources and support for that work to be compensated, to be appreciated, to be recognized, then you realize how much more people actually need in order to thrive in organizations.

And when you meet those needs—when you create space for people to take care of their families during the workday; when you create space for people to take meaningful vacations so that they get actual rest; when you create the conditions for really strong benefits and policies, so people's healthcare needs are provided for (and they're not worried about whether they can make their doctor's appointments on time, because they know that they have the time off to do that); when you create an environment where people aren't going to be pressured to deliver things at the last minute, because you build in time and space for thoughtful planning so it doesn't end up on somebody's plate (often a Black woman's)—then you can create an organization where Black women can thrive. And if Black women are thriving, everybody is thriving. That's our fundamental belief.

Building pro-Black organizations means going beyond challenging structures to designing new structures with the values and needs of Black people at the center. Derias says,

Building pro-Blackness and building power require much more than just defending ourselves against anti-Blackness, and much more than just asking white folks in the organization to take a training. It's really about moving the needle with respect to looking at Black people as the folks who develop our governance, as the folks who, by virtue of our values, lead the development of the systems, policies, practices, and procedures at the organization.

Some organizations institute sabbaticals, which give staff members much-needed time to reflect and consider their next move in the work. At Faith in Action, staff members who have been there for 10 years or longer are eligible. Moses explains,

Depending on what they need, [a sabbatical can be] anywhere from three to five months. And they can put together a plan for the time. Our colleague Denise Collazo used her time to write a book, Thriving in the Fight. *Denise has been organizing for twenty-five years and is now our chief of external affairs. And she talks a lot about how that sabbatical was one of the ways in which she got the space that she needed to do the reflection for that book. So, she was able to use that time off to get clear about how it was that she was able to stay in the work.*

Denise was an innovator of our Family–Work Integration program, where we strive to reduce meetings on Fridays and limit email. It's not a day off, but it is a day that you can use to meet whatever needs you have—to catch up on any work from the week that didn't get done, or sleep in a little and go to a gym class, or take your mom to a doctor's appointment, or take care of that errand that you've been meaning to do—so that you don't end up feeling like there's no time for those activities that are really important for one's well-being. If you center well-being, then you create more opportunity to do better work. . . . And people are happier. We have a much happier culture.

Building pro-Black organizations also includes resourcing Black programmatic work. Derias shares,

We had a plurality of Black staff [members] for the first time in CompassPoint's 47 years. . . . . This is important to note, because what we found is that it's really hard to build pro-Blackness when you are the sole Black person at the organization. I mean, it's like moving a mountain. And so that plurality provided an opportunity for the Black staff [members] to get together and really interrogate pro-Blackness internally. And as we did that, we really built unity—we built across our values. And that's when we decided that it was really important for us to resource our Black programmatic work.

Moses agrees, and she shares how being a recipient of a MacKenzie Scott gift makes it possible:

We want to make sure that our teams are resourced. With the gift that we got last year from MacKenzie Scott, we now have the resources to make sure that people can work reasonable hours. If there's a gap in the organization, we can create a job description and recruit for it. We don't have to operate out of scarcity; we can operate out of abundance. And that's so exciting.

This type of pro-Black change in an organization usually requires having Black leadership.

Moses says,

I have a hard time seeing how folks who aren't Black can understand what Black folks need in an organization. Truly. And how they would be able to resource it at the level that's required. That doesn't necessarily mean the top people all need to be Black; it just means you have to have meaningful representation of Black folks in leadership, in order for that ethos to get rooted all the way through the organization. I've worked in organizations where there were Black staff [members], but we didn't have enough power for things to change.

Supporting Black leaders is also critical. I, and others, have written extensively about how they do not have the support they need and often face the sector's most pressing challenges.[1] Derias says,

---

[1]See, for example, Cyndi Suarez, "Leaders of Color at the Forefront of the Nonprofit Sector's Challenges," *Nonprofit Quarterly*, February 3, 2022, nonprofitquarterly.org/leaders-of-color-at-the-forefront-of-the-nonprofit-sectors-challenges/.

Now that we have Black people who are taking up positional power, it's really important to support them. I think what would strengthen the sector is giving time and space for Black people in positional power to learn skills, to network, to vent, to pool resources.

The challenges Black leaders face come from systemic, sectorwide forms *and* from within organizations and Black staff members, many of whom want to be experimenting with alternatives to hierarchy.

CompassPoint provides an example. The organization recently underwent a leadership transition that included an interim period during which it tried the holacracy method of decentralized management. It then decided to move forward with a codirectorship model. As Derias describes it,

At the core for [CompassPoint] as we were building a pro-Black organization was experimenting with a new governance model. Holacracy was useful, but it didn't meet our needs—so, we're developing a new kind of governance model. There's nothing really new under the sun—but what it does is push us to center our values.

Smith, who was at CompassPoint during this time of change, adds nuance.

I'm just gonna speak plainly: There was a sense of a commitment to holacracy and shared leadership, and the Black folks on staff [members] were doing some of the implementation and evaluation of that work, and it increased their responsibility and created visibility [for] their leadership—my own included. And when the organization committed to moving away from that, that was one of the few instances that I would say CompassPoint unintentionally perpetuated anti-Blackness.

Supporting Black leadership can appear to be in conflict with what Smith refers to as Black self-determination. He asks, "What does it look like to have autonomy and agency in an organization that intrinsically depends on collaboration?"

Ross sees this conflict about leadership and forms in his work, too.

What can come next can only come next if we allow for something that has not been allowed, has not been given space to really, really breathe. When I think about organizations, they're still not giving space to breathe. . . .

How I see that showing up primarily right now is in many ways centered on the question of how we organize ourselves as an entity. And so you're seeing a lot of folks contesting the model of hierarchy that organizes and cements power in this very concentrated place at the top of the organizational chart. People really want to contest that and find out what are the distributive ways in which we can organize ourselves. . . .

Pro-Black creates the space for that which needs to evolve to evolve. Pro-Black, to me, is connected to the notion of adaptation. It's connected to, and very much rooted in, the notion of interdependence. It is connected to and rooted in the notion of ideas [about] vulnerability, and different forms of knowledge and knowing. All of those are invitations to do the exploratory work that is necessary to find out what is next.

There is an opportunity for nonprofit organizations to evolve by learning from Black people's history and victories, particularly in how to build liberatory identities. Ross says,

A lot of organizations are in the midst of an identity crisis right now. After two years of racial reckoning, they are really deeply asking, "Who are we?" It's being asked at the generational level. We have younger folks asking the organizations who they are, and it's causing older folks to ask the question of themselves. . . .

And who in our country has had their identity contested again and again and again, and has had to figure out who they are again and again and again? Black folks. Identity has always been a question: "Are you really human?" "Are you American?" That question of identity has always been at the core of how we have had to orient ourselves and survive. . . .

What can nonprofits learn from folks who've had to go through that and answer that question repeatedly over their history in this country?

One way that Black people have defined liberatory identities is by moving beyond binaries to hold multiplicity. This can be a challenge for everyone, including Black people. Ross says,

I spend a lot of time looking at Patricia Hill Collins's work [about] Black feminist epistemologies. . . . I find myself referring repeatedly to an article she wrote 36 years ago. . . .

She was pushing against binaries in her work. She says—and I paraphrase—"Don't use what I am proposing here as a world, as

*the replacement for what currently exists, because that is a problem
as well." That's still the binary. . . .*

*It's much more complex and nuanced to recognize and be able
to hold the multiplicity [about it]. . . .*

*And, to be quite honest, one of the things that I find in organi-
zational spaces right now—that is, I think, a developmental
process—is that the calling out of white supremacist culture is
being used as its own kind of bludgeon. It's becoming now its own
orthodoxy, and so everything has to line up in that way.*

For Matthews, becoming a pro-Black organization depends on the
people in it doing difficult, personal work. For this, the organization needs
to be providing political education. She says,

*There is no way to enter movement and genuinely advocate for
radical ideas without interrogating your allegiances to oppressive
systems. So, if we're not offering political education to our staff and
board [members] to understand the complexities and history of
anti-Blackness, not only in the United States but also globally—so
that they can have enough context to be able to authentically make
some of the political decisions and commitments that they want—
then we're missing the mark.*

*The debate [about] critical race theory illustrates just how
hard it is for us to educate people in America about the history of
atrocities that this country has perpetrated against Black people.
So, we have to make that commitment in our organizations.*

There is tension or conflict not only within organizations, and
between organizations and movements, but within movements as
well. Matthews shares that movement spaces aren't always pro-Black
either. She admits, "Our movements can be inhospitable to people who
are growing."

What Would a Pro-Black Sector Sound, Look, Taste, and Feel Like?

Imagining a pro-Black sector did not come easily to the writers with
whom I spoke. However, the contours are beginning to take shape. One
thing is for sure: people want more humanity. At the center of it is Black
comfort and joy.

The sound would be that of a space ringing with the laughter of Black solidarity. Ross says,

> *There's laughter, there's commiseration. [Leaders of color are] finding community with each other, and they're not seeing one another as competitors or as people they need to feel threatened by. They're defining their tribe.*

It would look like trust. Ross says,

> *It looks like people being trusted to have a sense of what's needed but also of what's comfortable and what's connected to impact. Because if it's not connected to impact—if it's not connected to what our mission is—why are you putting it on me? . . . My presence and how I show up in the world shouldn't be making you comfortable or uncomfortable.*

. . . And the trust would extend to foundation partners really resourcing this work. Derias says,

> *It's really important that we not be beholden to projects or initiatives that have concrete, predetermined outcomes driven by our foundation folks. . . . Allow us to do the work of building the capacity of staff [members] to play with this vision of pro-Blackness, to experiment with it internally, to experiment with it externally. That's really important for our sector.*

It would taste like the deliciousness of complexity. Ross imagines,

> *It would taste like some kind of fruit that sort of explodes in your mouth, and each bite provides you with something distinct that you never imagined before. You've had that flavorful dish that starts off tasting one way with that first bite, and then the second bite adds another flavor, and the third bite another, and it produces a sensory joyfulness that you want to keep processing. You're not trying to just get to the next bite—you're really enjoying the bite that's in your mouth, what's going down.*

It would feel relaxed. Ross says,

> *There's a lot of haste in the work. A lot of unnecessary urgency pervades. And I think pro-Black space, pro-Black identity, pro-Black work, and folks who are centered in pro-Blackness are very clear—we need to slow down sometimes.*

Different cultures can have different relationships with time. For people of color, it can be more qualitative than quantitative.

Moses shares how Faith in Action has instituted rituals that are familiar to staff members of color, such as spending considerable time in meetings checking in. She says,

> *We recently had an hour-long meeting with twenty-five people, and we spent 25 minutes of the meeting with everyone calling in the ancestor that they wanted to bring into the space. And then we spent 35 minutes getting all the business done that we needed to do. And when you spend 25 minutes hearing each other's personal stories, that's a way of centering Blackness, centering Black culture, and centering the fact that we are more than the people in this room. We are all the people who came before us. We are all of the wishes and aspirations that our ancestors had for us, and often have exceeded those. . . . And when you really create space for that conversation, it builds community, it builds deeper trust, it builds deeper relationship, and it allows for better conditions for the work.*

For Matthews, pro-Black is ultimately an aspiration:

> *If you look at the trajectory of the Black liberation movement throughout the twentieth and the twenty-first centuries, there are some clear indications that the movement is becoming more pro-Black. . . . One of the major distinctions between the civil rights movement and the Black Power movement of the 60s and 70s and this current iteration of the Black liberation movement is that our leadership is decentralized and queer- and women- and nonbinary-led. Some people would say, "What does that have to do with being pro-Black?" Well, if Black people who are nonbinary, transgender, and/or women do not have power in your movements, then you cannot proclaim to be pro-Black, because you are only pro-Black for some.*
>
> *Even now, there are important critiques about this iteration of the Black liberation movement—and our job is to listen, repair harm, discuss, and course-correct. . . .*
>
> *There is no pinnacle of pro-Blackness at which one will arrive. . . . We are changing, and our material conditions are changing, all the time. And we have to evolve with those changes. Every single day, there are new ideas we have to contend with— and that means constantly evolving our strategies, our thinking, and our behaviors to be commensurate with those new ideas.*

When Blackness Is Centered, Everybody Wins

A Conversation with Cyndi Suarez and Dax-Devlon Ross

In this conversation about defining pro-Blackness, Cyndi Suarez, *Nonprofit Quarterly*'s president and editor in chief, talks with Dax-Devlon Ross, author, educator, and equity consultant, whose latest book, *Letters to My White Male Friends*,[1] is garnering well-deserved attention.

The conversations that ensued can be found in full in Spring 2022 of *NPQ*.

***

CYNDI SUAREZ: It's always great talking to you, Dax, because I love the work and analysis you're doing out there in the field on race and power, racial justice, DEI, and whatever else people are calling the work as it evolves. The recent articles that you've done with *NPQ—A Letter to My White Male Friends of a Certain Age* (which became a book that came out last year) and *Generational Differences in Racial Equity Work—* have really resonated with our readers as well.[2] So, when we landed on the topic of building pro-Black organizations for this issue of the magazine, I knew

---

[1] St. Martin's Press, 2021.
[2] Dax-Devlon Ross, "A Letter to My White Male Friends of a Certain Age," *Nonprofit Quarterly*, June 5, 2020, nonprofitquarterly.org/a-letter-to-my-white-male-friends-of-a-certain-age/ last accessed March 09, 2023; Dax-Devlon Ross, *Letters to My White Male Friends* (New York: St. Martin's Press, 2021); and Dax-Devlon Ross, "Generational Differences in Racial Equity Work," *Nonprofit Quarterly*, April 29, 2021, nonprofitquarterly.org/generational-differences-in-racial-equity-work/.

we had to include you in the mix. You were one of the first to start naming the generational differences. We both know that the field has been doing this work on race and power, in different iterations, for the last 30 years at least, right? And we're only now starting to have this conversation at this level in the sector. We're hosting this conversation for the whole year at *NPQ*, and we're already getting a lot of response. I wanted to bring you in to talk a little bit more about the article you wrote for this edition—"Resistance and Radical Love: The Call-Forward of a Pro-Black Sector"—as well as to delve more into what it means to be pro-Black.

DAX-DEVLON ROSS: I appreciate that. So, I was very inspired by the fact that you used the term *pro-Black* in your call-out to writers for this edition. It made me really think about what is being asked here. It made me think of Black Power and discomfort—how when the phrase *Black Power* was created, not just as a term, but as a call to action, it created discomfort for a lot of Americans half a century ago. And when I meditated on your questions: What does this call for pro-Black mean, here and now? What does a pro-Black sector look like? What do pro-Black organizations look like? It also made me feel a certain level of challenge. I thought, Oh, they want to go there with this! And it literally sent a sensory experience through my body. And I thought, Okay, let's go; let's actually explore this and try to forget about all the people who might be offended, or who might say, "Oh, but what do you mean, and who are you leaving out?"

Let's just name and center this right here as *pro-Black*. It's not just a place where Black folks can thrive and be. It's a place where *all* folks can thrive and be. Because in my understanding, and how I have referenced and thought about history, whenever Blackness is centered, everybody wins.

And I feel like that's what's always missing from these conversations in organizations. Leadership is always saying, "If we focus too much on race, who are we forgetting, who are we leaving out?" But if we look at the history of this country, whenever we are focused on race in this way, the benefit has accrued to so many other groups of people. So, let's not get caught up in this conversation centered on fear of being too up front [about] race because that might be perceived as not intersectional or not taking into consideration other experiences. Because the history of Black folks has never been one where we have not looked at and thought about other folks on the journey.

So, when you put out that call for folks to think about what pro-Black would look like in the organizational (and intersectoral) world, my feeling was, Let's think about this not just as a place where Black folks can be and thrive but also a means of thinking about where and how the values that have persisted within Black freedom struggles become the values that get mapped onto the sector. For example, what do we know to be true about emancipation? What do we know to be true about the fight to end Jim Crow? What do we know to be true about Black Lives Matter? These are movements that developed worldviews, epistemologies, forms of knowledge-making and creation and ways of knowing that allowed for these movements to be successful in advancing in the face of all sorts of terroristic threat. And yet, we've never really thought about how we could adopt some of what they did and do—the things that they learned and had to build around as a worldview, as a philosophy, as ideology—and apply it to our work in our sector. I hear sometimes, "Let's get some Black folks in here. Let's bring in Black folks or folks of color into the organization." But I never hear, "How do we develop and evolve our worldview [from] the intelligence they bring?" Because that worldview exists already. We've seen plenty of evidence of its power and its ability to shift power, but it never gets adopted and brought in as legitimate and serious forms of organizing and developing and building in the mainstream context.

What I landed on was that I wanted to be able to help folks to think about a way forward, because a lot of organizations are in the midst of an identity crisis right now. After two years of racial reckoning, they are really deeply asking, "Who are we?" It's being asked at the generational level. We have younger folks, folks of color, folks of different identities asking the organizations who they are, and it's causing older folks to ask the question of themselves. People are struggling with their identity.

And who in our country has had their identity contested again and again and again, and has had to figure out who they are again and again and again? Black folks. Identity has always been a question: "Are you really human?" "Are you American?" That question of identity has always been at the core of how we have had to orient ourselves and survive. And if I see a sector right now really having a challenge [about] its identity, it's the nonprofit sector. What can it learn?

What can nonprofits learn from folks who've had to go through that and answer that question repeatedly over their history in this country? There's something to be learned there.

CS: There are so many directions we can go here—there's so much in what you've said. Take this idea of identity. A couple of years ago, I wrote a piece called "A Cult of Democracy—Toward a Pluralistic Politics."[3] It asked, How do you build a cult of democracy, where that becomes the most important thing over any other kind of difference in ideology? And when I set out to do research, I looked at what the political scientists and philosophers were saying, and it was all [about] creating subjectivities—how the most important thing right now is to create a new understanding of identity and bigger identities for people to step into. Last week I wrote a piece called

[3] Cyndi Suarez, "A Cult of Democracy—Toward a Pluralistic Politics," *Nonprofit Quarterly*, January 7, 2021, nonprofitquarterly.org/a-cult-of-democracy-toward-a-pluralistic-politics.

"Examining Whiteness," which looks at whiteness as an identity that's formed against Blackness.[4] Black people have had their identity contested repeatedly, but also defined for them and us, right? So, there's a lot there. And at the end of it, when I was doing my research, I was surprised to find that a woman, a psychologist, Janet Helms, had created a framework for white identity as a developmental process.[5] It always amazes me how many fields of knowledge are out there that are yet to be discovered.

DDR: Oh, yeah.

CS: For some reason, when I first saw her name—she was referred to repeatedly by her last name in the literature—I thought it was a guy, a white guy. I thought, Who is this person? Helms turned out not only to be a woman but a Black woman, and one at my old school. She teaches at Boston College! So I thought, A Black woman created a typology for white identity! And when I read about how she did it, I discovered that she had built on a different typology that had come out in 1971, developed by William E. Cross Jr.—one on Black identity, called the *Nigrescense model*. And it was all about integrating your identity in a society that has it in opposition. Both versions comprise five phases each, and both culminate—in terms of development—at a point where you can interact with someone who is different from you without asserting that you're superior. And for the Black person, this means to be able to be free of that kind of framing and interaction—to know how to live healthily in a world that does that to you. And so it's very interesting, this question of identity—and I saw that it is something that psychologists have been taking up because they felt it was important and that they have a role to play. And I thought, Well, why don't we see ourselves as a field that has a role to play

---

[4]Cyndi Suarez, "Examining Whiteness," *Nonprofit Quarterly*, January 27, 2022, nonprofit quarterly.org/examining-whiteness/.
[5]Janet E. Helms, *A Race Is a Nice Thing to Have: A Guide to Being a White Person or Understanding the White Persons in Your Life*, 3rd ed. (San Diego, CA: Cognella, 2019).

in identity? And what are we constructing now, if we take on a role in constructing identity? Would it be beyond race? Would there be something higher that ties people together around liberatory identities?

DDR: To build a little bit off of what you're saying, I want to frame whatever I write very clearly in the understanding that I am building off of and building for additional work, thinking, whatever else can evolve. I spend a lot of time looking at Patricia Hill Collins's work [about] Black feminist epistemologies, for example. I find myself referring repeatedly back to an article she wrote 36 years ago as I think about this work.[6] And it is often the case, of course, that Black feminism in particular is a place where we can go to get a sense of a lot of things—because it has had to orient itself in such opposition to what it is always encountering in the academy, in the world, in the workplace. And one of the things that she talks about and plays with in her work—and I think this is really important—is the notion of *standpoint theory*. The idea that, rather than us starting to develop a sense that our role, our objective, is, as Black feminists (that's her context) to decenter the white male hegemonic order and replace it with a Black feminist frame, let's use standpoint theory as a way to understand that this is *one* way of interacting and understanding the world, *one* form of identity—and that there are many, many other ones as well.

She was pushing against binaries in her work. She says—and I paraphrase—"Don't use what I am proposing here as a world, as the replacement for what currently exists, because that is a problem as well." That's still the binary—it's still this notion that we

---

[6] Patricia Hill Collins, "Learning from the Outsider Within: The Sociological Significance of Black Feminist Thought," *Social Problems* 33, No. 6 (October-December 1986): S14–S32. And see Patricia Hill Collins, *Black Feminist Thought: Knowledge, Consciousness, and the Politics of Empowerment* (New York: Routledge, 2008); and Patricia Hill Collins, *Black Feminist Thought: Knowledge, Consciousness, and the Politics of Empowerment (Perspectives on Gender)*, 2nd ed. (New York: Routledge, 1999).

have to replace one with the other. It's much more complex and nuanced to recognize and be able to hold the multiplicity [about] it. And what I want to name—and am always resisting, even in my own work—is that I don't want it to be perceived as arguing for doing away with what has existed and bringing in a new thing that is the complete opposite of it. Because, for me, that doesn't necessarily move us forward. It gets us another frame that's valuable, but it also has its own potential shortcomings, its own foibles. And it keeps us in that same binary, either/or construct that we're trying to push ourselves out of and push through.

And to be quite honest, one of the things that I find in organizational spaces right now—that is, I think, a developmental process—is that the calling out of white supremacist culture is being used as its own kind of bludgeon. It's becoming now its own orthodoxy, and so everything has to line up in that way. So, if something in any way checks that box, it's bad, and we need to get it out of here. But that's not necessarily the world I'm in. My lived experience, my history, is complex. For instance, I was educated in a variety of institutions, some of which were white, and for me there is value in a lot of the knowledge that I developed at those institutions. What I am trying to challenge is the notion that this is the default and the only way, and that it is the one that has to be honored as *the* form, and in opposition to any other form of knowing and knowledge and ways of being in the world. And I'm presenting these Black freedom struggles as a worldview that has had to evolve in constant reaction to—in relationship with—that dominant frame.

So, it's not the way out, but it *is* a way forward. What can come next can only come next if we allow for something that has not been allowed, has not been given space to really, *really* breathe. When I think about organizations, they're still not giving space to breathe. I keep finding as I write and read, such as in pieces I've seen at *NPQ*, that folks have recognized that a lot of the ways in which organizations have tried to address the conflicts and crisis is by finding Black folks to become the leaders. And what they find again and again is that this puts those Black folks in a very vulnerable place. They're often pulled in multiple directions, because not only do they have to be the leader of the organization—the face of it— but also [they] have to respond to all the crises within it. And it's not a fair place to put them. So, knowing that, this sort of superficial transition of power to a different body isn't the solution; we have to dig deeper. The problems are the systems, the operating principles—the more foundational stuff that I think historically has never really been touched. We don't really like to go beneath the hood and really dig in and figure out and ask ourselves, "Why do we do it this way?"

How I see that showing up primarily right now is in many ways centered on the question of how we organize ourselves as an entity. And so you're seeing a lot of folks contesting the model of hierarchy that organizes and cements power in this very concentrated place at the top of the organizational chart. People really want to contest that and find out what are the distributive ways in which we can organize ourselves. Which, again, leads us back to, What are the most recent iterations of Black freedom struggles demonstrating to us? What are other forms of leadership models, other forms of organizing, that we can learn from?

Not to say that Black freedom struggles are the only ones that have done that. I think a lot came out of Occupy that was really fascinating. I think anarchist movements are important, which is why I refer to [David] Graeber and [David] Wengrow's new book *The Dawn of Everything*.[7] I think this book is so transformative. And it's because it presents the notion that our accepted ideas [about] how hierarchy has to

---

[7] David Graeber and David Wengrow, *The Dawn of Everything: A New History of Humanity* (New York: Farrar, Straus and Giroux, 2021).

be the guiding principle for all organizing structures isn't necessarily true. There can be other ways that we can be together, and for our organizations to succeed. But we have to be willing to test things out a little bit, and I don't know if folks are comfortable with that yet. I *know* they're not comfortable with it yet. Because we have all been socialized to believe that the only ways that we can possibly move anything forward is through the models that we have been steeped in—which is to say, that there's somebody at the top making all the decisions. And what organizations are finding—and what I think young folks are asking for, leaders are asking for, people of color are asking for—is *something different*. We want to try something different. We don't necessarily know what that's going to always look like, but we know that this thing that we have right here doesn't feel like it's nourishing us organizationally, and it doesn't feel like it's serving us professionally and personally. What else can we try?

And that's all it is: a question. It is an opportunity. And some folks will feel that as a threat. And naturally, whenever power is contested, people do feel threatened by it. But I'd see that as a way for a sector like ours to lead. It's to lead and in many ways to *not* be the ones to lead this. I think it's showing up—it's gonna show up all over the place. But it's a call to leadership.

CS: I like that you use the word *multiplicity*, because that's one thing that I've been exploring as one of the five characteristics of Edge Leadership. This idea is something that I'm very committed to—that you don't have to choose between one or the other, and that everyone doesn't have to agree on the same thing. There's really no need for that most of the time. And it's interesting, because I was going to ask you, "What does it mean to be pro-Black? And what are the characteristics of a pro-Black organization?"

And in terms of how you're talking about it, it kind of overlaps with this generational question, with the question of hiring. In a conversation we had in late January that you were a part of—about generational conflict in this work—Black leaders were felt to be at the forefront of a sectorwide challenge. And this is something that [Michael] Hardt and [Antonio] Negri talk about in their book *Assembly*—that the biggest challenge right now for leaders who care about social justice is the new type of organization that will hold a participatory democracy.[8] And I've been looking at that, because we've been hearing from the field repeated questions [about] hierarchy. I did my master's in nonprofit management, and my thesis was on alternatives to hierarchy. So, I've been looking at this question for a while, and there are many ways in which hierarchy is a part of nature, and many ways in which hierarchy overlaps with other forms. An author I really like, Caroline Levine, explores four key forms in nature in her book *Forms*, and hierarchy's one of them.[9] She says that almost never do you find a form by itself; usually they overlap. You have multiple forms in the same space. You might have a hierarchy, and you might have a network. So, this is another way to think about it. There never is just one form. And lately, I've been reading this piece about how we're evolving to a different worldview that also explores this point [about] structure, and it's articulated as *fractality*[10]—this idea that there is a structure, and that it replicates at different levels, but those levels don't have to be value laden. They don't have to be in an order of value. That they are *all* valuable. So, I guess the question that's intriguing me here is, Is pro-Black *that*?

DDR: I think pro-Black *could* be that—but I think pro-Black creates the space for that which needs to evolve *to* evolve. Pro-Black, to me, is connected to the notion of adaptation. It's connected to, and very much rooted in, the notion of interdependence. It

---

[8] Michael Hardt and Antonio Negri, *Assembly* (Oxford, UK: Oxford University Press, 2017).
[9] Caroline Levine, *Forms: Whole, Rhythm, Hierarchy, Network* (Princeton, NJ: Princeton University Press, 2015).
[10] Grant Maxwell, "'Symmetry Across Scale': The Fractal Quality of Process," chap. 7 in *The Dynamics of Transformation: Tracing an Emerging World View* (Nashville, TN: Persistent Press, 2017), 84–92.

is connected to and rooted in the notion of ideas [about] vulnerability, and different forms of knowledge and knowing. All of those are invitations to do the exploratory work that is necessary to find out what is next. What I think is true, in my experience, is that one of the barriers to trying these—to allowing, to inviting—is that there is a fixedness that is often aligned and associated with predominantly white-dominant structures, right? That's part of what we are contesting, I think: that this notion of fixedness, of how individuality is centered as the paragon, is the ideal. And what we know has challenged that, and has presented different pathways for something other than that, has lived—at least in the American context—in the bodies and movements of Black folks.

So, again, I am not saying that Black folks have all the answers. I am saying that there are some clues to this new world that I think people are trying to break us into that can be found with regard to folks who, historically, have been trying to break us into a new world *all the time.* And so why would we not try to understand what those folks have done from a historical perspective and gather the things that have helped to sustain and nurture?

Also, there is a trust crisis in organizations right now that's connected to power and connected to structures. Across organizations—and I hear this from leaders—there's a desperate desire to regain trust, or maybe not even *regain* but *gain* trust. And there's a desperate desire, I think, from people who are in organizations, to be trusted. And when I think about it, I think about how central trust was to organizing resistances to slavery. If I couldn't trust you—if trust wasn't present in our relationship—there's no way we could have organized and built an underground railroad. So, trust is this feature that I think is missing in a lot of organizational contexts, because of the ways in which power has manifested itself and the way power often operates as a means of keeping people out of information flows, a means of concentrating decision-making authority, and a means of centralizing spaces. All those, I think, are features that have invariably been components of the hierarchical structures that have evolved in the Western Hemisphere, in particular. I don't know the entire world, but that's my experience.

Regarding other forms, I've been reading about *wirearchies*. If you look at networked organizations now, it is not necessarily from your manager that you gain your knowledge. You gain it also from your peers, from people who are located in other parts of the country. And that's who you're *wired* to. If you look at org charts, traditional organizations take the form of lines that ladder up. But that's not how people are actually functioning in a lot of these organizational contexts. They're diagonal *here*, they're dotted *there*, they're circling, they're connected.

And I'll never forget this one experience that I had when I was working in an organization. I met with this young man, a young Black man, who didn't report to me. I had a position that was sort of dotted in his world. We didn't have a formal connection, but he and I built a strong work relationship. I was a Black man, a few years older than him, who was in the work; and he was like, "Yo, I want to learn from you and build from you." After we had spent some time together doing some work, I got a phone call from his boss—also a leader of color, by the way—who said, "Yeah . . . I'm uncomfortable with the ways you-all are starting to kind of interact." And it hit me—there was a sense that I was disrupting this person's authority, because they were oriented to think that their power and their ability to lead their work was contingent on a kind of strict structure of power and hierarchy. And I was disrupting that in some way. I wasn't doing it intentionally; I was just building with this person. But that threat was a real thing, because I was disrupting something that this other leader held in deep value. I tried to communicate to them that (a) I'm not trying to threaten you, (b) I think that the work is being enhanced, and (c) this is actually how folks in a networked environment interact: We get information and insight from all over, not just from you who sits as my manager on the org chart. I get it from, maybe, your colleague, or this person over here, or that person—people who we should be engaged with, and who should be trusted and invited in to partner on building something. I think that's what people are craving and asking for, because they're looking for growth and development and learning, and to have more impact in their work. And I think that's a real challenge to leaders.

CS: It's interesting that you say it was a person of color. I've had similar experiences, when if I talk about what happened, the person will assume the person's white. And I say, "No, actually, it's a person of color doing this." So it speaks to this idea that pro-Black isn't always the perfect answer, right? It speaks to the fact that this is a project for the sector—and, I think you're saying, pro-Black opens up the space. Because when I think about that leader who you just mentioned, who has that reaction, can you imagine the forces making them feel like that's how they have to be? When do *they* get the space? And where do they go to design something different? Because when you describe this kind of organization, I try to imagine what that chart would look like, and I think, Who would even know how to build a chart like that? I used to work at a networking organization, so we did actually build things like that. But that's not really how people think of this. And even if you could, how do you fund it? Everything's a question, when you look at it like that. How do we change that at that level, so that the individual leader isn't trying to figure it out on their own?

DDR: Oh, my goodness.

CS: And, usually, what they have is a peer group with other leaders like themselves.

DDR: Oh yeah—trying to figure it out. I identify in this way as well. My training, formal and otherwise, has often been within the very structures that are being challenged. I've been rewarded in many ways throughout my career for having navigated not the structures that I create or even desire but those that have been presented to me as the only way. And I think this speaks to what is experienced by a lot of these leaders of color. These are amazing folks who've been exceptional in everything that they've done throughout their careers. And now they're in this position of decision-making and authority and resources, and they have to raise money, and they have to manage all these people, and they have boards, and they have staff [members]. And they're being asked to do something they've never done before.

CS: And that you can't hire someone to do. I mean, can you imagine finding a consultant [who] could come in, if that was the answer? [Who] could actually come and help build the organization?

DDR: There are two things that I find really interesting. I'm working with an organization that has an interim/transitional leadership team in place, and the organization is using the benefit of a lot of vacancies at the leadership level to do some experimenting. And I think that it can be interesting to work in that kind of interim space, because you have people who are wed[ded] to an outcome in terms of what benefits the organization and not in terms of their positionality. Their job isn't on the line, because they're very clear that they are practicing in a transitional space, for a 6- to 12-month period, to help bridge what the organization has been and what it needs to become. They can help make decisions in a spirit that's not necessarily connected to being the beneficiary of what happens next.

I think the challenge for a lot of folks is, What happens to me? Where do I go? If we do shift the way we organize ourselves and the structures that we have, what does that do to me? Where do I sit in that? I think these are very important and fair questions to ask. And I don't pretend to say that I have all the answers. But I do suggest that there's something powerful in organizing temporary teams to do this kind of work. In *The Dawn of Everything*, Graeber and Wengrow show, through their own research and looking at the historical record, that there were societies that spent half the year in hierarchies and half the year in autonomous kinds of arrangements.[11] And it was often aligned with what the needs of the community were in a given moment in time. Wengrow is an archaeologist, and Graeber was an anthropologist—he passed away about a year and a half ago. (Some folks might be familiar with Graeber's name because he was one of the more visible characters from Occupy. He wrote a book called *Debt: The First 5000 Years* that is really fascinating.)[12] In *Dawn*, Graeber and Wengrow present a notion that challenges the view that once we discovered agriculture and the agricultural revolution began, humans went from being hunter-gatherers to agricultural beings. They're saying it's more complicated than that. That it's more iterative. That there were offshoots of communities that were experimenting with other forms of living and organizing.

So, to bring that back to what we're talking about, I think about what it would mean for organizations to consider and play with different organizing structures for different points of a cycle. It already implicitly happens. Cycles and flows already exist within organizations, such as when work ratchets up at one point during the year because it's a critical fundraising period or a big event is happening or a new program is being introduced. But what I'm presenting and suggesting is, What does the next step of that look like? How might that work more intentionally? So that we go beyond recognizing that, say, this part of the year we're ramping up or working harder,

[11] Graeber and Wengrow, *The Dawn of Everything*.
[12] David Graeber, *Debt: The First 5000 Years* (Brooklyn, NY: Melville House, 2011).

to *organizing* ourselves a little differently for that period in time—whether it's for six months, three months, or whatever. And it could be because there are different needs, or different challenges we're presented with. I know that requires a very high level of organizational intelligence—not individual intelligence, *organizational* intelligence—and organizational awareness and even resources. You can't do this without resources. But it's intriguing to consider that there have been social arrangements that have existed where people have consciously adjusted themselves based on what is being presented to them regarding their needs. And folks can say, in this context, "*This* is what we need," and in this other context, "We need *that*."

Therefore, this notion of fixedness—that we are this way all the time, at all times—is not the thing we're going to root ourselves in, because in order for us to have the greatest impact, or for us to survive (which was the case several thousand years ago), we need to shift. And I am saying that I think, in some sense, some organizations—and I think the sector more broadly—are encountering something of an existential challenge.

For the past two generations, the nonprofit sector has been able to say, "We're always going to get these really talented young folks who come into this space because they want to do good and because they don't want to go to the private sector, or they don't want to go into private industry." What I think has happened, interestingly enough, in the last couple of years—partly because of George Floyd, partly because of Black Lives Matter—is that we are seeing private sector and private enterprise starting to learn that, to attract talent, they have to have an orientation. And then they can draw some of those people in who might otherwise have gone into the nonprofit sector. We're seeing these companies recruit with that in mind. *I* came to this sector because I wanted to do good in the world. Where else would I go?

But I don't think that's going to be the case, moving into the future. I think people are going to see a variety of opportunities and ways in which they can express themselves in the world, and that to do good in the world does not mean having to go into the sector that you and I, because we are children of the civil rights movement, grew up believing is the place you go if you want to have impact. I think younger folks are saying, "I can have impact in a lot of places. Moreover, I don't need to get underpaid; get treated X, Y, and Z; get overworked. I can make more money and still have social justice be something that's part of my ethos and identity. It might not show up explicitly as the mission of the work, but it's connected to the work that I'm doing." I think that's a burgeoning challenge that needs to be named and navigated by our sector.

CS: Thank you very much, you've given us a lot here. I have one last question. What would a pro-Black sector sound, look, taste, and feel like to you?

DDR: That's a great question. I think that on a very basic level, it would sound like some of the conversations that are happening among leaders of color and in the peer group spaces that are emerging. It would sound like that, where there's this sharing of information, sharing of challenges. There's laughter, there's commiseration. They're finding community with each other, and they're not seeing one another as competitors or as people they need to feel threatened by. They're defining their tribe.

And I think this exists to some extent—and it's kind of emerging because people are demanding it—but it would look like folks being able to show up as they are and as they feel called to show up in their workspaces. I am one who believes there's a time and place for everything. And these interesting questions that people are raising [about] what professionalism is and looks like, are, I think, at the heart of race and identity—because it's often young folks of color who are challenging what we call "the politics of respectability" that are sort of encoded into us and which we're expected to just assimilate ourselves into. Folks are saying, "Nah, I don't feel like that's necessarily how I need to show up at work to get my job done."

I think that it looks like people being trusted to have a sense of what's needed but also of what's comfortable and what's connected to impact. Because if it's not connected to impact—if it's not connected to what our mission is—why are you putting it on me? If this is just about me presenting in a way that makes you feel comfortable, then that's something we need to talk about—because my presence and how I show up in the world shouldn't be making you comfortable or uncomfortable. That's not what we should be up to right now.

I think the taste—man, I would have to go more into a space of metaphor for that one. I think it would taste like some kind of fruit that sort of explodes in your mouth, and each bite provides you with something distinct that you never imagined before. You've had that flavorful dish that starts off tasting one way with that first bite, and then the second bite adds another flavor, and the third bite another, and it produces a sensory joyfulness that you want to keep processing. You're not trying to just get to the next bite—you're really enjoying that bite that's in your mouth, what's going down. And that's something that I would really like to see. Because there's a lot of haste in the work. A lot of unnecessary urgency pervades. And I think pro-Black space, pro-Black identity, pro-Black work, and folks who are centered in pro-Blackness are very clear—we need to slow down sometimes.

This pace that has been created is unnecessary. It is not required. It does not get us to where we're trying to go. I think pro-Black is focused and centered on, Where do we get our rest? So, I love the work that people are naming in social spaces and social media spaces: rest, naps, the nap ministry. I want to lift that up. I think that this is part of what a pro-Black sector would feel like. People can name and get the rest they need—so that they can do the work with full impact and not as tired people doing more and more and more, because they keep being asked to do more and more and more.

The last thing I would add is that when we talk about a pro-Black sector, I would include the folks at the philanthropic level. Pro-Blackness can't come into being, can't be manifested, without real coordination, alignment, understanding, space—all the things that I think the philanthropic sector has demonstrated in a very tepid way that it might be open to, but is still moving way too slowly. I'll close with this: I've had three calls in the last 12 hours—each from clients, none of whom know each other, who have received money from MacKenzie Scott. And I think, on one level, it's really sad that one person in a three- or four-year time frame can have that kind of impact—because it throws a light on everybody else. It means all you other wealthy folks could have been doing more—a lot more—if you would just let go. Release. Release the money, and release the need to control outcome. Let go of this need to feel like because this is your money, you need to be able to determine the outcome. That possession? Folks don't want that. They don't need that. That does not drive the outcome. That's not going to create the kind of world that folks are trying to live in. I bring that into this space because if the *philanthropic* space could just lean more into that sort of trust, into belief, and just release this need to control, so much could get done.

Black folks don't want to be controlled. Our history shows we gonna get free. Whatever you put on us, we're going to find and seek freedom. That's who we are. That's how we're built. And we want that for everybody, not just for ourselves. Freedom is something that we have brought to this country and given real life to and brought real, deep meaning to. That is a part of our legacy.

CS: Well, Dax, you said it all. Thank you so much. I really appreciate you.

DDR: Cyndi, I just want to lift you up before we close this out. I met you just a couple of years ago, and I emailed you out of the blue because I'd read your articles and I had got your book. And I was just so blown away by how you think and the ways you write. I just hadn't seen it. I honestly hadn't seen it. No one I was reading in that space in our sector was writing and thinking the way you were. I'm so glad that you're in the role that you are now, and that you haven't let up in any way. You're just pushing it even further, and you're inviting people like me to be part of this work with you at the edge—whether through Edge Leadership work or in the magazine. I'm just so grateful that you exist. And I think the sector is so blessed to have you be a part of it. Folks need to know your greatness. You are a wonderful, beautiful, generous, trusting, brilliant human being. And I'm just grateful to know you and be a partner with you in the work.

CS: Oh, thank you. I feel very lucky to be here, and to be with people like you, and to make my time here be about creating what we want, for real. So you're part of that. You have been from the beginning. Thank you. Please stay with us. I hope to continue this conversation. I want to host this conversation on pro-Black organizations for the rest of the year. I want this to be the start. And I want to do a call to action to the community. I want people to start really holding space to define this, to get funding for leaders to create these models and these case studies, and to create a reader at the end that collects all the work into one place. That's my goal for the year. So, I hope that you stay with us and that you keep naming this stuff.

DDR: Let's do it.

CS: All right.

DDR: We got this. It's what we do.

Leading Restoratively

The Role of Leadership in a Pro-Black Sector

Sequoia Owen

Nonprofit organizations pledge to serve communities through powerful missions. Often, those missions are about empowerment, restoration, safety, and wholeness for the marginalized within our communities. Since 2021, racial reckoning has led the nonprofit sector to examine the ways in which white supremacy lives in our organizational systems. Increasingly, nonprofits are publicly showing support for Black causes—at times, to distance themselves from the appearance of condoning racism. Operating as pro-Black, however, involves much more than releasing a statement of support for Black and Brown lives. It may not even require a change in organizational mission or new programming—an organization can make such changes and still operate with a white supremacist structure.[1]

Being a pro-Black organization means internalizing our missions and extending energy and resources to our frontline staff members who serve our communities. It calls for the antithesis of divisiveness and destruction and a movement of restoration. Nonprofit leadership must build thriving workplace environments in which staff members have the permission and tools they need to become their best selves. A pro-Black organization ensures staff member well-being, safety, dignity, and advancement by practicing trauma-informed, collective care; prioritizing psychological safety; and restoring worker dignity by providing equitable living wages and building leadership pipelines.

---

[1] https://coco-net.org/wp-content/uploads/2019/11/Coco-WhiteSupCulture-ENG4.pdf

Our Promise to the Community

Ask anyone in the nonprofit sector why they came to work, and you will get a variation of the same answer: belief in the mission. Nonprofits have beautiful and inspiring missions that make one's heart leap at their audacious optimism. They envision a world without hunger, disease, strife, or lack. In 2020, Insight Center for Community Economic Development introduced a framework for centering Blackness.[2] A key element of their framework is *shared abundance*. They insist that, to create a world where the marginalized lack nothing—and therefore, abundance is shared by all—our sector must center Blackness.

Some nonprofit leaders are concerned that centering Blackness will require a whole new direction for their organization. They ask whether centering Black people is "mission aligned" or if their organization is prepared to tackle something so vast. The answer to both questions is yes. No one can deny the intersection that race has with our missions. Black people are overrepresented among domestic violence victims,[3] prison inmates,[4] and the homeless[5] and underrepresented in educational attainment[6] and economic security.[7] It is absurd to think that any one of these intersecting issues stands alone, and that, for example, we can end homelessness without centering the people largely affected by it. As legal scholar and activist Kimberle Crenshaw says, "If we aren't intersectional, some of us, the most vulnerable, are going to fall through the cracks."[8] We fall out of alignment with our missions when we do not serve the most vulnerable. Centering Blackness may seem like a large and intimidating ask, but it is no larger than our bold ambitions to eliminate poverty or end world hunger. It's the first step toward truly realizing our missions.

Some nonprofits have acknowledged that challenging systemic racism is mission-aligned work; they have started by making statements in support of Black lives and examining how to structure their programming to better serve Black and Brown communities. Statements and programming are a first step toward diversity and inclusion, but they do not move the sector toward Black liberation.

---

[2] https://medium.com/economicsecproj/centering-blackness-the-path-to-economic-liberation-for-all-f6c2c7398281
[3] https://www.cdc.gov/violenceprevention/pdf/NISVS-StateReportBook.pdf#page=135
[4] https://naacp.org/resources/criminal-justice-fact-sheet
[5] https://endhomelessness.org/homelessness-in-america/what-causes-homelessness/inequality/
[6] https://nces.ed.gov/pubs2019/2019038.pdf
[7] https://www.americanprogress.org/article/systematic-inequality/
[8] https://www.jstor.org/stable/1229039

If we want to center Blackness, we must be authentic in our execution. We must recognize that standing with the Black lives closest to us—the ones we employ—is the most authentic expression of a pro-Black organization. Our missions are a promise to our communities that we cannot fulfill without first internalizing this promise ourselves.

Pro-Black Organizational Leadership

A pro-Black organization requires pro-Black leadership that dismantles white supremacy internally and replaces its structures by rebuilding an organization that paves the way for the liberation of all people. Such leadership requires an understanding of the anti-Black origins of modern management. The idea of viewing humans as capital originated with slave owners. And as economic historian Caitlin Rosenthal explores in her book, *Accounting for Slavery: Masters and Management*,[9] modern workforce management techniques emerged out of plantation slavery. Pro-Black organizational leadership must therefore reject capitalism's tendency to view workers as producers of capital and focuses instead on workers' humanity.

To lead restoratively, leaders need to shift from simply managing personnel to fostering an environment that encourages staff members to thrive. This means rethinking the way we lead. We must examine whether our actions detract from or contribute to staff members thriving. When setting grant outcomes, for example, pro-Black organizational leadership considers the quality of the services provided as well as the resources needed for staff members to carry out and sustain the work. These leaders inquire about caseload size and its effect on staff members' overall workload and time for professional development because they understand that burned out staff members who do not grow cannot effectively carry out the organization's mission. In other words, pro-Black leaders extend the organizational missions on our doors to those who serve our communities—our frontline staff members.

A thriving environment will look differently across different types of organizations. However, common indicators across all staff levels include

- Staff members who are empowered and equipped to do their best work
- High retention rates with clear opportunities for growth

[9]https://www.hup.harvard.edu/catalog.php?isbn=9780674972094

- A culture where mistakes are viewed as learning opportunities
- A sense of ownership of organizational priorities
- A culture that allows staff members to be themselves without fear of retaliation or negative consequences for their self-worth and career

Before white nonprofit leaders jump ship, this call to pro-Black leadership involves you. A pro-Black sector does not call for the mass exodus of white leaders; it calls for the creation of a pipeline of growing, thriving Black and Brown leaders. It will take all of us to make good on this promise.

Reimagine Staff Wellness

When we hear *staff wellness*, we may think of initiatives undertaken by the corporate sector, but on-site fitness centers and weekend-long staff relaxation retreats are unattainable luxuries for the nonprofit sector. We simply do not have the funds. Grant-funded projects may also place restrictions on how staff members can use their time. What would it look like to reimagine wellness through a pro-Black lens in a nonprofit context?

The pro-Black nonprofit leader views staff member well-being as an anchor that guides the way decisions are made and how actions are carried out, in contrast to an approach that uses wellness programming to attract new talent to a stressful work environment. This leader's commitment to staff member well-being is centered on the wholeness of their workers as they give of themselves to their community.

A pro-Black organization is one in which direct service workers employ SAMHSA's trauma-informed approach to care[10] with clients, and managers use this same approach with staff members. Service workers recognize that clients need specific support to recover from trauma. Likewise, managers recognize that staff members—and direct service workers in particular—require supervisor support to prevent burnout and secondary trauma. A pro-Black organization understands the importance of educating and equipping every manager with trauma-support skills and holds leadership accountable for modeling trauma-informed care to "restore a sense of safety, power, and self-worth"[11] to every worker.

---

[10]https://www.samhsa.gov/sites/default/files/programs_campaigns/childrens_mental_health/atc-whitepaper-040616.pdf
[11]https://www.gobhi.org/trauma-informed-care#:~:text=Trauma%20Informed%20Care%20(TIC)%20recognizes,power%2C%20and%20self%2Dworth

In other words, a pro-Black organization rejects trauma-informed care as simply a term to place on a grant application to gain extra points. Instead, it views trauma-informed care as an organization-wide initiative where leadership supports staff members in dealing with secondary trauma, rather than penalizing or discarding them.

When service delivery must be changed to improve the client experience, simply replicating a model that has worked elsewhere—without staff member input—can disempower staff members. Pro-black leadership asks, "How can we leverage staff members as experts and collaborate to adjust this model to best serve our community?"

A pro-Black organization also believes in and practices collective care. When a tragedy touches the community, leadership pauses to create a safe and intentional space for staff members to process their thoughts and feelings in a group setting and support one another, instead of continuing the workday as though there is no connection between the personal and professional. Just as the African proverb states, "It takes a village to raise a child," a pro-Black organization acknowledges the toll that community service work can take on employees and draws from the healing power of the collective to mitigate burnout. Pro-Black leaders and organizations believe that collectively grieving the hardships that occur in pursuit of the mission is just as important as celebrating the victories. They also understand the importance of offering safe space for staff members to do so. In practice, these safe spaces to develop mutual support can take the form of affinity groups or wellness circles facilitated by an outside, neutral party.

Prioritize Psychological Safety

Another element of centering Blackness[12] is redefining safety. There is no denying that physical safety is important in the workplace. While federal and state laws exist to protect employees from physical harm, our sector offers little to protect the mental health of our staff members. Because pro-Black organizations prioritize the safety of their staff members as whole people, they understand that mental health is an important part of overall well-being.

Psychological safety[13] is the ability to "show and employ oneself without fear of negative consequences of self-image, status, or career." Though

---

[12]https://medium.com/economicsecproj/centering-blackness-the-path-to-economic-liberation-for-all-f6c2c7398281
[13]https://journals.aom.org/doi/10.5465/256287

the term has recently gone mainstream, the concept of psychological safety is not new to Black people who feel its absence and experience negative consequences when they show up as themselves at work: from employers questioning the professionalism of natural, kinky hair to being perceived as less qualified than white counterparts with the same credentials. Pro-Black organizational leadership takes up the charge to build psychologically safe environments as a moral imperative. Because leaders have the power to deal out consequences and perpetuate fear, they are responsible for restoring mutual respect and acceptance in the work environment. A McKinsey Global Survey[14] backs this up, arguing that "a climate conducive to psychological safety starts at the very top of an organization."

Once psychological safety is established within an organization, staff members in a thriving environment will exhibit four qualities that lead to high performance and innovation, as outlined by Dr. Timothy Clark:[15]

- The feeling of connectedness and belonging
- The ability to ask questions and make mistakes
- The assurance that their contributions are meaningful
- The ability to think constructively to improve processes

Restore Worker Dignity

Many nonprofit leaders would agree that their workers deserve to be paid a living wage. However, nonprofits need more funding to provide better pay. Without increased funding, leaders face the dilemma of maintaining low staff wages or providing fewer services. But it doesn't have to be this way: funders and foundations must recognize that operational costs are essential to programming, and we must educate elected officials on the need for increased resources.

Though nonprofit leaders did not create the economic system that underpays workers, through our silence, we have been complicit in denying our staff members the wages they deserve. Indeed, many nonprofits do not raise wages until state laws mandate a minimum wage increase. Pro-Black organizational leadership does not wait for wage increases to

---

[14]https://www.mckinsey.com/capabilities/people-and-organizational-performance/our-insights/
psychological-safety-and-the-critical-role-of-leadership-development
[15]https://www.leaderfactor.com/4-stages-of-psychological-safety

become mandatory. Rather, pro-Black leaders advance pay equity, a central demand of Black liberation movements: Dr. Martin Luther King Jr., who advocated for pay equity, was quoted as saying, "We're coming to get our check,"[16] before the Poor People's March on Washington in 1968.

Pro-Black organizational leaders understand that messaging is their most powerful tool. They choose to restore worker dignity by refusing to fundraise for the lowest possible cost. You won't find a pro-Black organization advertising that a child can be fed for less than the cost of a cup of coffee because they understand that feeding a child requires the labor of frontline personnel who purchase, pick up, and serve the food. Pro-Black organizational leaders do not shrink their visions to make them more palatable to others. When designing a program, they ask, "How many staff members are needed to effectively provide this service?" instead of, "What is the lowest number of staff members required to get this program running?" They unapologetically present the true cost[17] of programming to individual donors—including living wages, benefits, and professional development for all workers—because they know that staff members deserve more.

Build Leadership Pipelines

It is no secret that Black and Brown leaders are underrepresented in positions of power within the nonprofit sector. A study from BoardSource[18] reports that only 13% of nonprofit CEOs and 22% of board members identify as non-white. The reasons for this underrepresentation include Black and Brown workers receiving less support from managers to gain promotions[19] and nepotism within board recruiting.

Pro-Black leaders offer leadership development to all staff members because they value potential leaders at every staff level. They understand that true leadership doesn't come with a title, and they embody shared leadership[20] as an approach to distributing power. Pro-Black leaders encourage growth instead of tempering it for fear that an employee will

---

[16] https://www.facebook.com/jacobinmag/videos/mlk-were-coming-to-get-our-check/404314146818198/

[17] https://www.bridgespan.org/bridgespan/Images/articles/nonprofit-cost-analysis-toolkit/NonprofitCostsAnalysisToolkit.pdf

[18] https://leadingwithintent.org/

[19] https://womenintheworkplace.com/

[20] https://www.businessnewsdaily.com/135-shared-leadership-social-media-fuel-business-growth.html

threaten someone else's job or outgrow the organization. They make liberal investments in leadership development, knowing such investment creates a more equitable leadership pipeline.

Pro-Black leaders use the leadership pipeline as a tool for succession planning. They have a plan to replace themselves and acknowledge that the lack of such planning leaves a gap in organizational growth, resulting in unintended consequences for the organization and community, including "additional staff turnover, missed opportunities, decreased funding, and diminished service."[21]

Conclusion

Simply put, a pro-Black organization demands more from its leaders than an organization operating with white supremacist ideals: it calls for leaders who understand that they have a responsibility for staff member well-being. Pro-Black leaders treat staff member wellness as an opportunity to restore relationships and build community instead of confining such work to a program. They acknowledge their power and how their actions contribute to an environment in which staff members burn out or flourish. Pro-Black leaders are also unapologetic about giving their staff members the tools to succeed, including equitable living wages and leadership development resources.

It is time for the nonprofit sector to center our missions in everything we do—including how we treat and invest in staff members. It is time for us to be just as intentional with our staff members as we are with our clients and donors. We cannot expect to change our communities without first changing our internal work environments, and we cannot expect to change our work environments without our leadership teams changing the way we lead. It is our responsibility as leaders of the nonprofit sector to take up the cause of recognizing and restoring the dignity, wholeness, and humanity of every worker. Then, and only then, will we see sustainable change within our organizations and communities.

---

[21] https://ssir.org/articles/entry/the_cliff_of_unintended_consequences

II

Building Pro-Black Institutions: Narrative and Forms

What It Looks Like to Build a Pro-Black Organization

Liz Derias and Kad Smith

Always bear in mind that the people are not fighting for ideas, for the things in anyone's head. They are fighting to win material benefits, to live better and in peace, to see their lives go forward, to guarantee the future of their children. National liberation, the struggle against colonialism, the construction of peace, progress and independence are hollow words devoid of any significance unless they can be translated into a real improvement of living conditions.

—Amilcar Cabral[1]

The conversations that ensued can be found in full in Spring 2022 issue of *NPQ*.

Amilcar Cabral, Pan-African leader of the Guinea-Bissau and Cape Verde national independence struggle, wrote and spoke extensively about the need to fight for tangible, material changes for our communities. For Cabral, the wave of global independence movements by Africans and other (Western-titled) "Third World" peoples was always about returning power from imperialist and colonial forces to everyday people. Today, this aim for social change workers remains the same, if not more pronounced.

---

[1] *Return to the Source: Selected Speeches of Amilcar Cabral*, ed. African Information Service (New York: Monthly Review Press, 1973).

Our work is always to build power, not engage in ideological debates that only advance a few.

At CompassPoint (CP), we define power as the capacity (which includes will, resources, time, access, and more) to shape the outcomes of one's circumstances. Our work has been on a six-year-long antiracist path that has led to power building rather than challenging anti-Blackness or building for diversity, equity, and inclusion.[2] As an objective of our racial justice goals, we seek to grow power for our staff (and community) members who are marginalized, with a focus on Black women. In February 2019, Building Movement Project released the report *Race to Lead: Women of Color in the Nonprofit Sector*, by senior research associate Ofronama Biu, which surveyed more than 4,000 nonprofit staff members (women of color made up 32%, about 1,280 respondents).[3] It describes the all-too-familiar status quo:

Women of color described being passed over for opportunities for new jobs or promotions, often in favor of white and/or male candidates with fewer qualifications. They observed that men, particularly white men, tended to advance faster—even if they were underqualified—and were given more professional development opportunities. They wrote that directors did not see women of color as leaders and withheld projects and advancement opportunities.[4]

The report yielded three major findings: (1) racial and gender biases create barriers to advancement for women of color, (2) education and training are not enough to help women of color advance, and (3) the social landscape within nonprofit organizations can create conditions that undermine the leadership of women of color.[5] All of these issues require a shift in power in order to transform.

These findings and assertions—and more—are no surprise for BIPOC leaders in the sector; after all, organizations are a reflection of the broader white settler colonial project that drove the genocide of Indigenous peoples and the enslavement of Africans. The colonial project is premised on stripping BIPOC people of the power in their lives. Thus, our social change work must be focused on dismantling the white settler colonial project and

---

[2] Although the title of this article uses the phrase *pro-Black organization*, it could just as well be *pro-Blackness* ("What It Looks Like to Build for Pro-Blackness") or *pro-Black power* ("What It Looks Like to Build for Pro-Black Power").
[3] Ofronama Biu, *Race to Lead: Women of Color in the Nonprofit Sector* (New York: Race to Lead, Building Movement Project, February 2019).
[4] Ibid., 9.
[5] Ibid.

building power for all people oppressed by the project's subsequent systems. As a result of building power for Black people, we build power for all oppressed peoples (inside and outside our organizations); that is, when we center Black people, we uplift all people. The Haas Institute for a Fair and Inclusive Society's *Targeted Universalism* primer describes this, asserting that when those most marginalized build power to shift policy that benefits them, it has the capacity to benefit other marginalized peoples.[6]

We have experienced this truth at CP. Our former staff members set off on a journey to redefine CP as an equity and social justice organization back in 2016.[7] When we began to move past equity as a frame and introduced a more nuanced pro-Black power stance (surfaced by our former codirector Lupe Poblano), we began to see the potential of understanding and expanding power. For instance, in 2018, we examined dependent insurance coverage for our staff members, predicated on the principle of supporting the Black mothers in our organization. In 2022, CP passed a 100% dependent coverage provision for all staff members, regardless of number of dependents. When Black staff members developed an affinity group to build unity and discuss experiences of anti-Blackness within the organization, affinity groups for all staff members commenced. Affinity groups have created a critical reflective space for relationship building for participants, for white and BIPOC staff members to understand and dismantle their participation in anti-Blackness, and for staff members to be able to surface requests to the organization safely. It was our affinity group of coordinators who led the way to CP bringing all our workshops online during COVID and emerging with a how-to manual for virtual learning. These examples and many more have been at the crux of several structural, policy, and procedural changes at CP, including reimagining staff compensation and employee benefits,[8] increased program monies for Black programming (including for our Self-Care for Black Women in Leadership program, which evolved from a program funded internally to one that has so far graduated five cohorts with the support of multiple funders),[9] and hiring our first Black (woman) executive in CP's nearly 47-year history.

----

[6] John A. Powell, Stephen Menendian, and Wendy Ake, *Targeted Universalism: Policy & Practice* (Berkeley, CA: Haas Institute for a Fair and Inclusive Society, May 2019).

[7] "A Vision for Belonging," CompassPoints of View (blog), CompassPoint, April 3, 2019, compasspoint.org/blog/ vision-belonging.

[8] "Reimagining Compensation Decisions Through an Equity Panel," *CompassPoints of View* (blog), CompassPoint, December 11, 2019, compasspoint.org/blog/reimagining-compensation -decisions-through-equity-panel.

[9] "Self-Care for Black Women in Leadership Program," CompassPoint, accessed February 6, 2022, compasspoint.org/self-care-black-women-leadership-program.

The Failures of Diversity, Equity, and Inclusion (DEI)

Examples like CompassPoint's and other organizations' pro-Black efforts provide a way forward and data to help others with their power-building efforts. A good start for an organization wanting to take on pro-Black power building is to redirect one's attention away from two current popular approaches and frames: organizational anti-Blackness and diversity, equity, and inclusion (DEI). Organizations advancing the theory and praxis of building pro-Black power include Tides Advocacy, whose mission statement reminds us that "Our Focus on Justice Requires Us to Be Pro-Black Every Day";[10] Equity in the Center, which is partnering with the BIPOC Project to deliver a training titled "Building Black Power: Dismantling Anti-Blackness in Our Institutions and Movements"; and Essie Justice Group, which in 2020 took on an intersectionality lens to develop a webinar and tools titled "Black Feminist Institution Building: Employee Policies in the Age of COVID & Uprising in Defense of Black Life."[11]

The presiding concentration on confronting anti-Blackness often requires that Black staff members define, defend, and solve their own experiences of oppression within organizations. Using pro-Black power as a frame draws in white staff and staff of color to interrogate their own anti-Black bias, as well as drawing the organization into challenging the systems, processes, policies, and practices, not just interpersonal behaviors or attitudes. It also enables us to center our efforts on solutions that materially shift the conditions of Black people, instead of diagnosing whether anti-Blackness is "actually a problem" within our organizations (a dangerous phenomenon that we see all too often).

Analogously, DEI initiatives often miss the interdependence of organizational components. This is not to say that the many DEI staff members and officers who we admire, work with, and champion aren't doing work that is fundamental. It is to say that diversity, equity, and inclusion frameworks and initiatives miss the mark, because they consistently fail to clearly identify the fundamental need to shift power in an organization.

----

[10] "Leadership Transitions: Liz Derias and Shannon Ellis Are CompassPoint's Co-Directors," *CompassPoints of View* (blog), CompassPoint, July 28, 2021, compasspoint.org/blog/leadership-transitions-liz-derias-and-shannon-ellis-are-compasspoints-co-directors.

[11] "Our Focus on Justice Requires Us to Be Pro-Black Every Day," Tides Advocacy, accessed February 6, 2022, tidesadvocacy.org/news/our-focus-on-justice-requires-us-to-be-pro-black-every-day/.

In 2019, the *Harvard Business Review* published the article "Does Diversity Training Work the Way It's Supposed To?," detailing the results of their experiment to measure the effectiveness of diversity training.[12] According to *Harvard Business Review*, the results (published in the *Proceedings of the National Academy of Sciences)* found "very little evidence that diversity training affected the behavior of men or white employees overall—the two groups who typically hold the most power in organizations and are often the primary targets of these interventions."[13] We would venture to say it is indeed working as it's supposed to—to intentionally *not* shift power. DEI initiatives have ignored the centrality of power, rather heavily focusing on diversity training—among other interventions—as *the* antidote to challenge (interpersonal) anti-Blackness. Additionally, DEI staff are isolated with few resources to do more than address one issue at a time, usually focusing on interpersonal relationships between staff members wherever anti-Blackness is embedded.

We are inspired by several alternative approaches and frames to DEI. Namely, we draw from Dr. Angela Davis, who tells us, "If we do not know how to meaningfully talk about racism, our actions will move in misleading directions."[14] The work of building pro-Black power enables us to journey in the right direction to meaningfully dismantle the vestiges of white settler colonialism that produce power disparities in our organizations. We also draw from Aida Mariam Davis (Dr. Angela Davis's niece-in-law), CEO and founder of Decolonize Design, whose article "Diversity, Equity and Inclusion Have Failed. How About Belonging, Dignity and Justice Instead?" clarifies, "The DEI industrial complex came into existence as a pre-emptive defense to avoid litigation by members of protected classes, particularly under Title VII of the Civil Rights Act of 1964."[15]

Finally, we rely heavily and unequivocally on bell hooks's *Feminist Theory: From Margin to Center,* in which she asserts that in order to shift power, we must examine (1) how power has historically oppressed groups

---

[12] "Building Black Power: Dismantling Anti-Blackness in Our Institutions and Movements," Equity in the Center, accessed February 6, 2022, https://equityinthecenter.org/services/culture-trainings/building-black-power/.

[13] "Black Feminist Institution Building: Employee Policies in the Age of COVID & Uprising in Defense of Black Life," Essie Justice Group, August 14, 2020, essiejusticegroup.org/2020/08/black-feminist-institution-building-employee-policies-in-the-age-of-covid-uprising-in-defense-of-black-life/.

[14] Edward H. Chang et al., "Does Diversity Training Work the Way It's Supposed To?," *Harvard Business Review*, July 9, 2019, hbr.org/2019/07/does-diversity-training-work-the-way-its-supposed-to.

[15] See Edward H. Chang et al., "The Mixed Effects of Online Diversity Training," *Proceedings of the National Academy of Sciences* 116, no. 16 (April 16, 2019): 7778–83.

of people who are at the margins (in organizations, this is often BIPOC women and others who hold identities from traditionally oppressed communities) and (2) those who are at the center (in organizations this is often people who hold positions of authority, such as an executive director or a board member).[16] hooks advises that to shift power, we must bring people from the margins into the center. This theory is integrated into all our workshop and training offerings and has proven invaluable when starting conversations that examine power and privilege.

Interrogating Governance to Construct a Pro-Black Organization

Since 2016, CP has engaged in reexamining our entire organization to dismantle white supremacy. This has required an active and intentional redesign of every detail of CP.[17] In 2020, we stepped more deeply into this liberatory work—that is, we moved beyond equity to build a pro-Black organization. And in 2021, we realized that in order to build a pro-Black organization, we needed a more comprehensive framework. To help us continue evolving our praxis as a pro-Black organization, we developed an organizational model premised on a governance framework. Developing this model has enabled us to live into our core strategy, which is to live liberation from the inside out.[18] We build structures, cultural practices, business strategies, and approaches to organizational change that bring us and the people with whom we work closer to liberation. We try on practices from the inside so that we can practice and then share what we're learning. At the same time, we study ways in which leaders outside our practice are living into liberation, so that we can bring new learning in, creating a cycle of mutual reflection, practice, and change. We use the definition of governance from the Indigenous Governance Toolkit, which defines governance as "how people choose to collectively organize themselves to manage their own affairs, share power and responsibilities, decide for themselves what kind of society they want for their future, and implement

---

[16] Angela Y. Davis, *Freedom Is a Constant Struggle: Ferguson, Palestine, and the Foundations of a Movement* (Chicago: Haymarket Books, 2016), 88.

[17] Aida Mariam Davis, "Diversity, Equity and Inclusion Have Failed. How About Belonging, Dignity and Justice Instead?," *World Economic Forum*, February 23, 2021, weforum.org/agenda/2021/02/diversity-equity-inclusion-have-failed-belonging-dignity-justice/.

[18] bell hooks, *Feminist Theory: From Margin to Center*, 2nd ed. (Boston: South End Press, 2000).

those decisions."[19] This framework includes several interrelated components: values, principles, structure, decision-making, culture, and community engagement.

We are developing practices about values that our Black staff members hold in high regard, such as communalism, self-care, authenticity, distribution of power, transparency, and healing. These practices are our principles, and our principles shape our structure—our systems, practices, policies, and procedures. Our organization is structured in three circles that allow for the sharing of power among staff members, regardless of titles (a form we experimented with years ago, before endeavoring to build a pro-Black organization, when we explored the holacracy model).

For example, our internal resilience circle, which coordinates all things traditionally understood as "operations" and "human resources," manages our hiring processes for staff members. Equipped with our commitment to distributing power, staff members whose titles are *coordinator* or *associate director* in these circles often lead and participate in our hiring processes. Among other things, this builds confidence and a sense of ownership for all staff members. This structure directly lends itself to the democratic decision-making processes we embark on at CP, because using modified consensus on major decisions allows staff members—particularly Black staff members, who often have little to no space in society to shape their circumstances—to shape the circumstances of the organization. All of this—the values, principles, structure, and decision-making—shapes the culture of the organization, which at CP we articulate as the norms, traditions, practices, expectations, ways of being, histories of being (including ancestral knowledge), beliefs, and desires of our staff members. It also shapes how we engage with our communities. When we feel misaligned regarding any circle, we take the time to dissect why—often tracing back to our values—and construct a more aligned way forward. And we have found that when we've experienced a more aligned way forward, it's been when Black staff members are centered.

All of these components of governance, if done with the values that Black people hold at the center, can go a long way to shaping a pro-Black organization. What's additionally critical is to constantly build a foundational staff understanding of this governance approach. In fall 2021, we instituted organization-wide political education; using Cyndi Suarez's book *The Power Manual: How to Master Complex Power Dynamics*,[20]

---

[19]To read more about our journey, see "Putting Racial Justice at the Heart: How Did CompassPoint Get Here?," *CompassPoints of View* (blog), CompassPoint, March 6, 2019, compasspoint.org/blog/putting-racial-justice-heart-how-did-compasspoint-get-here.
[20]Suarez, Cyndi. *The Power Manual: How to Master Complex Power Dynamics*. Gabriola Island BC, CA: New Society Publishers, 2018.

we engaged in a five-part internal study to dissect power in our lives and our organization.[21] Fundamentally, we all now understand that ongoing political education builds power, because it builds the structural and conjunctive analysis of staff members—an essential ingredient for understanding and shaping circumstances. Indeed, political education is fundamental to building a pro-Black organization—just as fundamental as our external workshops and cohort leadership programs that aim to build power within our community of participants.

Supporting Organizations to Build Pro-Black Structures

CompassPoint designs and delivers intensive cohort leadership development programs, which bring leaders together in learning communities. These programs combine a set of core methodologies, including teaching, peer learning, coaching, and physical practice. In 2021, we launched our inaugural B.L.A.C.K. Equity Intensive to take the work we did to begin transforming CP into a pro-Black organization and share it with our community.[22] Twenty-seven participants, organized into nine teams of three, met online for six sessions between February and October 2021. We started with the premise that to catalyze change in an organization, it's important to have multiple people pushing from within. We aimed to build community, explore equitable structures, ground in a pro-Black political stance, and build agency, all while stepping into our power. We used principles of popular education to create learning experiences that uphold self-determination, democratize participation, and engage everyone as both a teacher and a learner—all fundamental components to building pro-Black power. Popular education, a pedagogical approach to teaching and learning developed by educator Dr. Paulo Freire, aims to transform society by centering the experiences of everyday people.[23]

A few key tenets embedded in this pilot program will continue to be central to our power-building practice and continued programs and our cohort leadership programs. The tenets are the following:

....

[21] "Our Vision and Values," CompassPoint, accessed February 6, 2022, compasspoint.org/vision-and-values.

[22] "1.0 Understanding Governance: 1.0.1 What Is Governance?," Indigenous Governance Toolkit, accessed February 6, 2022, toolkit.aigi.com.au/toolkit/1-0-understanding-governance.

[23] For more on the holacracy model, see "Holacracy," accessed February 7, 2022, holacracy.org/explore.

- Build intentional community among people who are working to dismantle white supremacy in their organizations. Meaningful racial justice work is deeply challenging and can be sustained most effectively when we come together and support each other as whole people—hearts, minds, spirits, bodies—who are actively in the struggle to create pro-Black organizations.

- Ground in the power of small teams. This program is designed with an understanding that small teams of deeply connected and aligned people can effect changes in the larger systems around them. The program relies on the power of small teams with diverse perspectives (in both social positioning and organizational hierarchy) working together to more deeply understand the nuances of how their specific organization perpetuates racism, and design equitable cultures, structures, and practices in response.

- Amplify existing momentum. All racial justice work has to start somewhere, and the systems of inequalities in our sector are both broad and deep enough that a wide variety of organizational interventions and supports are likely needed to shift the full system. At CP, we are currently focusing our efforts with teams and organizations where there is already explicit racial justice work under way—linking with folks who are not at the beginning of this journey but rather already on their way.

- Learn across organizations. Racial justice work requires multiple layers of learning—within ourselves, among our teams, and within our organizations. Our approach supports these and offers an additional layer—learning from people doing this work in other organizational contexts—that can sometimes help catalyze areas where a team may be stuck or help calibrate a team's understanding of where they are on their racial justice journey and how their particular struggles are both common and unique. This learning can be deepest and most impactful when it unfolds in an intentional community in which people have been invited to be whole, vulnerable, honest, and openhearted. Sharing directly and deeply about our experiences cross-organizationally opens up a deeper level of learning than does just reading others' stories or case studies.

- Challenge traditional dependence on expertise. We are active co-learners in our programs, advancing our own efforts to deepen racial equity at CP through our facilitation of and participation in this learning community. The CP facilitation team serves as another, 10th team in the cohort, as we are actively working on our own internal efforts to continue to grow racially just structures and practices while designing and facilitating this learning community. Given this, in addition to the processes named previously, we draw from our direct experiences with this work to offer inspiration, support, and practical tools to guide small teams in seeding new possibilities for pro-Black structures and practices in their organizations.

***

Building pro-Black organizations is a necessity if we are to achieve our goals of liberatory transformation. It requires us to depart from solely challenging anti-Blackness or engaging in DEI efforts that don't seek to shift power. Inspired by our theoreticians, fellow organizations in the field, and a community of participants, we are committed at CP to resourcing the time and efforts needed to build pro-Black power in our organization and with our partners and community of participants. We aim to grow and scale the impact of this work, increase its accessibility, and share learnings and tools with more organizations and with the sector more broadly. We invite our community, including the organizations we serve, partners in the field, and philanthropic partners, to join us on this journey.

To Build a Public Safety That Protects Black Women and Girls, Money Isn't the Only Resource We Need

Shanelle Matthews

This spring marks two years since Louisville, Kentucky, police killed 26-year-old Breonna Taylor. Officers shot 36 rounds of ammunition into her home in a bungled raid serving a "no-knock" warrant, realizing later that the suspect they were looking for was already in custody. The police who shot her could have intervened to save her, but they didn't; in Kentucky, as in most states, police are not obligated to deliver medical aid to people they've shot or maimed.[1]

In concurrence with the lynching of George Floyd, Breonna's death sparked nationwide uprisings and prompted vigorous debates about the police's role in public safety. Coalitions like the Movement for Black Lives (M4BL) and organizations like Black Visions brought attention to abolitionist arguments that the only way to prevent deaths such as Mr. Floyd's and Ms. Taylor's is to take power and funding from police and reinvest those resources into other public safety measures.

Note: This chapter was written on June 29, 2022.

[1] https://www.themarshallproject.org/2020/12/15/cops-could-use-first-aid-to-save-lives-many-never-try

Breonna's shooting was unusual in that, unlike most police shootings of Black women, it garnered significant media attention—although some argue[2] only after the avalanche of news about the death of Mr. Floyd.

Police in America have killed 366 people so far this year—roughly three people a day according to data from Mapping Violence,[3] a nonprofit research group. Their victims include Black women, amongst them Tracy Gaeta, a 54-year-old grandmother who was shot to death on February 22 in Stockton, California. Ms. Gaeta backed her car into police officer Kyle Ribera's police vehicle. In return, Ribera fired 30 rounds into Ms. Gaeta's car, killing her. Although Ms. Gaeta was unarmed, Ribera was unrelenting, stopping briefly to load more bullets into the chamber of his gun then continuing to unload his weapon.

Black female victims of police violence also include children like 16-year-old Ma'Khia Bryant, who was killed last spring in her hometown of Columbus, Ohio, after police officer Nicholas Reardon was dispatched to quell a fight among foster youth. Within seconds of arriving, Reardon shot Ma'Khia. As police often do to Black people, Reardon justified his use of excessive force by attributing superhuman attributes to the adolescent; he claimed that Ma'Khia appeared bigger than him so he didn't think mace or other non-lethal approaches would be effective.[4]

This kind of excessive force by police isn't the exception when it comes to deadly encounters with Black women. It's the norm. Yet, while media attention of police shootings of Black men has increased dramatically thanks to the Black Lives Matter movement, the grievous violence Black women suffer at the hands of police continues to attract little to no media attention.

Rather, at present, Black boys and men remain the face of police brutality and state-sanctioned violence in the United States. Their deaths and the organizing that follows have given rise to powerful mass uprisings for racial justice and Black liberation. Oscar Grant, Trayvon Martin, Philando Castile, Alton Sterling, Eric Garner, Mike Brown, George Floyd—we know their names. This is important. Black women and girls deserve the same recognition, rage, and people-powered response. As professor Brittany Cooper smartly asks, "Why does it remain so difficult for outrage over the killing of Black women to be the tipping point for national protests challenging state violence?"[5]

---

[2] https://www.nytimes.com/2020/06/04/us/breonna-taylor-black-lives-matter-women.html

[3] https://mappingpoliceviolence.org/

[4] https://www.npr.org/2022/03/12/1086283433/police-officer-cleared-makhia-bryant-shooting; https://www.theguardian.com/us-news/2014/nov/25/darren-wilson-testimony-ferguson-michael-brown

[5] https://time.com/5847970/police-brutality-black-women-girls/

The relative invisibility of Black women's experiences of policing in the United States is a product of Black women's social positionality: Black women sit at the intersection of patriarchal misogyny and anti-Black racism. Patriarchy deploys ideological and physical violence to objectify and repress women in the interest of male dominance, denying women's fundamental humanity. Anti-Black racism, an essential part of the racial capitalism that structures US (and global) society, involves, as a professor of African American studies Dr. kihana miraya ross explains, "society's inability to recognize our humanity—the disdain, disregard and disgust for our existence."

Existing at this intersection means Black women are doubly disregarded, and they are plagued by both hypervisibility—the experience of being overly scrutinized when our bodies are stereotyped or commodified—and invisibility—where violence against us is ignored or disregarded. This dualism makes talking about state-sanctioned violence toward Black women and girls hard, and it makes communicating about and organizing for a world that keeps us safe even harder.

The fight to defund the police and reimagine public safety is part of a larger, long-term social justice strategy to divest structural resources—that is, tangible recourses such as money, member networks, and organizational power[6]—from harmful institutions such as the police, and to reinvest those resources into common-sense approaches[7] to public safety. However, money isn't the only currency organizers must rest from the powerful. They must also take ownership of symbolic resources, which shape how we value—or fail to value—the lives of Black women and girls, including transgender women and girls.

Such resources include "words, signs, images, music and even bodies [which] shape our perceptions of reality and invite us to act accordingly."[8] Social movements use these symbolic resources to expose patterns, cultivate compassion, recruit members, inspire collective action, and build public will for sweeping social changes. The hashtag #BlackLivesMatter is a symbolic resource, as was Emmitt Till's open casket. Till's mother, Mamie, believed people should see what is often concealed—the ghoulish manifestations of white supremacy.

As we lay the foundation for new public safety infrastructure in the United States, the control and distribution of symbolic resources,

---

[6]Williams, R. H. (1995). Constructing the public good: Social movements and cultural resources, *Social Problems, 42*(1), 122–124.
[7]https://whitebirdclinic.org/cahoots-faq/
[8]Morris III, E. C., and Browne, H. S. (2013). *Readings on the rhetoric of social protest.* Strata Publishing.

including narratives, can be deployed to make the invisible visible. For Black women and girls that means exposing the underlying network of intersectional, systemic narratives, stereotypes, and myths that result in our hypervisibility, invisibility, and dehumanization in life and death.

Narratives as Symbolic Resources

Narratives are collections of stories, refined over time, through which we make meaning of the world. Narratives and stories differ. To quote the Narrative Initiative, "What tiles are to mosaics, stories are to narratives. The relationship is symbiotic; stories bring narratives to life by making them relatable and accessible, while narratives infuse stories with deeper meaning."[9] Such meaning frames our worldview and understandings of our daily experiences, including our relationships with others, people's behaviors, social structures, and global events. In sum, narratives are the foundation of our ideologies and belief systems, which shape our actions—and they're powerful.

In all societies, multiple, competing narratives circulate, but some narratives are hegemonic—or dominant—centering the desires, beliefs, and values of dominant groups. Hegemonic narratives deploy science, law, and cultural difference to devalue and dehumanize certain groups of people, normalizing inequality and exploitation. These beliefs are then reinforced in social institutions, including churches, schools, and the media, and in interpersonal interactions.

Throughout US history, hegemonic narratives have portrayed Black people as inherently inferior, deviant, and shiftless. One such narrative appeared in the widely circulated 1965 Moynihan Report.[10] Rather than focus on systemic employment and wage discrimination, the report argued that single-parented households and the "breakdown of the nuclear family" led to a "culture of poverty" in Black communities. This narrative of Black pathology—singling out Black people as the source of our own, and the country's, social problems—has old roots and persists today.

Anti-Black narratives are gendered, meaning they target Black women and men in different ways. In particular, they have consistently stereotyped Black women as sexual deviants and unfit mothers. Such narratives have accumulated power over time and hold sway over our capacity to

---

[9] https://narrativeinitiative.org/
[10] https://www.dissentmagazine.org/article/moynihan-report-resurrected-daniel-geary-black-power

empathize with Black women and our perceptions of who does and does not deserve to benefit from public safety measures.

Today, for example, more than a third[11] of Black women experience some form of sexual violence in their lifetime. Yet according to a Brandeis University study, prosecutors file charges against just 34% of attacks reported by Black woman, compared to 75% of attacks reported by white women.[12] According to research by the African American Policy Forum, the police are often perpetrators of sexual violence against Black women.[13] Former Oklahoma City police officer Daniel Holtzclaw, for example, raped and/or sexually assaulted at least 13 Black women over several years.

In a future where public safety includes the welfare of Black women and girls, we have to interrogate how narratives of sex and race determine who is considered part of the public and from what and whom they need to be kept safe. As NYU history professor Jennifer Morgan, author of *Reckoning with Slavery: Gender, Kinship, and Capitalism in the Early Black Atlantic,* writes, "you need so many lenses to see all the different ways in which we are still grappling with the legacies of hereditary racial slavery in this country that you can't just look at it from one perspective. You're going to miss so many other ways that this is being made manifest."

Oppressive Narratives That Shape Perceptions of Black Women in the United States

The narratives circulating about Black women in America contribute in essential ways to the hypervisibility and scrutiny Black women experience when alive, and to the erasure and invisibility Black women like Ms. Taylor, Ms. Gaeta, and Ma'Khia share in death. As Professor Cooper writes about police killings of Black women, "in a world where the pains and traumas that Black women and girls experience as a consequence of both racism and sexism remain structurally invisible and impermeable to broad empathy, these killings recede from the foreground quietly."[14]

---

[11] chrome-extension://efaidnbmnnnibpcajpcglclefindmkaj/https:/ujimacommunity.org/wp-content/uploads/2018/12/Ujima-Womens-Violence-Stats-v7.4-1.pdf

[12] https://www.brandeis.edu/projects/fse/slavery/united-states/slav-us-articles/kennedy-full.pdf

[13] https://scholarship.law.columbia.edu/faculty_scholarship/3226/

[14] https://time.com/5847970/police-brutality-black-women-girls/

The narratives that shape how we value—or fail to value—Black women and girls have their roots in slavery; over time, they have accumulated immense power. To justify slavery, European and white settler experts exploited science's growing influence, developing theories that argued that Black people were the result of an evolutionary diversion. According to such scientific racism, while white people evolved thanks to their environments and inherent biological traits, Black people remained evolutionary stagnant or regressed, resulting in a host of inferior qualities, including laziness, stupidity, hypersexuality, and deviancy. In other words, Black people were more akin to beasts of burden than people, and it was justifiable if not laudable to treat them as commodities from which enslavers extracted value.

The slave plantation was essential to the national and global economy, and it took shape within a patriarchal society that reduced women of all races to men's sexual objects and breeding machines. While white women's sexuality was policed to ensure the purity of the white race, Black women's reproduction became a brutal business enterprise designed to perpetuate the institution of slavery. Stated otherwise, the first role of Black women in US society was not that of a mother, let alone citizen, but as producers of an enslaved labor force.

While white women bore responsibility for transferring superior whiteness to their offspring, Black women bore responsibility for passing down inferior Blackness. As professor of law, sociology, and civil rights, Dorothy E. Roberts, writes in her classic book, *Killing the Black Body*,

> *For three centuries, black mothers have been thought to pass down to their offspring the traits that marked them as inferior to any white person. Along with this biological impairment, it is believed that black mothers transfer a deviant lifestyle to the children that dooms each succeeding generation to a life of poverty, delinquency, and despair. . . . A popular mythology that portrays black women as unfit to be mothers has left a lasting impression on the American psyche.*

In other words, according to hegemonic narratives, Black people were to blame for their own problems, and this blame resided in particular with Black women, the producers of Black children.

After emancipation, this myth that Black women were—by virtue of their reproductive power—the source of Black inferiority continued to permeate US culture, and stories of bad Black mothers were ubiquitous. Eventually, these stories gave rise to the welfare queen narrative, according to which Black women took advantage of social programs, misappropriating the tax dollars of hardworking Americans. Given that anti-Black racism barred many Black women from accessing public services, this narrative, which had no factual foundation, rendered Black female welfare recipients hypervisible. It also burdened Black women with the stereotype of the welfare queen who, as the Frameworks Institute writes, "is portrayed as a pathologically greedy, lawbreaking, deviant, lazy, promiscuous, and 'Cadillac-driving' Black woman who cheats the system and defrauds the American people."[15]

Black People and the Police

For much of US history, law enforcement meant implementing laws designed to subjugate Black people and uphold white supremacy. The first slave patrols, created in the Carolinas in the 1700s, were made up of volunteer white men who hunted enslaved escapees and squashed rebellions led by enslaved people to free themselves. Such policing continued in Southern states through the end of the Civil War.

Even after emancipation, Southern plantation capitalism relied on cheap Black labor. So, although the 13th Amendment technically freed some four million Black people in 1865, Southern states swiftly implemented Black Codes—a combination of harsh vagrancy and contract laws—to keep Black people indentured. The police were responsible for enforcing these laws.

In 1868, the 14th Amendment was ratified, and Black Codes were abolished, theoretically granting Black people equal protection. However, Jim Crow laws that legalized racial segregation quickly took their place. Black people were forbidden from living in predominately white neighborhoods. Theaters, restaurants, pools, and even water fountains were segregated. Black people who violated these rules risked violent interactions with police, resulting in unjust arrests, beatings, or death.

As Jim Crow evolved so too did the violent and lethal relationship between police and Black women. During slavery, hegemonic constructions of Black womanhood invisibilized Black women's humanity, propagating stories that justified our rape and forced reproduction. Such stories alleged that Black women were "easy" and responded eagerly toward any sexual advance. During Jim Crow, the stereotype of the promiscuous Black woman converged with growing anxieties that promiscuous

---

[15] https://www.frameworksinstitute.org/publication/talking-about-poverty-narratives-counter-narratives-and-telling-effective-stories/

women destroyed families and communities. Increasingly, cities passed laws against public disorder, including vagrancy and prostitution. In her book, *The Streets Belong to Us: Sex, Race, and Police Power from Segregation to Gentrification*, Anne Gray Fischer argues that the police who enforced these laws targeted Black women, whom they viewed as both sexually deviant and likely to produce "a new generation of criminals." According to Fischer, sexual policing—"the targeting and legal control of people's bodies and presumed sexual activities"[16]—disproportionately affected Black women, as did the "mass misdemeanor policing" that followed in its wake.[17] In other words, by virtue of racist patriarchal narratives, Black women were hypervisible to police, with often violent results.

As the cases of Breonna Taylor, Tracy Gaeta, and Ma'Khia Bryant reveal, today, when Black women interface with police, the outcomes are still violent—and sometimes fatal. According to reporting from the *Washington Post*, Black people are killed by police at more than twice the rate of white Americans, and Black women are fatally shot at rates higher than women of all other races. Since 2015, police have fatally shot 247 women. Of these women, 48 were Black, accounting for 20% of the women killed.[18]

Though pervasive, however, police violence against Black women—and to a more severe degree against Black transgender women—remains structurally hidden. This means that when you look at the most obvious places these stories and experiences should be documented and contended with—in the media and policy documents—they're absent. This invisibility is a product of long-standing narratives that rupture empathy and compassion with Black women and exclude Black women from the public.

A Framework for Making the Visible Invisible

Narratives are part of the activist's toolbox of symbolic resources, and indeed, the Black Lives Matter movement has changed many of the narratives about Black people, crime, and policing. The movement has embraced a framework of narrative power, whereby social movements

---

[16]Fischer, A. G. (2022). *The streets belong to us: Sex, race, and police power from segregation to gentrification.* University of North Carolina Press.
[17]https://www.theatlantic.com/books/archive/2022/04/police-sexual-policing-streets-belong-to-us-review/629611/
[18]https://www.washingtonpost.com/graphics/2020/investigations/police-shootings-women/

take advantage of political opportunities to construct counter narratives that disrupt hegemonic thinking and expand collective perceptions of what is socially, economically, and politically possible. Narrative power goes beyond a cursory understanding of a problem, using symbolic resources—including ethical storytelling—to radically shape the rules and norms by which we live.

This type of analysis has its roots in Black feminism. A framework that insists on the simultaneous eradication of racism, sexism, and classism, Black feminism articulates Black women's experiences where the feminist and civil rights movements failed to do so, making the invisible visible through intersectional analysis and storytelling. Indeed, Black feminism inspired intersectionality, the recognition that many of us hold concurrent identities that affect our lives. Today, Black feminism continues to expand as a framework, as organizers and thinkers like Charlene Carruthers build on it by making explicit the influence of queerness in the politic of reimaging society away from patriarchal sexism and anti-Black racism.[19]

The Black Lives Matter movement has followed in the footsteps of Black feminists. In an interview[20] with Jacobin Radio, historian Donna Murch[21] argues that through the use of symbolic resources, the Black Lives Matter movement delegitimized narratives of Black pathology that were used to justify the wars on poverty and drugs and the militarization of police in Black communities. In turn, the movement put the blame for Black suffering where it belongs—on the state—recasting Black pathology as "state-sanctioned violence," which includes "any forms of harm produced, promoted, and/or institutionalized by the state to the detriment of Black women, their families and communities."

Through decentralized organizing, policy making, electoral justice, a narrative power strategy, and other tactics, M4BL—an ecosystem of Black-led organizations—is using symbolic resources to reframe how we understand Black suffering in America and offer a vision[22] for how to reduce it.

Increasingly, organizers and scholars are also intervening into the erasure of Black women and girls. One such intervention is the #SayHer-Name campaign launched by the African American Policy Forum in 2014.

---

[19] Carruthers, C. A. (2019). *Unapologetic: A Black, queer, and feminist mandate for radical movements*. Beacon Press.

[20] https://podcasts.google.com/feed/aHR0cHM6Ly9mZWVkcy5hY2FzdC5jb20vcHVibGljL3 3Nob3dzLzYxOWJlNWMwNzA1MTM4MDAxYjljODQ3OQ/episode/NjI2N2YzNWVkOWMy YmMwMDE1M2ViMmM5?hl=en&ved=2ahUKEwino8nO67T3AhWclIkEHdEcDIMQieUEe gQIAhAI&ep=6

[21] https://history.rutgers.edu/faculty-directory/249-murch-donna

[22] https://m4bl.org/policy-platforms/

#SayHerName is a symbolic resource that provides communities routinely excluded by mainstream media institutions with a platform from which to speak our truths and replace narratives that reflect a single subjective angle with those that include our voices, stories, and lived experiences.

BYP100s She Safe We Safe[23] is another campaign to put an end to violence against women, as well as gender non-conforming people. She Safe We Safe uses counternarratives to call for the reallocation of funding from the police to community-run programs that address gender-based violence in Black communities. In 2021, in collaboration with Times Up, me too international launched[24] We, As Ourselves, a narrative power campaign to make visible the stories of Black survivors of sexual violence and to reshape the narrative about sexual violence and its impact on Black survivors. These are critical interventions by Black-led organizations—and we need more.

The humanity, freedom, and self-determination of Black women and girls are directly connected to the symbolic resources and power we have to define the problems we are working to solve. Who we collectively agree has the power to define both these problems and their solutions matters.

---

[23] https://www.shesafewesafe.org/
[24] https://www.glamour.com/story/the-new-initiative-uplifting-the-stories-of-black-survivors-of-sexual-violence

Combatting Disinformation and Misinformation

A Struggle for Democracy and Racial Justice

Kitana Ananda

In 2022, *NPQ* hosted a dynamic conversation about a critical problem of our time: the role of disinformation and misinformation in civil society.

The webinar, "Combating Disinformation and Misinformation in 21st-Century Social Movements," centered on the nature of disinformation and misinformation, their impact on democratic struggles for justice, and strategies for fighting false narratives in a complex information ecosystem.

The event was organized by Shanelle Matthews, the Movement for Black Lives' director of communications and founder of the Radical Communicators Network. Matthews drew on her knowledge of radical social movements and her wealth of experience as a communicator and organizer to convene a thoughtful panel on a topic that couldn't be more relevant given everything happening in the United States in 2022: the January 6th hearings and investigation into last year's failed insurrection, voter suppression ahead of upcoming midterm elections, a spate of mass shootings, the coronavirus pandemic, inflation's impact on people's everyday lives, and talk of a looming recession.

A rich and insightful conversation ensued among the panelists, threading together several urgent issues for leftist and progressive social movements: the growth of white supremacist movements in the United States and, with them, anti-Black violence, anti-Semitic conspiracy narratives, anti-trans legislation and rhetoric, attacks on abortion rights and reproductive justice, the scapegoating of immigrant workers, and so much more.

Framing the Problem

The problem of disinformation can feel vast and overwhelming. Matthews began by acknowledging this, noting that she was eager to learn from the panelists and share best practices.

The conversation then moved to an overview of disinformation's and misinformation's various forms, which can include everything from viral misinformation to deep fakes, conspiracy theories, and state-sanctioned propaganda. These false narratives generate political and social conflict, as Matthews pointed out: "One of the aims of the contemporary disinformation movement is the erosion of democratic ideals. And one of the aims of the progressive and leftist social movement is to realize democratic and socially democratic ideals, so we are at odds."

Matthews invited a specialist in the field, Jacqueline Mason, the director of programs at Media Democracy Fund, to explain the difference between disinformation and misinformation before diving into how they affect social movements and democracy.

Misinformation, according to Mason, is "false content, but the person sharing doesn't realize the content is false or misleading." She provided an example of this: false information about cures and remedies for COVID-19 pre-vaccine distribution. The people who shared this misinformation on social media were trying to help themselves and others. By contrast, she defined disinformation as "content that is intentionally false and designed to cause harm within communities." Often spread to make money or for political gain, disinformation creates chaos within an information ecosystem.

The lines get blurred, however: because of the way that content is rapidly disseminated and shared—in traditional media and social media—disinformation can quickly turn into misinformation shared by well-meaning people. Although the distinction between disinformation and misinformation rests on the political intentions of those who are sharing false content, they both result in significant harm.

Online Disinformation's Racist Impact

On this point, Mason noted that misinformation and disinformation have disproportionate effects on communities of color.

First, the media often frames people of color as being more susceptible to misinformation—whether through targeting or being more prone to believing it—but she says this is "an extreme falsehood." Given the history of racial injustice in US medicine, Mason said, "Black, Latinx, and Indigenous communities have legitimate reasons to be skeptical of information given the legacy of historical traumas we faced in our communities related to vaccines and civic participation." That trauma is compounded by ongoing medical racism: Mason cited examples of people who were turned away from the hospital during the pandemic and the death of Dr. Susan Moore, a Black medical doctor who cared for COVID patients but was denied treatment and died.

Combatting misinformation requires trust. Mason described how the Disinformation Defense League—a network of organizations dedicated to fighting disinformation that affects communities of color—develops trusted sources by working with people who are grounded in community spaces, like barbershops and churches, and training them in best practices for narrative change on issues like voting and healthcare.

Then, Mason zeroed in on a particularly dangerous form of disinformation identified by information experts and academics. "Online racialized disinformation" is false content about racial justice issues that is shared online and designed "to deceive or manipulate the public for the purpose of achieving profit, political gain, and/or sustaining white supremacy." Its proponents wield many different tactics—including incitements to hate, stereotypes, wedge issues, harassment, and infiltrating groups—to undermine democratic institutions and movements for social justice. Noting how bots were used to impersonate Black people online ahead of the 2016 US presidential election, Mason said, "Online racialized disinformation not only creates and reinforces inequalities; it also consolidates power among politicians, wealthy individuals, and media and technology companies."

Old Narratives, New Tactics

The discussion continued with Matthews tracing the ways in which the US government used disinformation in the 20th century to delegitimize radical social movements, beginning with the Federal Bureau of Investigation's (FBI) "radical division," created after World War I for counterintelligence and investigations used to dismantle the Communist Party, to 50 years later, when the FBI used anonymous mailings to create and exploit conflicts among Black liberation organizations in the late 1960s—ultimately leading to the violent deaths of Black Panther Party members.

Much of that same strategy and infrastructure has continued to be used in the 21st century, Matthews noted. Of the FBI's counterterrorism unit's designation of the Black Lives Matter activists as "Black Identity Extremists," she said, "They used acts of violence that were wholly unrelated to BLM to justify targeting Black dissident voices. And their goal, broadly, was to categorize Black activists as threats to national security, justifying an intensification of government surveillance, domination, and punishment."

Tackling disinformation today requires nuanced political analysis and strategic communication because "the use of propaganda to delegitimize social movements is not a new tactic, but we're living in different times and under different conditions."

Although disinformation is not new, the scale of the problem has grown with the rapid spread of digital communication technologies over the past three decades—and it's become especially apparent in the past 10 years.

As a result, Black liberation movements are contending with new forms of disinformation in the 21st century. Matthews says, for example, that "Russian operatives were working overtime to stir discord related to America's long standing racial divides by infiltrating online communities of the Black Lives Matter movement and, even to a more severe degree, the online groups frequented by ordinary people."

Still, newer forms of disinformation continue to use an "obstinate and ubiquitous" element of mis- and disinformation: racist, homophobic, sexist, and transphobic tropes that "dehumanize and justify oppression, violence, and social exclusion."

The Rise of Anti-Trans Disinformation

The next speaker extended the discussion of disinformation tropes by focusing on sexuality and gender. Kris Hayashi, executive director of the Transgender Law Center—the largest national trans-led organization in the United States—discussed how the resurfacing of old homophobic and transphobic tropes in public discourse affects today's trans liberation movement.

Hayashi connected the fight for trans liberation to society's broader failures. While the coronavirus pandemic, climate change, and the rise of white supremacist and anti-democratic forces all reveal the failure to value people and their humanity, trans communities were already struggling to survive and have their basic needs met while facing high rates of discrimination and violence.

The growing visibility of trans people in the past decade has, in fact, been accompanied by increased anti-trans violence. The details Hayashi provided were sobering: "Every year for the last few years has been the most reported murders of trans people in the US, of which the majority are Black trans women and femmes." The bombardment of anti-trans rhetoric and legislation also has disturbing psychological consequences for trans children and their families and trans people more broadly—especially for a community that already faces high rates of suicide and other mental health conditions. Hayashi said that trans leaders in Texas have already observed an increase in suicides that can be pinpointed to the state's criminalization of gender-affirming care. Such overt antipathy to trans and queer people has emboldened hate groups, including white nationalists who attacked drag queen story hours at Pride celebrations last month.

This is not a question of individual bias; it's a backlash organized at the state level. Hayashi described how the conservative right mobilized two disinformation narratives to promote anti-trans legislation and policies more than a decade ago.

In the first example, anti-trans activists and legislators ramped up their efforts in 2014–2015 with so-called bathroom bills in states like North Carolina, creating a moral panic by presenting images of men in girls' bathrooms. These images invoked an old homophobic trope, now updated for 21st-century transphobia: trans women as potential sexual predators or "groomers"—a term that refers to "someone who builds a relationship of trust and emotional connection with a child or young person so that they can manipulate, exploit, and abuse them." In anti-trans rhetoric, this false narrative frames parents, teachers, and "anyone who cares for, supports, loves a trans child, as being a groomer."

The second example is a newer disinformation narrative emerging about trans participation in competitive sports. It posits that trans girls and trans women have an unfair advantage in girls' and women's sports. Whether the battlefield is women's bathrooms or sports, anti-trans narratives and their claims rely on essentialist notions of gender to falsely assert that "trans women are men, that trans women are not women."

After Trump was elected, Hayashi recalled, the right-wing attack on trans people moved to the federal level. The administration rolled back the few rights and protections available to trans people in an attempt "to deny our humanity and ultimately to deny our very existence, as they did for so many communities" at that time. But with a new Democratic administration, these attacks have moved back to the states. Hayashi explains that the amount of legislation is unprecedented: in the past year alone, 33 states advanced 150 anti-trans bills—seven times the number of bills introduced at the height of the "bathroom bills" panic. The proposed bills—and those that have passed—range from those that deny gender-affirming care to trans children and youth, to bans on trans participation in women's sports, to prohibitions on naming the existence of queer and trans people in schools, as with Florida's so-called Don't Say Gay bill.

The Mainstreaming of White Supremacist Ideology

Matthews noted another false narrative, the great replacement theory, "a racist and xenophobic, often anti-Semitic conspiracy narrative that falsely asserts that there is an active and ongoing covert effort to replace white populations in current white majority cities with people of color through either immigration or reduction of birth rates for white women." Past iterations of this narrative have led to forced sterilization, racial quota systems, and restrictive federal immigration laws. And it's been used more recently to justify mass anti-Black violence: the Buffalo shooter was an obsessive online proponent of replacement theory.

Joseph Phelan, executive director of Reframe, spoke about the impact of this white supremacist propaganda on leftist and progressive social movements.

Modeling one strategy for combatting disinformation, he began with a story about the political trajectory of a former mentor. As an unpaid organizer activist and self-described "working-class kid from the suburbs of New York City," Phelan worked in carpentry and construction to pay the bills. His mentor was an older white man, and as their conversations and relationship deepened, Phelan encouraged his mentor to take greater action to fight white supremacy; this included marching with a coalition of people against the war in Iraq in the early 2000s and facing down the police, engaging other white people in conversations about racism, and at a local level, learning to speak Spanish and employing day laborers at more equitable wages.

Over the years, however, as Phelan became a nonprofit professional and stopped making cabinets, he and his mentor saw less of one another. They grew apart, and his mentor's views shifted further and further to the right. Considering why this happened, Phelan explained that the (re) emergence of right-wing narratives—like replacement theory and the scapegoating of immigrants and women—is appealing to working-class white men like his former mentor because they tell him that "his failures are not his." The interlinking of these false narratives, he argued, is how white supremacist ideology gets mainstreamed.

In telling this story, Phelan emphasized the importance of organizing, which he characterized as "contesting for power at the individual and group level." The contest for power is a struggle over meaning, which means that "Organizing is going to be the best defense and offense," as it's "the construction of authentic relationships where we share worldviews."

Noting that delegitimizing dominant narratives is core to building narrative power, Matthews raised important questions about the gap between understanding the problem of disinformation narratives and taking concrete actions to undermine such narratives' legitimacy: is the right information getting to the people it needs to reach? How do we communicate with mass engagement in mind?

Reframing False Narratives

Turning to these questions, the next speaker discussed the importance of reframing false narratives. Sabrina Joy Stevens, an expert in using values-driven narrative techniques, discussed how to help organizers do a better job of spreading information and narratives that neutralize misinformation and disinformation.

Despite growing awareness of the power of stories and increased boldness in telling them, many people assume that "truth will cancel out misinformation." On the challenge of persuading those "who are trying to beat back the disinformation monster with their fact club," Stevens reiterates that "it doesn't work the way people want it to work." Continuing to make the point, she said, "We need to be able to situate those facts, those statistics, within the context of stories that actually help people understand things in human scale terms."

Stevens explained why this is important. "When we're constantly kind of trying to push back against the provocations of people who are spreading false information, that often puts us in the position of actually amplifying the very information we're trying to help people understand the truth about." Instead of reacting to disinformation designed to undermine civil society, Stevens encouraged participants to "share things in our own terms according to our own values." Instead of constantly debating facts and trying to change people's minds, the goal is to think about how, through conversations with the people around us, we can "uphold narratives that are going to help people find, claim, [and] use their power well." By doing this, Stevens said, movement communications can do "double duty," neutralizing disinformation while moving a progressive agenda forward and building the world we want to see.

How to Combat Disinformation

Given the trap of reinforcing false narratives by repeating them, is it ever appropriate to correct disinformation and its spread as misinformation?

The question, as it turns out, is not whether to correct it, but how this is done. Stevens identified "three As" for effective messaging: "Make sure your content is accurate, actionable, and aspirational. If you're hitting those three things every single time you're communicating, chances are you're also not doing the things that are going to uphold mis- and disinformation." She encouraged movement communicators and organizers to pause and reflect when someone repeats bad information. Paying attention to what's missing from a narrative enables us to "re-present what we want to present in a way that replaces instead of repeats the misinformation."

Wrapping up, Matthews asked each of the panelists for three things they would want to say to movement workers, academics, and others about combating disinformation. The panelists reiterated key points from the discussion, with Mason identifying three key interventions: building networks that plug people into ongoing efforts to combat disinformation through narrative analysis and solution building; holding Big Tech accountable through advocacy and legislation to advance a racially equitable digital society; and diversifying media, tech, and academic institutions that are working on these issues to center the analyses and needs of affected communities.

The Q&A period, which was facilitated by *NPQ's* editor in chief, Cyndi Suarez, revealed the audience's overwhelming interest in learning how to have conversations about disinformation. The questions ranged from talking about disinformation in a personal way, to teaching college students how to avoid misinformation and disinformation in social research, to effective methods for communicating outside one's own circle, to facilitating discussions in group spaces and understanding how infiltrators use technology to spread disinformation that targets individuals and groups online.

The discussion also reiterated the importance of understanding the power dynamics behind disinformation's corrosive impact on civil society. Stevens responded to an audience question that asked the panelists to speak to the claim that "disinformation is thriving across the political spectrum" by picking up Phelan's point about disinformation's uneven playing field. She clarified that, while there is a problem across the board, "we're all impacted by it differently," as groups with short-term interests in profit and political power deliberately mislead people "to basically deprive us of the ability to have good faith conversations across disagreement and difference."

Despite the magnitude of the challenges of fighting disinformation, the conversation concluded on a more hopeful note. Mason urged people to focus on creating scalable solutions. Hayashi encouraged participants to check out the work of trans organizations and the "bold and beautiful and powerful ways that we are organizing, that we are telling our stories, that we are creating our vision." Picking up on this note, Phelan reminded the audience that, at the end of another Pride month, "What we can learn from the queer liberation movement is celebration and love and joy in the face of extinction. And finding connection and community that allows for the creation in real time of something different than [what] currently exists." Stevens echoed this sense of possibility as she discussed the importance of building relationships and shared trust: "There is so much power in us coming together and sharing these really accurate, aspirational, actionable stories of what we can do."

Energized by the conversation, Matthews reminded everyone that reclaiming narrative power doesn't happen by itself. To combat disinformation, "we have to fight to give people the information they need to be free."

Forms

A New Theory of Power

Cyndi Suarez

You've probably noticed that social change practitioners often repli-
cate the structures they, or we, seek to oppose. One of the reasons
I wrote *The Power Manual* is that I often couldn't tell the difference
between my activist peers and the people they were organizing against.
Oh, sure, we had different goals and maybe even different values, but we
used the same structures and were surprised that we often unwittingly re-
created the same challenges.

I recall a young woman of color who contacted me a few years ago.
She was hired by an organization that had undergone a racial justice
change process. It was now led by a Black person and had a primarily
people-of-color staff. But they realized they were still a white supremacist
organization. She was using my book as a guide in redesigning toward a
liberatory organization and was inquiring about any help I could provide.
Her story is a perfect example of why diversity doesn't work to shift power.
Eventually, we have to consider the forms we inhabit, which oftentimes
are the source of so many problems in our work.

The conversations I've had with readers of my book have had a theme:
*How do leaders of color redesign historically white organizations—or away
from white supremacist culture?*

Organizations are working on their own trying to figure out how to
restructure themselves, as they are also taking on more complex work,
often with a philanthropic field that is steps behind them. Thus, this work
is often unfunded.

So, I was intrigued when I first came across Caroline Levine's book
Forms: Whole, Rhythm, Hierarchy, Network, in which she proposes a new
theory of change:

If forms always contain and confine, and if it is impossible to imagine societies without forms, then the most strategic political action will not come from revealing or exposing illusion, but rather from a careful, nuanced understanding of the many different and often disconnected arrangements that govern social experience.[1]

Edge Leadership (a social change R+D platform hosted by *NPQ*) recently invited Caroline Levine as the first special guest of our new online show. (See excerpts here[2] and here.[3]) Levine's proposition has been key to the design of the Edge platform. Her work and mine intersect on forms and power. She looks at forms and asks questions about power. I explore power and ask questions about forms.

Levine's theory of forms offers two things: an analysis of how forms shape power and an outline of the four most important forms shaping us. There are at least five key ways that forms shape power:

1. **Forms constrain.** They impose "powerful controls and containments."

2. **Forms differ.** There are "rich vocabularies and highly refined skills for differentiating among forms."

3. **Forms overlap and intersect.** Various schools of thought (including intersectional analysis) have "developed methods for analyzing the operation of several distinct forms operating at once."

4. **Forms travel.** Forms move in two ways: they "can survive across cultures and time periods" and they move "back and forth across aesthetic and social materials."

5. **Forms do political work.** Forms matter because they "shape what it is possible to think, say, and do."[4]

The four main forms are whole, rhythm, hierarchy, and network. Although some of these have positive reputations and others negative ones, all forms have positive and negative uses. And reality always exceeds form.

WHOLE is totality, unity, containment. It is a unifying power, the "capacity to hold together disparate parts."[5] It is also "a broader desire to regulate and control—to dominate the plurality and heterogeneity of

---

[1] Levine, Caroline. *Forms: Whole, Rhythm, Hierarchy, Network* (Princeton, NJ: Princeton University Press, 2015), 18.
[2] https://nonprofitquarterly.org/perspective-on-forms/
[3] https://nonprofitquarterly.org/exploring-hierarchy-as-form/
[4] Ibid., 4.
[5] Ibid., 24.

experience."[6] So it is both the desire for unity and the desire for control. The power to hold things together requires violence. However, "no single ideological or political whole successfully dominates or organizes our social life."[7] So instead of focusing on deconstructing or disrupting wholes, we can multiply them. We can introduce more wholes, curtailing the totaling power of any single whole. The goal then is "to think about how one might put bounded wholes to work for strategic ends."[8]

RHYTHM is temporal order, repetitive patterns that impose constraints across time. It is particularly effective for social cohesion. Levine notes that "the attempt to impose temporal order has certainly been a hallmark of large-scale modern uses of power."[9] Periodization, the process of categorizing the past into discrete blocks of time, is a rhythm.

Historical time is transhistorical organizing. Institutions also comprise rhythms or "patterns of duration and repetition over time."[10] They endure because participants "reproduce their rules and practices."[11] However, more often than not, institutions have repetitive patterns that do not align but are uncoordinated.[12] As a form, rhythm tends to be plural and conflicting. Levine concludes, "In order to understand the political and social power that temporal forms exert—their capacity to regulate and organize our lives—we need a kind of analysis capable of revealing how temporal patterns collide."[13]

HIERARCHY is the arrangements of bodies, things, and ideas in order of importance. According to Elliott Jaques, one of the leading thinkers of the model, 75% to 90% of working people in "economically developed nations" work in "managerial accountability hierarchies" where work is done by means of specialization of functions in vertical organizations, where each level is able to hold more complexity than the level below.[14] At least, it should be. When it doesn't, the hierarchy becomes dysfunctional.

Hierarchies also abound in nature, in knowledge, and functional organization. Genes are organized in our DNA this way, the expression of one being necessary to activate another. Knowledge in the human brain appears to be hierarchically organized. And living systems are organized

....

[6] Ibid., 25.
[7] Ibid., 39.
[8] Ibid., 37.
[9] Ibid., 50.
[10] Ibid., 56.
[11] Ibid., 58.
[12] Ibid., 65.
[13] Ibid., 51.
[14] Jaques, Elliott. *Requisite Organization* (Fleming Island, FL: Cason Hall & Co. Publishers, 2006), 4.

in successive organization levels, from genes to ecosystems. There are also developmental hierarchies, where the next level of development includes the former, but the former does not include the next, like nested dolls.

What underlies hierarchical thinking is binaries or dichotomous thinking, which doesn't just distinguish but ranks two polarized terms, such that one becomes privileged and the other subordinated. In *The Power Manual*, I describe how a perception of difference is what triggers power dynamics. It is not surprising, then, that hierarchies "foster an obsession with advancement at the expense of other values and purposes."[15] Or that "the most consistent and painful affordance of hierarchical structures is inequality."[16] Thus, hierarchies "play an important role in modern understandings of power."[17]

However, on closer study, Levine finds that hierarchies "exert a far less orderly and systematic kind of domination than we might expect."[18] She cites social scientists who are discovering that hierarchies are "surprisingly fragile, unpredictable, and vulnerable to breakdown."[19] Ultimately, hierarchies break down not because of internal contradictions but due to encounters with other hierarchies that unsettle them. Thus, the most strategic approach to addressing the power exerted in hierarchies is not to seek to flatten them, but to overlay them with other forms that disturb their power.

Finally, **NETWORK** is the form that most affords connectedness. It links bodies, ideas, and things. It is "a set of connections that link [discrete] elements."[20] However, recent network theory research finds that "these connective configurations [also] follow knowable rules and patterns."[21] Further, "networks can jeopardize, stabilize, or reroute bounded unities."[22] The power of a network to organize depends not only on its pattern but also on the way it collides with other forms, including other networks. "The network provides a way to understand how many other formal elements—including wholes, rhythms, and hierarchies—link up in larger formations."[23] Therefore, "attention to the patterns governing

....

[15] Levine, 101.
[16] Ibid., 82.
[17] Ibid., 99.
[18] Ibid., 85.
[19] Ibid.
[20] Ibid., 113–114.
[21] Ibid., 112.
[22] Ibid., 120.
[23] Ibid., 113.

networks will allow us to think in newly rigorous ways about political power and social experience."[24]

Thus, *wholes contain space, rhythms regulate time, hierarchies differentiate and stratify, and networks connect disparate elements and disturb wholes.*

In addition to offering us this simple, powerful, and practical theory of forms, Levine also suggests what we could call a sister theory when she notes that "there are many events and experiences that do not count as forms—and we could certainly pay close attention to these: fissures and interstices, vagueness and indeterminacy, boundary-crossing and dissolution."[25]

The concept of forms is universal and elegant. It enables us to talk about a lot of things in a coherent and strategic way. And it gives us a more nuanced way to talk about systems. Levine concludes her exposition on forms with this important point:

> *"The system" is less an organized or integrated single structure than it is precisely this heaped assortment of wholes, rhythms, hierarchies, and networks.*[26]

The study of forms offers us a new understanding of how power works. As systems around us shift—and at times collapse—it is increasingly important for social change practitioners to pay attention to the forms that we enliven and to see their design and redesign as an opportunity to advance liberatory power. But let's do this without preconceived and unexamined notions about what they are and what they actually do.

....

[24] Ibid., 113.
[25] Ibid., 9.
[26] Ibid., 148.

Hierarchy and Justice

Cyndi Suarez

In today's organizational climate, where leaders are being held account-able for shifting their organization from a white supremacist culture to a more justice-oriented one, critiques of hierarchy are a key leadership challenge. I often hear leaders express frustration at not knowing how to respond to these staff critiques of an organization's system, and staff members are often eager to lead even if they don't fully understand the system. However, this does not need to be the paradox it appears to be. Justice-oriented hierarchies are not completely unknown. Organizations that use an organizing approach are often designed for leadership development, often with a membership model.

However, in my 30 years of experience in the nonprofit sector, I have never worked at an organization that exhibited a functional hierarchy. The observable hierarchy was often a racial one, with white people toward the higher end of the hierarchy as leaders, and staff members of color toward the bottom as frontline staff—if there were any staff members of color at all. Often, the lower-level staff members do not understand how the whole organization works, don't trust that it works at the higher levels, and are stressed by the need to work around dysfunctions. Sometimes, the higher-level staff members do not understand or see the whole organization either and are not able to offer a value for their benefits in the system. And, un-fortunately, often the highest-level staff members are not capable of con-structing complex systems that support staff members in seeing the whole system and their role in it, or even view such work as their responsibility.

The ability to construct fair and transparent complex systems is a criti-cal leadership skill, no matter what its form.

Hierarchy as a Form

At the simplest level of discussion, hierarchy is a form, a basic organizing structure, and like any form, it can be used to advance justice and injustice.

In her book *Forms*, Caroline Levine argues that all forms are political, in that they organize power. They all have affordances, things they make possible. She identifies four key forms:

Whole	A unified form, or the desire for unity
	It requires control of difference, the domination of "the plurality and heterogeneity of experience."[1]
	"It is created and maintained by acts of exclusion."[2]
Rhythm	A form across time, temporal order
	The "time-bound workings of political power"[3] or the way time is used in preserving or demanding power.
	Such workings are techniques of normalization; they afford portability (the borrowing of temporal forms), but also interruption and transformation.
Hierarchy	A form that allows the arrangement of "bodies, things, and ideas according to levels of power or importance"[4]
	"The most consistent and painful affordance of hierarchical structures is inequality."[5]
	It is built on binaries: masculinity/femininity, public/private, mind/body, Black/white.
Network	A set of connections that "follow knowable rules and patterns"[6]
	"Their power to organize depends on the particular patterns of each network and the way its arrangements collide with other networks and other forms."[7]

Levine points out that none of us lives within a single form but rather within overlapping forms. For example, when it comes to rhythm, we may struggle "to balance work and school schedules."[8] And, although Levine considers hierarchies "the most troubling of all the forms,"[9] she points out that when you actually look at how forms play out in real life, "the most

---

[1] Levine, Caroline. *Forms: Whole, Rhythm, Hierarchy, Network* (Princeton, NJ: Princeton University Press, 2015), 25.
[2] Ibid., 31.
[3] Ibid., 53
[4] Ibid., 82.
[5] Ibid.
[6] Ibid., 112.
[7] Ibid., 115.
[8] Ibid., 49.
[9] Ibid., 82.

strategic approach to the power exerted by hierarchies . . . is not always to dismantle, flatten, or upend them" but to disturb them with intersections of other forms.[10]

In fact, according to Levine, "hierarchies turn out to be surprisingly fragile, unpredictable, and vulnerable to breakdown," and "if we consider closely the workings of hierarchical forms, we will find that they exert a far less orderly and systemic kind of domination than we might expect."[11] This happens because hierarchies are built on more basic hierarchies, binaries, such that there is never one hierarchy but a concatenation of hierarchies that sometimes contradict. Levine calls instances where hierarchies do not lead to the outcomes expected by domination "slippages."[12]

Hierarchies are fragile not just because of these internal contradictions, or "their encounters with other hierarchies [that] unsettle them," but also their encounters with the other three core forms.[13] Levine calls encounters *between* forms *collisions* and proposes that they "afford multiple outcomes" that can either reinforce dominant power or disturb it.[14]

The goal then is to put forms "to work for strategic ends," intentionally designing forms to advance social justice.[15] This requires studying forms, particularly how they overlap and collide.

But, keeping our focus on hierarchy, it is important to also distinguish between functional and dysfunctional hierarchies.

Functional Hierarchies

In *Requisite Organization: A Total System for Effective Managerial Organization and Managerial Leadership for the 21st Century*, Elliott Jacques proposes a systems approach to hierarchy, which he call *stratified systems theory*.[16] It is based on four factors:

> "First, the capability of the individual, in terms of the modes of maturation throughout life of a series of higher and higher levels of that capability"[17]

---

[10] Ibid., 85.
[11] Ibid.
[12] Ibid.
[13] Ibid., 91.
[14] Ibid., 97.
[15] Ibid., 37.
[16] Jacques, Elliott. *Requisite Organization: A Total System for Effective Managerial Organization and Managerial Leadership for the 21st Century*, rev. 2nd ed. (Fleming Island, FL: Cason Hall & Co. Publishers, 2006).
[17] Jacques, Page Pair 12.

"Second, a series of higher and higher levels of inherent complexity in work which correspond to the levels of capability in individuals."[18]

"Third, a series of higher and higher levels of organizational structure which reflects both levels of work complexity and of individual capability."[19]

"Fourth, a wide range of processes, including managerial leadership practices, to be applied with accountability and consistency."[20]

In functional hierarchies, levels correspond to task complexity; that is, each level is able to manage more complexity than the level below it. Thus, each level delivers a value in the system. Jacques argues that, as there are only seven levels of task complexity in a system, the maximum number of levels a hierarchy should have is also seven. He offers a framework for systems that focuses on the ability to discern, form judgments, and make decisions—at various levels of complexity.[21]

Stratified Systems Theory		
Individual Maturation Bands	**Levels of Task Complexity**	**Organizational Strata**
Mode VII	Construct complex systems	Chief executive officer Chief operating officer
Mode VI	Oversee complex systems	Executive vice president
Mode V	Judge downstream consequences	Unit president
Mode IV	Parallel process multiple paths	General manager
Mode III	Create alternative pathways	Unit manager
Mode II	Diagnostic accumulation	First line manager
Mode I	Overcome obstacles, practical judgment	Shop + office floor frontline staff members

....
[18] Ibid.
[19] Ibid.
[20] Ibid.
[21] Ibid.

Of course, most organizations are not large enough to have seven levels of hierarchy. More likely, they have fewer levels with decision-making coupled across levels.

For Jacques, an organization that designs for both efficiency *and* the development of capability is composed of

A universally applicable organizational structure
A system of detailed managerial leadership processes
An equitable differential structure using pay levels tied to the structure of managerial layers
A newly discovered system of evaluation of individual potential capability[22]

Though the structures for a functional system are few, they require focus and commitment. Applying them is an ongoing process and the responsibility of leaders. The fourth factor includes a deep understanding of human potential and the process of transformation, a worthy task for those of us who care about justice and liberation.

Forming Justice

Thus, there is a significant difference between functional hierarchies and dysfunctional ones. Many of the challenges to hierarchy that we hear in nonprofits, and civil society in general, are related to dysfunctional hierarchies, or hierarchies that do not correspond to levels of complexity or leadership. Although power is stratified in hierarchies, so is, or should be, mastery. The difference between functional and dysfunctional hierarchies is the gap between the two.

When I worked in a strategy center for political organizing, the most advanced networks had leadership ladders. The focus wasn't on the organizational chart, but on the levels of engagement of their members. Our biggest network had five levels of engagement: definitions, trainings and other capacity building, behavior that demonstrates that members are ready to move up to the next level, and a process for doing so. The structure clarified and made transparent the duties and benefits of engagement. Although this organization had a hierarchy in both its staff and membership structure, it closed the loop by drawing its board from its members.

....

[22] Ibid., Page Pair 2.

During the process of creating a system that clarifies levels of participation, or levels of leadership, we considered:

1. The various ways that members participate
2. What members need to participate well at each level
3. How organizers interact with members to support them at each level
4. How organizers discern when members are ready to increase participation/leadership and provide them with relevant support and opportunities

At each level members have both rights and responsibilities. They are entitled to certain opportunities—like coaching, training, leadership, and resources. They also are expected to honor the organization's guiding principles and processes, taking increasing responsibility for those. In particularly effective organizations, the levels are integrated strategically, so that the work of more entry or peripheral levels is led by those at higher or inner levels. Jacques's framework for what comprises a requisite organization is not very different from this.

I've seen leaders use collaborative processes to camouflage manipulation and hierarchy to advance justice. There are surely times when a nonhierarchical model is the best for an organization or system. There is a need to better understand when that is and what characteristics signal it. In my experience, nonhierarchical models have a high bar and require something other than hierarchy to hold the group together, such as a super clear goal, a high level of complementary skills, a history of strong relationships based on trust and accountability, and commitment to reflection and radical personal growth.

Ultimately, power is beyond form. Form is what holds power, and there are many ways to do that because power is not just one thing. Yes, power is privilege in a system. It is also mastery, clarity of vision, the attractive force of integrity, the ability to see and design for multiplicity, the ability to connect across difference, and the ability to imagine a better world.

It's time to move beyond the stalemate concerning hierarchy and become more competent with forms.

A Journey from White Space to Pro-Black Space

Isabelle Moses

How do you infuse racial and gender equity throughout organizational culture and practice? How do you make it a shared responsibility rather than one person's job?

Not unique to my job or my organization, these are questions that I wrestle with every day. For nearly five years, I have worked at Faith in Action, the nation's largest faith-based, grassroots community-organizing network. I previously served as a management consultant and executive coach to Faith in Action's leadership team, and came on staff to bring that expertise in-house. My current role as chief of staff requires me to think daily about how to build an organization that ensures that Black, Indigenous, and people of color—and Black women and women of color, in particular—are set up to thrive. A large part of my responsibility is working with our leadership teams to address our internal systems and structures that have perpetuated inequities and inhibited our team from fully living into our talents and aspirations.

One might like to believe that an organization like ours—one that has a 50-year track record of building power in low-income communities of color across the country—might have had a head start in this area.

Not so.

The reality is that Faith in Action, like many historically white-led organizations, has had to undergo its own internal change process so that our organizational leadership and staff teams truly reflect the communities in which we live and work. As an organization, we have grappled with the truth that systemic racism is the fundamental obstacle to our collective liberation, and when we really grappled with that truth, our whole organization had to change to reflect the aspirations we have for society.

This challenge is hardly unique to Faith in Action. Like many of our peers, we have experienced the consequences of shifting to more intentionally recruiting and hiring leadership and staff members of color without fully addressing underlying systemic inequities. These inequities often inhibit us from thriving when we're offered opportunities we haven't been offered in the past.

When I was hired, it was largely because of organizational failings in this area. By the middle of the 2010s, Faith in Action, which back then was called the PICO National Network, might have been practicing "race-conscious organizing" externally, but internally the transformation had yet to fully manifest.[1] We were hiring more frontline staff members of color, but when it came to the organization's leadership, even five years ago this was still a white-led nonprofit, including a majority of the board of directors.

We have come a long way, but we have hardly figured it all out. Our journey includes both the lessons we are learning and many open questions.

And given the scale and scope of our network, it is an important story to tell. The Faith in Action network operates in 27 states, El Salvador, Haiti, and Rwanda. Our network includes 45 affiliated federations that are independent organizations. Our national organization collaborates with federations by offering leadership development in the form of training and coaching, political analysis, and deep partnership in developing and executing organizing plans and strategies. We also raise and regrant millions of dollars each year. We focus on a range of issues, including voting rights and voter engagement, immigrant justice and citizenship, and economic and criminal justice.

The Dam Breaks

In spring 2017, a group of 14 Black directors—all of whom had leadership roles with national staff members and affiliated organizations of the Faith in Action network—gathered in Dallas, Texas, for a retreat. The agenda was designed to focus on opportunities for collective fundraising. But this would prove to be no ordinary fundraising retreat.

During the discussion, several Black women raised a red flag: in recent years, a disproportionate share of Black women had quit or were transitioned out of affiliated organizations or national staff in the network.

---

[1] See Steve Dubb, "National Network Leader Looks Back on 40 Years of Community Organizing," *Nonprofit Quarterly*, May 2, 2018, nonprofitquarterly.org/national-network-leader-looks-back-40-years-community-organizing/.

The conversation shifted to the question of how a faith-based, grassroots community–organizing network lives its values and ensures that Black women and women of color more broadly are set up to thrive—knowing that when Black women are thriving, it's more likely that everyone is thriving (as the theory of *targeted universalism*, developed by Dr. john a. powell, articulates).[2] It became clear that, although fundraising still mattered, understanding and addressing the experiences of Black women was an even higher priority.

As the Black directors explored the catalysts behind the departures of Black women, several demands of the leadership of national staff members emerged. These included carrying out an external assessment of the state of Black women across the network, hiring a human resources director to instill values-aligned systems and practices, ensuring access to professional development for Black executive directors, adding a Black woman to the executive leadership, addressing racial and gender disparities in allocation of regrants from the national organization to affiliates, and creating a Wisdom Council to bring restorative justice practices to personnel (and other) conflicts that arose within the network.

I joined Faith in Action's national team soon after this retreat. My position was in large measure a response to a call from Black directors who wanted to see greater focus placed on setting Black staff members up for success, especially Black women. Over time, my role evolved to become the director of organizational development and, more recently (as noted), chief of staff.

My own path to Faith in Action was somewhat unusual. I completed an MBA degree—not your typical training for a community-organizing network—and spent the first couple of years of my postgraduate career in management consulting with for-profit corporations, identifying opportunities to increase profit or operational efficiency. Getting laid off in the middle of the 2008–2009 financial crisis was the wake-up call I needed to recognize that a job that contributed to racial and economic inequity was not for me. For the past decade, I've supported strong and vibrant organizations at the leading edges of racial and economic justice. Although Faith in Action still has a long way to go in our process of becoming, we are striving every day to create an internal culture that lives our values of justice, power, and love.

---

[2] "Targeted Universalism," Othering & Belonging Institute, University of California, Berkeley, accessed January 22, 2022, belonging.berkeley.edu/targeted-universalism.

New Leadership Sets an Audacious Vision—and Offers a Framework for Action

Faith in Action had been led by two white men—first, Father John Baumann, the founder of then-PICO, and second, Scott Reed—for its first 40 years. Both had many accomplishments. At the same time, Reed's retirement opened up space for new leadership and new thinking. In May 2018, Rev. Alvin Herring was hired as the network's new executive director and the first Black person to lead the organization.

When Rev. Herring arrived, the organization faced a number of issues. Among these were:

- Financial challenges
- Women of color throughout the network feeling slighted and unseen
- A culture of silos without shared vision and direction
- An unwieldy national network that had grown out of existing systems and structures
- A need to reshape governance and develop a collective approach to organizing that centers wisdom and lived experiences of people of color

One of Rev. Herring's top priorities was to take the time to deeply listen to the pain of Black and Brown women on staff who felt that our contributions to the organization were undervalued. The network engaged a consultant to complete a report on the state of Black women in the organization that sought to understand the underlying themes behind the disproportionately high rates of turnover of Black women, both on national staff and within our federations. (More recently, we have completed a similar study with our Latinx staff members.) Our organization took all of these actions because we believe that to change organizational culture we first have to understand it.

After the initial listening round and about a year into his tenure, Rev. Herring set an explicit goal that Faith in Action would become the best possible place to work for people of color. This was not a small declaration.

The last three years have been all about moving from vision to implementation. This meant a comprehensive effort to transform the culture of the national staff team through self-examination about race and gender, and riding the national momentum that is asking leaders to operate with greater accountability to the communities we care about. The vision offered by Rev. Herring has guided much of our approach to ensuring that our organization lives our values.

Several changes have been implemented regarding national staff over the past three years:

- Strong fiscal responsibility and a renewed focus on fundraising have propelled us to the healthiest balance sheet we've had in the organization's history.
- People of color now serve in all seven positions on the executive team (five women, two men).
- To recognize the leadership and talent that already resided in the organization, key staff members of color who had labored in the network for years received significant promotions. This freed up long-tenured team members who weren't always in positions of power and influence to bring their deep learning and ideas to life.
- Throughout the organization, we have implemented the Zulu concept of *sawubona*. Literally, the phrase means, "I see you," but more broadly it means an organizational commitment to respecting our common humanity.[3]

In addition, within the network, more than half of our affiliate organizations are now led by people of color, of which a high percentage are Black women and Latinas.

The goal, in short, has been to shift from a white-dominant and patriarchal culture to one where more people of color, especially women, have access to decision-making rights and influence over the continued evolution of both *what* we work on and *how* we work collectively. It's about considering every day how to design an organization for liberation and not oppression.

Organizing Human Resources as If People Matter

In this process of internal organizational transformation, we are learning many things. One perhaps obvious—yet sometimes hidden—point is the

[3] Valeria Sabater, "Sawubona: An African Tribe's Beautiful Greeting," *Exploring Your Mind*, last modified November 15, 2021, exploringyourmind.com/sawubona-african-tribe-greeting/.

need to recognize that racial trauma affects a large portion of our staff members. This means we have found that we need to intentionally create space for healing and well-being. This has many practical human resources implications that community organizing networks—and, dare I suggest, other nonprofit and for-profit organizations—ignore at their peril.

Our chief people officer, Crystal Cumbo, has been a steadfast champion of this work. In response to the set of requests from Black directors, she also joined the national staff as the first human resources professional in our organization's 50-year history. She has made it her mission to ensure that Faith in Action practices its values through our organizational systems, structures, and policies. For example:

> **Compensating staff equitably.** One of our big wins over the past 18 months is the completion of a compensation and benefits study, so that all staff are paid equitably and competitively relative to the market for similar positions at similarly sized organizations. This was a huge feat and required the participation of the entire team in order to complete updated job descriptions that would serve as the basis for analysis. Ultimately, we landed on a new compensation framework that has structured salary bands by job function and guarantees that people who perform similar work are paid similarly across the organization. We are also ensuring that staff are paid at least at the median of the market. Due to our recent financial turnaround and strengthened balance sheet, we are also able to make salary adjustments to account for any inequities that emerged across our team.
>
> **Prioritizing staff well-being to avert burnout.** During the pandemic, we have made every effort to prioritize staff well-being and to make sure that our annual leave policies were not a barrier to staff getting the time off they needed. This builds upon our long-standing commitment to family–work integration that we piloted in 2019, with a practice of no meetings and no emails on Fridays.[4] While we aren't perfect at this, the program has greatly increased our team's ability to slow down, reflect, and handle personal priorities.

We've regularly surveyed our staff members during the COVID-19 pandemic to hear feedback about what's working and what additional supports are needed to ensure staff member well-being. As a result of

---

[4]Denise Padín Collazo, "Tackling Family–Work Integration Head-On to Keep Women of Color in the Work," *Nonprofit Quarterly*, August 20, 2019, nonprofitquarterly.org/

the feedback, we closed the office for a total of four weeks in July and December 2020 and January 2021, so that staff members could recharge and focus on themselves and their loved ones. And in 2021, we decided to implement a two-week holiday break in December (adding a second week to our usual holiday break) and have codified this as a standard practice going forward. Rather than pushing just a little bit harder, we recognized the need to take the foot off the gas, and that addressing burnout *required* time to recuperate. Ultimately, we believe that we will liberate ourselves *if* we create the conditions for everyone to stay in the work over the long term rather than creating conditions for constant churn in the mode of treating people like disposable parts. With the support of a diverse and dynamic leadership team, we can express our liberation by owning our ability to choose rest over work.

Investing in leadership development and caucus spaces. This meant engaging leadership development practitioners to support our leadership teams. It also meant working to strengthen our caucus and cohort spaces, including our Black caucus, Black women's caucus, Latinx cohorts, Asian Pacific Islander (API) caucus, and white caucus.

One of my proudest bodies of work over the last two years has been stewarding our Black women's caucus space to codesign and implement a curriculum focused on supporting Black women to own our power more fully while also healing harmful societal conditioning that has uniquely affected Black women through the intersection of misogyny and racism, known as *misogynoir*. We engaged Dr. Chanequa Walker-Barnes to understand and unlearn many harmful aspects of the Strong Black Woman archetype as described in her book *Too Heavy a Yoke: Black Women and the Burden of Strength*.[5]

Phyllis Hill, our national organizing director, has worked with Black women directors and organizers in the South to cocreate the Black Southern Women's Collective, which is a space for collective visioning, fundraising, professional development, community building, and healing. In this space of shared leadership and imagination, they have developed a strategy that recognizes that organizing is both about meeting the needs of everyday people in response to crises (such as in the aftermath of hurricanes) and about building long-term political power for Black and Brown communities (as demonstrated by high rates of voter turnout in Georgia during the November 2020 and January 2021 elections).

---

[5] Chanequa Walker-Barnes, *Too Heavy a Yoke: Black Women and the Burden of Strength* (Eugene, OR: Cascade Books, 2014).

The Need for New Thinking

The shift that has occurred at Faith in Action would have seemed impossible when I joined the organization five years ago. We have been working hard to walk our talk: centering the voices of those closest to the impact of issues we work on, both in our externally facing organizing as well as in our internal organizational practices. We are striving daily to move toward a deeper emphasis on self-determination and collective liberation. We are aiming to center the wisdom and experiences of people of color, especially women of color, at all levels of our organization.

This includes learning from organizing ancestors who look more like us—including Ella Baker, Cesar Chavez, and Fannie Lou Hamer—rather than only operating out of the frameworks of white organizers, such as Saul Alinsky. It also includes incorporating wisdom from living systems—such as that shared by adrienne maree brown in *Emergent Strategy*.[6] How do we move more like a flock of birds and share nutrients more like interdependent tree roots?

Since joining Faith in Action, my beliefs about organizational systems and structures have shifted significantly. I have begun to realize that many of the capitalist-oriented models and practices I was trained to implement were not working for our aspirations. For example, how do we think about a long-term shared vision and shorter-term goals that are defined more at the team level than at the organizational level? How do we hold healthy tension between the elements of "top-down" hierarchy that are needed for clear decision-making, while also responding to the "bottom-up" wisdom of our grassroots leaders?

Recently, in response to the receipt of an unexpected transformational grant from MacKenzie Scott, Rev. Herring tapped Denise Collazo, our chief of external affairs, to lead a networkwide commission to inform how best to use the funds. This is a first step toward taking on the challenge of engaging many stakeholder groups (grassroots leaders, network and national staff members, and boards) across language, distance, and many time zones in more democratic decision-making. Here are the commission's three overarching recommendations:

- Become the global spiritual and political home for BIPOC people and our coconspirators who aspire to build multiracial, multifaith democracies.

---

[6] adrienne maree brown, *Emergent Strategy: Shaping Change, Changing Worlds* (Chico, CA: AK Press, 2017).

- Invest in a new generation of community organizing leadership by amplifying the voices of Black and Brown women across the globe.
- Make this money make more money.

It seems they're off to a great start.

In short, internal transformation in the direction of racial justice does not occur merely by applying traditional methods. New thinking is required, and the leadership of Black and Brown women is an important part of the equation. There remains much work to do. We recently wrapped up a listening campaign to hear from leaders and clergy in our global network to build our vision for the next 10 years on our collective wishes and aspirations.

We know that Black, Brown, Asian, and Indigenous communities have the insights about what we need to thrive. Faith in Action wants to activate and equip people to be the authors of our own liberation. We believe wholeheartedly that we are the ones we've been waiting for.

III

Building Pro-Black Institutions: Philanthropy and Evaluation

The Emergence of Black Funds

Cyndi Suarez

In a recent article, part of a short report back series from this year's Association of Black Foundation Executives (ABFE) conference, I wrote about a leadership practice emerging amongst Black leaders, the exploration of Liberatory Leadership.[1] Another concept showcased at the conference was the emergence of Black funds, philanthropic vehicles controlled by Black communities.

In a session titled "Centering Black Brilliance: How Community Foundations Have Created Impactful Funding Initiatives to Support Black-led and Serving Organizations," Jonathan Cunningham, senior program officer at the Seattle Foundation, appeared to be on the leading edge of the concept as the principal architect behind the foundation's new framework, **REPAIR**—Racially Equitable Philanthropy Aimed at Initiating Reparations—the only known philanthropic fund with the word *reparations* in its name.

The conception of Black funds is critically important to understand and learn from, in a context where, according to ABFE, 1.8% of philanthropic dollars go to Black-led organizations.

What is a Black-led organization? For Cunningham, it is an organization that has at least 50% Black leadership and board. Black leaders are the "brain trust" of Black funds, the informed, connected, respected (by their communities) leaders that make decisions.

A framework for redressing philanthropic underinvestment in Black organizations and communities, REPAIR is also a foundation-wide commitment to award $25 million to Black-led nonprofits and business contractors over five years, beginning in 2021, to support a Black economic

---

[1] https://nonprofitquarterly.org/experiments-in-liberatory-leadership/

ecosystem in King County, Washington. The release of a study[2] by Echoing Green and The Bridgespan Group, which revealed that the assets of Black-led nonprofits were 76% smaller than those of their white counterparts, influenced REPAIR's development. As the Seattle Foundation's web page states, with this data point, "philanthropy's historic role in gatekeeping resources from Black-led organizations becomes more clear." REPAIR is an effort by the foundation to repair the harm caused by such gatekeeping.

Cunningham shared that REPAIR's first year of development was focused on building deep relationships with the community. His team created a feedback loop with the community that allowed Cunningham's team to tell the foundation, "This is what Black people said. . . ." His team was also guided by the field; it went on a listening tour of other organizations engaged in similar efforts, like Borealis and the East Bay Community Foundation.

Cunningham said that during this early phase, there was a need to heal past harms and relationships because some Black organizations did not get along and were competing with one another. It also emerged that staff members at Black-led organizations—especially smaller, grassroots organizations—were overwhelmed and exhausted. Cunningham said, "they were often one paycheck away from being a client." In response, the Seattle Foundation created a Black-led Joy and Wellness Fund, providing all the organizations that applied to the fund with up to $20,000. Some organizations used this to provide paid time off.

Cunningham says it took years to develop the framework. The process began with an internal examination of foundation process, with a racial equity lens. The results of this analysis were published in a 2018 report titled, "The Case for Investing in King County's Black Led Organizations."[3] It found that

1. BLOs primarily focus on serving Seattle residents, and nearly half serve South King County residents.
2. Most BLOs have limited full-time staff and robust volunteer support.
3. BLOs' advisory structures are primarily boards of directors with predominantly Black membership.
4. BLOs address a wide range of issues that impact the Black community.

---

[2] https://www.bridgespan.org/insights/library/philanthropy/disparities-nonprofit-funding-for-leaders-of-color
[3] https://cardeaservices.org/resource/the-case-for-investing-in-king-countys-black-led-organizations/

5. BLOs most commonly reported strong missions; skilled leadership, staff, and boards; and longevity as key strengths.
6. Reported budget size varied widely, with BLOs most commonly reporting an operating budget less than $250,000.
7. Nearly two-thirds of survey respondents reported three months or less of operating cash reserves.
8. Funding sources vary widely among BLOs.
9. Insufficient staff capacity was identified as a primary challenge in securing funding.
10. Insufficient funding is a common challenge.
11. BLOs reported dramatic and immediate impacts related to COVID-19 that amplified existing systemic inequities.
12. Trust, clear communication, and desire to collaborate emerged as the most important facilitators of partnership.

These findings paint a picture of what systemic racism looks like in the nonprofit sector. They also point to what is needed.

In 2019, REPAIR launched a pilot project to build relationships with Black-led organizations in King County by supporting them with general operating grants. This group of organizations developed into the Black-Led Organizations Cohort, or BLOC, which convenes monthly, builds partnerships in the community, and advises the foundation. BLOC developed REPAIR's framework "to provide catalytic support for Black-led nonprofits in this region through strategic investments."[4]

Though REPAIR was originally conceived of as a one-year pilot, COVID, the prominent murders of Black people across the country, and the intentional relationships developed with the community led the Seattle Foundation to deepen its commitment to supporting King County in a sustained way. REPAIR uses the targeted universalism[5] approach developed by john a. powell of the Othering & Belonging Institute at UC Berkeley, which, by orienting all racial groups toward universal goals, helps create support for its efforts.

The Community Foundation of Richmond, Virginia, also has a Black fund called the Amandla Fund for Economic and Racial Justice. Stephanie Glenn, vice president of diversity and engagement, leads it. Similar to Cunningham, Glenn highlights that the foundation could not be the decision-maker, so it partnered with SisterFund and Ujima Legacy Fund, two Black giving circles. Green shared that 95% of the work

[4]https://www.seattlefoundation.org/blueprint-for-impact/repair
[5]https://nonprofitquarterly.org/beyond-equity-targeted-universalism-and-the-closing-of-the-racial-wealth-gap/

went into creating the fund, and data were important. So, the Community Foundation also started with a report,[6] which took two years to complete and identified two initial focus areas that are critical to Black economic mobility:

1. Increasing Black homeownership
2. Expanding Black leadership

Within the foundation, the team working on the fund is cross-functional, composed of five staff members lent to the project. Their focus was engaging Black leaders within their legacy of giving. The team found that Black people don't give like traditional philanthropists. Similar to emerging, Black-led funds, Black donors are not focused on bridging gaps, but on removing systemic barriers. Glenn said, "Bridging the gap is imperative for surviving, but now is the time to deal with systemic, racist barriers to wealth."

Amandla focuses on Black voice, and it values both expertise and lived experience. No report is due at the end of each year. In fact, Glenn said, "There are not a lot of metrics because we're not talking about deficits but assets." The fund has a goal of raising and awarding $10 million by 2025. It is currently at $2.5 million. Glenn shared, "We weren't ready when we started. The process developed through the work, implementing and adjusting. So just start."

A third Black fund featured in the ABFE conference session was the Hampton Roads Community Foundation, also in Virginia. Vivian M. Oden, vice president for equity and inclusion, shared that the foundation also began with a report, this one titled, "Missing Voices in Philanthropy"[7] and published in 2019. The report was necessary because when it came to thinking about Black-led, Black-serving organizations, the foundation "didn't even know who these were." Through the exploration process it found 150 such organizations, 50% of which had never engaged with the foundation. "Even Black board members didn't know about these Black organizations," she said.

Oden led an equity assessment, created a board/staff committee, and "put community leaders in front of the board." As a result, the foundation created a Black giving circle and endowed it with $500,000. In 2021, Oden led the development of another report, "Giving Black: Hampton Roads/

---

[6]https://www.cfrichmond.org/Portals/0/Uploads/Documents/Publications/Amandla
Fund 2022 Report.pdf
[7]https://higherlogicdownload.s3.amazonaws.com/AFPNET/7d5fdbea-23b8-42fc-b3c2
-b7d58554eba5/UploadedImages/Oden_AFP_Presentation_-_Missing_Voices_20190521.pdf

The Genesis of American Black Philanthropy,"[8] which explored Black giving in Hampton Roads, "the oldest continuous Black community in the United States" and "the site of one of the first free Black communities that created economic systems based on traditions from their homeland."

The findings of the Giving Black report include the following:

1. The top-ranking issue for Black donors is economic stability/wealth building, with racial and social justice ranked second.
2. Black donors tend to see their fate as linked to the Black community as a whole.
3. According to survey respondents, the majority of Black donors are "well-educated, mid- to upper-income Black women who are employed full-time and married or in domestic partnerships."
4. The top ranked organizations receiving money from Black donors are Black churches.
5. Seven out of 10 Black donors rely on social media for information on giving.

Not surprisingly, a key recommendation was to "develop a regional strategy of economic stability and wealth building to strengthen bonds between different Black donors and communities of Hampton Roads." Oden said, "the Giving Black report was data for the foundation *and* the community."

Finally, LaDawn Sullivan, director of the BRIC (Black Resilience in Colorado) Fund at The Denver Foundation, said about setting up a Black fund, "It's hard work. There are roadblocks. White staff don't understand." So, in doing this work, you have to "protect your peace."

BRIC is a grants program that addresses systemic racism across the seven-county Metro Denver region. The fund awards general operating grants and allows a community-led advisory committee to identify funding priorities. Grants typically range from $5,000 to $25,000.

Glenn agreed that this is hard work. She added, "You have to show up as your best self, as hard as that is. Sometimes it feels like we're in a battle, infiltrated all the time. I take a rest when I can't indulge in a meeting or conversation."

These leaders shared that they have to be very careful when developing these funds. Sullivan said, "You have to understand internal dynamics. You're challenging traditional philanthropic hierarchy."

Glenn adds, "The process is how the work gets done."

---

[8] https://issuu.com/hamptonroadscf/docs/giving_black_hampton_roads_report_2021

Oden said, "It's a journey; code-switching, conforming. You will hear my voice, my true self, but I will pick my battles. I have to bring my colleagues along."

These leaders have had to create the conditions that honor Black leadership in their foundations. They agreed that COVID and the Black social justice movement contributed to the development of these funds. There was also a general desire to move out of a scarcity mindset into one of abundance, of understanding that Black communities have unique assets. They are opening up space for Black leaders to be real, share expertise, and not have to fit into nonprofit boxes.

What's next for Black funds?

1. Moving into policy space, advancing bills that appropriate money for intermediaries to mobilize resources for Black communities
2. Becoming endowed, free-standing, community-owned and supported
3. Maintaining and elevating Black funds nationally (national funders to support local efforts)
4. Giving larger grants
5. Creating a Black funds network

Reimagining Philanthropy to Build a Culture of Repair

Aria Florant and Venneikia Williams

The movement for reparations in the United States—a Black-led movement that began even before slavery's end—is making unprecedented strides forward, and governments across the country are beginning to act. In October 2020, California became the first state to initiate an official task force[1] to study and develop a reparations plan[2] for Black Americans harmed by slavery and its legacies. In March 2021, the city council in Evanston, Illinois,[3] approved the Local Reparations Restorative Housing Program to address racial discrimination in housing. In April 2021, HR 40 was voted out of committee[4] for the first time in its 32-year history. If passed, the bill would establish a commission to study the negative effects of slavery.

These initiatives represent just a few of the many forms that advocacy for reparations can take. Other activities include grassroots power-building, research, narrative change, and stakeholder mobilization. There is an enormous amount of work to be done, and it needs real investment to be successful.

A new philanthropic model, in the form of asset transfers coupled with a comprehensive racial repair framework, would deepen investment in Black communities while reflecting the reparations movement's goals. In addition, it would move the philanthropic sector into a liminal space (i.e., a transitional opening for social change) that could decrease the need for philanthropy in the first place.

---

[1] https://oag.ca.gov/ab3121/members
[2] https://nonprofitquarterly.org/californias-plan-for-lineage-based-reparations-for-slavery-is-it-enough/
[3] https://www.cityofevanston.org/government/city-council/reparations
[4] https://www.hrw.org/ReparationsNow

A New Philanthropic Model

The engine of philanthropy runs on hoarded wealth. Many—if not most—foundation benefactors earned their fortunes through the exploitation of people, land, and resources. Once accumulated, this wealth is maintained—often in perpetuity.

As is well known, foundations with endowments generate returns by investing those endowments, whether in the bond or stock markets or through hedge fund placements in private equity. They usually limit their giving to the federally mandated minimum of 5% of overall assets and have boards of trustees who make investment decisions but are far removed from the problems those investments aim to solve.

Many within philanthropy contend that limiting giving in this way is important to ensure that foundations can continue to finance mission-driven work. However, this approach has downsides. If foundations spent the money currently locked away in endowments, it might be possible to transform the systems that create the societal problems that foundations are dealing with. In short, although foundation leaders believe that preserving foundation assets in perpetuity serves the public interest, movement leaders involved in systems change hold a different view.

The United States is seeing a resurgence of white supremacist rhetoric and violence, and despite many efforts, the racial wealth gap is not closing—it is widening. Our criminal justice system continues to target Black people, and Black communities have been hit hardest by the pandemic and a slowing economy. A new model of philanthropy is needed to address this at scale and with speed.

What would it look like if, instead of grants, philanthropy took the form of asset transfers that shift funds to reparations movement organizations to spend or steward as they see fit? What if the power dynamic was dramatically flipped, and reparations movement organizations didn't have to worry about sustainable funding? And what if philanthropy wasn't just about financial investment but also about reckoning with the systems that created concentrated wealth[5] in the first place, and understanding how to transform those systems to make them more just for all?

---

[5] https://nonprofitquarterly.org/freeing-ourselves-from-colonial-white-savior-models-of -philanthropy/

Rooting the New Model in Repair

We believe that a culture of repair must be embedded into all institutions we create—including philanthropy—to ensure Black people can thrive.

At Liberation Ventures,[6] we define repair as an iterative, cyclical process with four components: reckoning, acknowledgment, accountability, and redress. This framework was developed through a study of frameworks across disciplines—from transitional and restorative justice, to prison-industrial complex abolition, to psychology and religion. It is a living framework; as more individuals and organizations try it out, it will evolve in tangent with our lived experiences. It can apply to all sectors, but here we use it to ask: what might a comprehensive philanthropic approach to repair look like?

We can begin with the obvious—financial redress. MacKenzie Scott has received a great deal of attention for giving a ton of cash to many incredible Black- and Indigenous-led organizations. What she has not done is shifted her assets—or given movement leaders control over whether to invest those assets or spend them down as informed by their proximity to the challenges at hand. Such a move would mean sharing not just cash, but power.

Control of money is important, but it is not the only component of repair. The choice to shift assets stems from an understanding of the unjust systems that enabled a privileged few—including donors and foundations—to amass great wealth while depressing the wealth of so many others, especially Black and Indigenous folks.

Public acknowledgment of this reckoning process models the process for others. Acknowledgment makes reckoning visible, which changes culture—and, in the process, helps communities that have been harmed feel seen. Although donors like Scott may have important reasons for wanting to stay out of the limelight, sometimes donors' public presence can upend the status quo by setting a new example for their peers.

Finally, holding donors accountable to grantees' needs ensures that Black-led organizations and their communities control the narrative. Scott has shifted her approach from announcing grantees, to creating space for grantees to share the news on their own terms, providing one example of what accountability to communities looks like.

---

[6]https://www.liberationventures.org/

What else might accountability involve? Some possibilities include organizing peers to make similar commitments and, as Evanston's aforementioned restorative housing program demonstrates, establishing local governance structures that create a new example for the field.

A Journey—Not a Destination

Trauma and theft at the scale of chattel slavery require time to heal. The redistribution of assets, paired with a reparative framework, would help bring more choice, freedom, and long-term sustainability to movement groups.

First, asset transfer would give reparations movement leaders control over how and when to invest or spend resources. When conditions are unfavorable to progress, movement leaders can use endowments to ensure sustainability; when conditions change, they can spend down to leverage windows of opportunity to create the most impact possible. This would enable those who are closest to the issues—and who have the clearest view of what is needed to win—to modulate levels of investment in the movement with more flexibility, agility, and speed.

Second, such an approach would enable movement organizations to upset the existing power dynamic, which favors philanthropists over those receiving funds. Giving movement leaders the choice to use endowments as a strategic tool would enable them to engage in long-term planning without worrying about funds being withdrawn due to a change of philanthropic fashion. This type of financial sustainability and security would result in widespread mental health benefits and increased organizational impact, and it would enable groups to operate from an abundance mindset rather than one of scarcity.

Third, asset transfers would help BIPOC-led organizations build durable infrastructure that prioritizes healing and wellness, instead of getting bogged down by short-term challenges and burnout. In short, asset transfers make possible a baseline level of capital that leads to a more sustainable and flexible strategy for movements.

Finally, asset transfer could contribute to building trust across lines of racial and class difference. Such trust-building creates healing for those who have historically been harmed by unjust systems and for individuals who have long benefited but who also need to heal from these systems. As James Baldwin reminds us,[7] "It is entirely up to the American people

---

[7] https://americanarchive.org/catalog/cpb-aacip-15-0v89g5gf5r?proxy_start_time=1400.843612

whether or not they are going to face and deal with and embrace this stranger whom they maligned so long. What white people have to do is try to find out in their own hearts why it was necessary to have a [n-word] in the first place. . . . The future of the country depends on that."

Toward a Liberated Future

We want a liberated future: a just, multiracial democracy and an economy that values people and our planet over profit. Repair is the pathway to this future, and all of us—especially Black and Indigenous communities—deserve it.

New models of philanthropy are critical to bringing this vision to fruition. We need philanthropists who are willing to share power. Asset transfer, paired with the ongoing work of comprehensive repair (reckoning, acknowledgment, accountability, and redress), could provide a framework for large-scale, flexible resourcing that heals our communities and benefits us all.

This is only one step toward a world where philanthropy is unnecessary because our economic and democratic systems create just outcomes for all. In this world, wealth isn't hoarded; it's invested in ways that meet all people's needs. A reparative model of philanthropy creates the liminal space needed to move closer to this new world.

How Philanthropy Can Truly Support Land Justice for Black Communities

Savi Horne and Dr. Jasmine Ratliff

The question of land (and its loss) has been prominent throughout African American history. After the US Civil War, many formerly enslaved Black people made tremendous efforts to acquire land. Even though the Union promise of "40 acres and a mule" was not honored, African Americans bought land where they could. By 1910,[1] Black farmers owned somewhere about 14% of all US farmland—with estimates of land holdings exceeding 15 million acres.[2]

These gains have since been largely reversed. Nearly 12 million acres[3] of Black-owned land has been lost in the United States over the last century. In Mississippi alone, between 1950 and 1964, Black farmers lost nearly 800,000 acres,[4] the equivalent of a $3.7 billion loss today.

How did this dispossession occur? Via the efforts of private and public actors, programs, and policies, including discriminatory loan programs, market forces, intimidation, and terrorism. Today, many Black farmers who retain land ownership face foreclosures or lawsuits from white farmers, among other challenges.[5] In the face of so much loss and opposition, asset reallocation can be a powerful tool for achieving self-determination for Black farmers and Black agricultural communities.

---

[1] https://theconversation.com/land-loss-has-plagued-black-america-since-emancipation-is-it-time-to-look-again-at-black-commons-and-collective-ownership-140514
[2] https://nonprofitquarterly.org/what-would-a-pro-black-farmer-policy-regime-look-like/
[3] https://eji.org/news/one-million-Black-families-have-lost-their-farms/#:~:text=Illegal%20pressures%20applied%20through%20USDA,acres%20from%201950%20to%201969.
[4] https://www.theatlantic.com/magazine/archive/2019/09/this-land-was-our-land/594742/
[5] https://www.nytimes.com/2022/02/21/us/politics/black-farmers-debt-relief.html?partner=slack&smid=sl-share

It is too late to restore all the land from which Black farmers have been dispossessed. But if philanthropy focused on asset reallocation—that is, the direct transfer of real estate holdings—it could help reverse the decline of Black-owned land holdings, especially if such a new focus was backed by investment in new agroecological infrastructure to support Black communities.

Such land transfers would also enable Black farmers to engage in climate change mitigation practices and would enhance Black people's food sovereignty. Food can act as medicine, especially when grown and maintained by community members. With control over food systems, Black communities would be able to better prevent and mitigate long-term health problems that affect our communities at disproportionate rates. In other words, landownership, food access, and healthcare are intertwined.

Working toward land rights and self-determination for Black communities also means working toward environmental justice and a just energy transition.[6] A new asset reallocation model, paired with grassroots organizing, would facilitate such a transition at both the local and national levels. Such a model would also fundamentally shift economic and hence political power.

Federal legislation and the US Department of Agriculture have long blocked these goals.[7] For this reason, we call on funders to prioritize land transfers and invest in BIPOC-led food economies.

Self-Determination and Land Justice

The Black liberation struggle has always sought Black self-determination. Unrestricted access to capital would enhance such determination, giving Black communities a real choice of whom to support and how they engage with social change work and funders—choices they often lack, as the decisions of funding recipients are frequently dictated by institutions far removed from those recipients and their needs. The ultimate goal of asset reallocation is to free Black communities from funders' mandates by creating a stable asset base that provides Black communities with the economic resources needed to build a self-determining economy that is, as much as

---

[6] http://usfoodsovereigntyalliance.org/food-sovereignty-and-energy-democracy-in-just-transitions/
[7] https://docs.google.com/document/d/18rDgNMAVvRVzfA0Dj4c8xRi5wkrAtl6O1S Yqd-Ex5s0/edit

possible, independent of the current, extractive economic system—with new tracts of Black-stewarded land held outside of the speculative real estate market.

Given that the number of Black farmers in the United States has fallen by an estimated 9% since 1920, we must demand asset reallocation. We must also galvanize our movements, organizers, funders, and institutions to learn from our ancestors, elders, and scholars so that we may carry forward the intergenerational knowledge needed to confront and mitigate the climate crisis facing Black farmers and land stewards.

Blackademics' cultivators[8] working group and other supporters of the National Black Food Justice Alliance[9] (NBFJA), a research arm composed of academic and research partners that anchors NBFJA's projects, have identified a critical need for an agroecological hub to gather data about Black farmers, disseminate information, develop innovative solutions to the problems Black land stewards face, and provide cross-institutional support.

The members of the Blackademic working group are committed to deepening our capacity, growing our body of work, and carrying forward the critical legacy of regenerative agriculture and Black land stewardship. We have partnered with Florida A&M University (FAU) to establish the first center dedicated to such work, the Lola Hampton and Frank Pinder Center for Agroecology.[10] Spaces like this can help us remove land from the speculative market and develop sustainable land-use systems.

Currently there is no agroecology program at any of the historically Black colleges and universities created by the 1890 Land Grant Act. Nor is there a land tenure center, as once existed at the University of Wisconsin. The vital role of land grant universities and cooperative extension in supporting farmers in the United States since the Civil War has been well documented.[11] Today, in order to develop new farmers who practice regenerative agriculture, similar support is needed. And for this vision to be realized, the programs in agroecology and land tenure that are developed must be rooted in democratic principles; grounded in community-based, culturally relevant research; and backed by intergenerational knowledge.

We also need sustainable organizations led by Black farmers and their communities that can provide food-growing knowledge and wealth-building guidance to help Black people achieve long-term health.

---

[8] https://www.blackfoodjustice.org/cultivatormembers
[9] https://www.blackfoodjustice.org/
[10] https://www.blackfoodjustice.org/agroecology-center
[11] https://extension.usu.edu/news/purpose-and-benefit-of-land-grant-extension-universities

What would be different if these resources were in place? All people would have access to nourishing food, housing, and medical care—which are currently unavailable in many Black communities.

Our Freedom Dream

Black community leaders must be at the forefront of this work, and this requires Black community control of assets—including, critically, ownership of land. Too often, whether intentionally or not, philanthropy uses resources as a weapon. Funding is provided, but for a short-term grant cycle, undermining the ability of community leaders to plan for the long term. The transfer of assets is therefore critical. To support a shift in power, philanthropy must provide funding that has the cycle of life, not a grant cycle, in mind.

In philanthropy, grant deliverables are almost always designed for the funder's benefit, rather than the benefit of the person or organization receiving the funds. We call on philanthropies and individual funders to build relationships and investments that truly center Black leadership and liberation.

In short, there must be a radical shift in mindset and power, a new approach that centers the ecosystem—that is, supports a network of organizations working toward a common goal—and funds in alignment with recipient communities. The expertise of communities involved in this land justice work must not be ignored. Funder-driven solutions will not lead us closer to our goals.

Generational trauma and related health issues are a massive drain on Black communities. Healing and getting back to a healthy baseline is a long-term effort that requires long-term resource reallocation. A real Wakanda is possible, but only if Black people have the necessary resources at their disposal.

In the free world of which we dream, our communities are well fed, income is not a barrier to good healthcare, and new education systems are run by and for the community. People would not just survive—they would be able to thrive. Asset and land reallocation can help achieve this world by transforming Black people's access to economic resources across the United States.

What Does Black Feminist Evaluation Look Like?

Cyndi Suarez

E valuation approaches and practices are contested sites of power. This is not surprising because they are the processes by which we assign value to things.

In the nonprofit sector, evaluation is shaped by the needs of philanthropy, as philanthropists drive the field with their ability to pay and demands for proof of the soundness of their investments. Evaluation is also a site for knowledge creation and strategic direction setting, as the reports that result are used to articulate an issue and make the case for efforts and funding.

When I wrote "The Leechers,"[1] an article about knowledge and resource extraction in the sector, many evaluators of color wrote to share stories about the extent of knowledge extraction in the evaluation field. They told of evaluators of color leaving the field, frustrated with increased gatekeeping in relationship to the widespread movement for racial justice and the field's demands for equity-focused evaluation, which often leads to white evaluator "allies" extracting, competing, and protecting their privileged positions in the field and market.

So, it is exciting to see evaluators of color innovate the field in new, more potent directions, away from the philanthropic gaze.

In a session titled, "A Black Feminist Framework for Research Evaluation as a Tool for Black-led Social Change," Dr. Sydney McKinney, executive director of the National Black Women's Justice Institute (NBWJI)—which focuses on ending the criminalization and systemic punishment of Black women and girls—demonstrated how to use research as a tool for social change.

---

[1] https://nonprofitquarterly.org/the-leechers/

Dr. McKinney started by stating that rather than taking a stance of objectivity, NBWJI positions itself as an organization of researcher activists. The research it leads looks at how Black women and girls experience the police, focusing on not just fatalities, but the way everyday interactions are harmful. The Institute seeks to understand the following:

1. What pushes Black women and girls into the criminal justice system?
2. What do they need?
3. What do they do after?

NBWJI began its work on Black women and girls because even though they are "overrepresented among those incarcerated at the federal, state and local levels,"[2] there is very little data on this specific demographic group. Women are included in the criminal system's data, but they are not segmented. NBWJI researchers go into the data sets that exist when it can, but because it is not engaging in conventional approaches and is instead centering Black women and girls and asking different questions, partnerships are important.

The Institute partners with Black-led organizations, working with those who are affected to define its questions, create surveys, and integrate an ongoing relationship with data. Kenya Welsh, director of development and strategic partnerships, shared that the work begins with a pre-engagement needs assessment. NBWJI also looks for opportunities that are trauma informed,[3] meaning that partners are skilled, or at least committed to becoming skilled, at designing with the assumption that the work may include people with a history of trauma. This enables staff members to engage participants without retraumatizing them.

NBWJI projects integrate data design, collection, interpretation, and implementation into organizational project models in a seamless cycle of improvement.

For example, the Institute has a partnership with The Mentoring Center in Oakland, California. The executive director, Celsa Snead, joined the session to share how such a partnership works. The Center runs EMERGE,[4] an innovative school reentry program for girls aged 16 to 18 "who are returning to school from a condition of confinement or incarceration." The overarching goal is "'confinement to a college and career' pathway for young women." The specific goals are as follows:

---

[2] https://www.calwellness.org/news/cal-wellness-invests-13-million-to-meet-health-needs-of-women-of-color/

[3] https://www.cdc.gov/cpr/infographics/6_principles_trauma_info.htm

[4] https://mentor.org/emerge/

1. Repair girls' relationships with school.
2. Provide opportunities for accelerated credit recovery toward their completion of a high school diploma.
3. Facilitate their enrollment in an institution of higher learning and/or permanent employment.
4. Create a trauma-responsive environment that advances social and emotional learning and healing.

This is a pilot program, and Snead said, "We wanted to make sure we are doing it correctly." The program is exploring what it means to educate Black girls. It wants to expand the model, so the model has to be strong. Having the Institute as an original partner has significant benefits, Snead notes.

The Institute informed both program design and evaluation by accessing the girls' voices. Thus, the evaluation was considered a key component of the work from the beginning. Snead said, "We felt good about the recommendations to make the program better. They were precise, tangible, and clear. Just the process helped us learn. We already started implementing what we learned to make improvements."

How exactly did the evaluation process help? EMERGE made improvements to the model in both the curriculum and the school day. The evaluation also confirmed what program staff members thought: that mental healthcare is needed, as well as other supports. The evaluation was also an opportunity to reflect on the work the program had done in terms of outcomes and impact.

Welsh said, "Talking starts the process. People want to talk. They want to be heard, validated, included. And they are more comfortable talking to someone that looks like them."

Everyone who completes a survey is offered mental health support. Dr. McKinney said, "Paying people for their time is important, but so is mental health."

However, "There's not a lot of uptake from participants on the mental health services, so we have to figure out how to do it better," Dr. McKinney said. She suspects that there is work to be done in getting participants to prioritize their mental health.

Snead said that although evaluation is critical in social change work, "a luxury that should not be a luxury," it is important to find the right evaluator. However, although funders encourage and even require evaluation, Snead said, "It is rarely the case that evaluation is embedded in the program and supported by philanthropy. That's a mistake, particularly with direct services."

There are so many ways to leverage evaluations, but they require partnerships. Current practice is requests for proposals. There is no co-creation. Funders fund a person who gathers and analyzes the data. There is no continuous learning and no internal staff members. Dr. McKinney said, "We need to invest in the how, not just impact. How do you know you have impact if you don't have the right model?

"Funders could also do more with the public. Right now, most evaluations result in internal reports. Investing in data visualization is also critical. The work is to figure out how to get that information out more effectively."

Further, Black research organizations tend to work with small budgets. Dr. McKinney said, "We have to ask for what we need."

Dr. McKinney concludes, "A Black feminist approach to evaluation means that we own our bias, but our bias is supporting people and projects to be successful. The goal is to do the work so that organizations don't need us. The evaluation is to build capacity."

Thus, it appears that a Black feminist approach to evaluation states its bias up front: the betterment of conditions for a particular subordinated demographic group. Further, because the demographic group is subordinated, this approach centers group members and seeks to understand conditions from their perspective. And, although the work may be issue focused, it is also intersectional, seeking to understand the way different forces act on the issue. It is also trauma informed, with an understanding that oppression causes trauma and a commitment to not only not contributing to trauma but also alleviating it. Finally, it is partnered, always tied to real action in the world.

Nothing Is Broken

What Evaluation and Philanthropy Can Learn from Abolitionism

Dr. Aisha Rios

I want to, from the very jump, say something—something that my friends, comrades, and I like to say about ourselves is that we identify as students of abolition or practicing abolitionists. And we say that because we, one, recognize that we're in a constant state of learning and unlearning. But we also want to honor our commitment to creating an abolitionist world. And so, I say that because I want to invite you all into dialogue with me in a place of learning and unlearning. And . . . to the extent that you can, try not to get held up in this, "OK, if I do this and this and this and this, I'll be a perfect abolitionist," or, "I have to develop a perfect understanding or definition of abolition."

So, how this next 20 minutes or so is going to go is, I'm going to share two stories with you. I'm going to invite you all to engage with me a little bit around what you noticed, and then I'm going to share what I noticed about these stories. And then I want to tell you what I think we can do about it collectively.

So, here's the first story. I was working on an evaluation with a foundation. They wanted to understand teachers in the United States perceptions of working with students with disabilities. They wanted to understand, "Do teachers feel a sense of responsibility to teaching and working with students with disabilities?" And they wanted to understand if teachers felt confident and competent in their ability to do so. So, my team and I started

Transcript from 2022 GEO Conference Short Talk.[1]

[1] https://nonprofitquarterly.org/nothing-is-broken-what-evaluation-and-philanthropy-can-learn-from-abolitionism/ / last accessed March 09, 2023.

talking with teachers, and we learned that they do in fact feel a sense of responsibility for all students. But the next thing that happened was really, really interesting. The teachers wanted to talk about something much bigger than individual-level behavior and attitudes. They wanted to talk about systemic and institutional injustices that shape their work with students. They wanted to talk about how they struggled to navigate these and the supports that they needed to actually work with students in a way that they felt was liberating and supportive for their students. And so, my team and I brought these findings to the funder. And the funder told us, well, that doesn't map onto the original learning and evaluation questions, so it shouldn't go into the report. My team and I pushed back. And we were able to get those findings, convince the funders to put the findings into the report, but only as a supplement, so not the main section of the report. So that's the first story.

Here's the second. I was working with a nonprofit with colleagues. And the nonprofit leadership wanted to understand what it would take for their staff [members] to work and implement programming in a way that aligned with reflective practice. What I mean by "reflective practice" is bidirectional reflection and learning and dialogue rooted in a political analysis, not one-directional kind[s] of education formats. And so, my team and I wanted to do the work in a way that was collaborative. What I mean by that was we wanted to design and implement the work in a way that was in partnership with the people who would be most impacted by the work . . . in this case, it was young staff [members] of color.

My team and I started working with the staff [members] and started talking with other staff [members]. And very similar to the first story, what we learned was the staff [members] wanted to have a much bigger conversation. . . .What they wanted to talk about was [the way] that leadership, the way that they were advocating for reflective practice, was done in a way that felt more oppressive than liberatory. The staff [members] felt like they were being pushed to engage in reflective practice. Staff [members] of color described feeling tokenized. Staff [members] described feeling that they wanted to have space for directional learning with one another, but they were constantly being pushed to perform individually. And so, my team and I decided that we were going to lean into what the staff [members were] telling us, right, and broaden the scope of the evaluation. So those are the two stories.

So, what I want to ask you all now is, how many of you in this room have been in a situation like either of these stories before? Show me by raising a hand. A lot of you. For anyone who raised your hand, could you share a bit more about how you responded to that if you're up for it?

[*Inaudible response from audience.*]

Thank you for sharing. Yeah . . . so the big takeaway that I'm hearing in the story that you just shared is that you resisted, right? And . . . that to me is the heart of what I want to talk about today. And so, this act of resistance, and even in the two stories that I shared also, my colleagues and I did the same thing. And so, I want to really point out that I believe that we all in this room can resist, even when we're implicated in institutions of oppression, right, even more implicated in a lot of really challenging dynamics. But what I love about both what you just shared and then the two stories that I shared is that when we open ourselves up to the possibility of different ways of being and we open ourselves up to the possibility of different voices shaping the work that we do and shaping the evaluation work that we do, we actually create more opportunities for far more nuanced and complex understandings of whatever phenomen[on it] is that's a subject of the inquiry that we're engaged in.

And so, one of the things that these stories also tell[s] me about the evaluation field is that, as evaluators, we basically become implicated in a lot of these oppressive dynamics, and we don't question them, and we don't push back like you did. And so, I really want to talk about resistance and the ways that we can push back, rather than fixate on the problems, as our luncheon keynote beautifully articulated. What happens in the evaluation field is that when we stay laser focused on questions, assumptions—things that are all dictated by those who commissioned the evaluation—we end up reinforcing oppressive dynamics. And we often create and reinforce individualized ways of responding to injustice, inequality—individualized solutions or problems. Case in point, the two stories that I shared. In both cases, the funder wanted to focus on individual behaviors and attitudes.

The other thing that happens is that we start reinforcing one-directional, hierarchical accountability all to the funder, as opposed to, say, being accountable to community and movement leaders. And so, these three themes [run] across both stories—learning agendas that are dictated by those who commissioned the evaluation, individualized solutions and problem-solving, and then also one-directional hierarchical accountability. All three of those [themes] are actually characteristics of what scholars and activists refer to as the nonprofit-industrial complex. So that is, I know, a mouthful, but basically, it's a web of relationships [among] funders, nonprofits, government, and wealthy elites. There is a really awesome artist based in Laos, who designed this zine. You can check them out. Their website is on a WordPress called **zeeninginlaos.com**. They articulate how philanthropy functions within the nonprofit-industrial complex with this art. So far left, you see, wealthy capitalists steal wages to make profit, then divert money out of public funds—taxes—thereby controlling dissent through grantmaking processes into tax-shelter foundations. I flipped that. Controlling dissent through grantmaking processes, which makes money, pays out, and benefits the system, while keeping us—aka, the masses—down. So, what this means is that funders engage in managing and controlling communities of color, queer and trans communities, our unhoused neighbors, all communities who have the power when banding together to resist oppressive systems.

And so, the other thing that happens is that, through these mechanisms, we actually dictate the narratives that are told and those that are not told. So, let's take the first story as an example with the teachers. If my colleagues and I had just stuck to the program—if we had said, "Yes, what the teachers are saying about systemic-level issues, like, that's not really what we need to be talking about"—if we had done that, we may have created a report that would have told a partial story that may have been published. It may have been presented at a conference like this. And all the nuances and the complexity that were [these] teachers' real, lived experiences and that of their students would have been erased.

There was a 2021 *Foundation Review* article[2] by Tanya Beer, Patricia Patrizi, and Julia Coffman, where they talk about this very topic. They articulate how advocacy groups and philanthropic support networks like GEO have critiqued the ways that funders manage and control communities and grantees and the work that they do. And they make the case that the evaluation field perpetuates these oppressive dynamics, and we don't question them. And I agree with them. These mechanisms and management and control for me, I believe, are deeply interconnected with institutions of policing and incarceration.

So, you may have been wondering, wait, I'm following you. But, like, what does this have to do with abolition? I'm going to get us there. I'm going to get us there.

So, from my perspective, and a lot of other scholars and activists out there who[m] I madly respect, these are all interconnected. But that's just part of the story. The other part of the story is what abolition teaches us about organizing. So, you may have heard people say, prisons and policing are not broken. The prison-industrial complex is not broken. It's doing what it was designed to do, which is to control and manage dissent. And I argue the same is true for the nonprofit-industrial complex, of which all of us who work in evaluation and philanthropy are a part.

The other thing that I want to elevate is that people often think about abolition as defunding police departments and completely abolishing prisons, and that is true. So, thinking about the [conference] luncheon today, [about the] kind of language about destruction and disrupt, right?

---

[2] https://scholarworks.gvsu.edu/tfr/vol13/iss2/9/

The other part of abolition is the other side of that. It's about imagining and creating something different, something that we can't even fathom, because we're focused in this matrix, and we can't see past it, feel past it. Ruth Wilson Gilmore has said infamously, "Abolition is about presence, not absence. It's about building life-affirming institutions." And that's exactly what I'm talking about here.

So, when I talk about embodying abolition, I talk about my evaluation work and my consulting work. I talk about my interactions with friends and families, the ways that my responses to harm kind of lean into punishment rather than care and love. And so, it's much bigger. And it is about the prison-industrial complex, and it's about everything else that we do in our lives.

I wanted to share these two stories with you because I wanted to show how these mechanisms operate in real life. I also wanted to highlight acts of resistance, so we're not just focused on the problem, right? What I want to do now is create some space to talk about what I think we can do about it collectively. . . . I believe we all in this room—I said this earlier—we all have the space to act collectively and resist oppressive structures. Again, this really resonates with what Juliette was saying yesterday. What was the framing? It was so beautiful. I'm blanking on it. Someone help me out. Disruption—darn it, I forgot. It was really, really, really, really, really beautiful. But basically, it's speaking to organizing. And so, "practice science fiction" is language that the editors of *Octavia's Brood*,[3] adrienne maree brown and Walidah Imarisha, have articulated. So, what they're saying is that science fiction authors are practicing science fiction, right? And that's what organizers are doing. They're imagining and building a world that's different, that doesn't exist right now. But it does exist right now because we're building it today. And so, practice science fiction.

So, there's three ways that I want to encourage us to do this. And I want to say that this is not the end all be all, just some ideas I want to offer us. One of them is expand whose questions and assumptions we let drive evaluation, right? So, this really maps onto the two stories that I shared. And so, I think in order to do this, what we have to do is build some skills and capacity around generative conflict. We have to create room for us to make mistakes and acknowledge when we don't know something, and we have to know that it's okay to do that. And we're not going to be ousted for that, right? And so, building these skills around critique and contestation feel[s] super, super important.

---

[3] https://www.akpress.org/octavia-s-brood.html

Second, I'll just pause to say that if you were in the luncheon today and yesterday, you're noticing lots of similarities, which to me is just a beautiful indication of being in the right place at the right time. I want all of us to think about ways that we can engage in internal resistance organizing work within our institutions. Dylan Rodriguez and Dr. Carmen Rojas described this as counter-occupying spaces. So, what that means is find ways to engage in radical truth telling within your institutions.

So, many of us have to stay in our positions, right? We have to do that to survive, to support our families and make ends meet. I'm not saying that we should all leave our jobs. What I'm saying, though, and challenging us on is, how can we really think critically about the work that we're doing and our roles and our institutions? And how can we challenge the logic and legitimacy of the status quo, which is framed so much as just practical and realistic? And so that's the second piece. And then finally, I want us to support grassroots organizing outside of our institutions. This is really important to me. I started my own consulting practice about two and a half years ago. And before that, all I had space to do, working for other people, was to do everything that was about billable hours. Work 50-plus hours a week. There was no space for reflective practice. There was no space for me to engage in organizing work. And so, when I started my own practice two years ago, I insisted that half of my time be engaged in unpaid labor and organizing work. And since I've done that, I've learned so much. And engaging in that work has sharpened my analysis. And I know it would do the same for all of you. And so, I want us to be engaging in work outside of our institutions so that we can really, really, really build collective action and critical analysis that's necessary to do this work. And there's so many movement spaces to be involved in. . . . we need as many people as possible in all these spaces.

I want to leave you with a quote. I was talking with a dear friend. Their name is Phoebe. They are based in the Philippines; I met [them] recently. We were talking about abolition and having really hard conversations. And they shared a quote from Grace Lee Boggs. So, Grace Lee Boggs said this: "Transform yourself to transform the world." And what they meant by that was not hyper focus on [your] individual self, but to instead look at your individual spheres of influence—so, the places where you work, your paid and unpaid labor—look at those as sites for change, sites for you to embody something different, sites for you to practice science fiction.

Thank you.

IV

Implementing Reparations: Health and Well-Being

Revolutionary Black Grace

Finding Emotional Justice in Global Black Communities

Esther A. Armah

L oss is an intimate part of global Blackness. Britain was an empire. America became a superpower. Africa had kingdoms. All global Black people lost something through systems of oppression where the language of whiteness ruled under brutal lash, stolen native tongues, and charred skin.

Unfortunately, the issue is that global Black people compare and judge our losses. We tell one another that our loss is way worse than yours. We reach into the wounds of historical untreated trauma, wrap our pain around our mother tongue, fashion an insult, and target it at a man or a woman or child who looks just like us, or a shade of us. We are prosecutors, presenting damning evidence of deficit, intending to diminish and destroy. Devastatingly, we succeed.

Africans tell African Americans, "What do you know of our trauma? You're not African. You're American. Why must you always say racism, racism, racism?" African Americans tell Africans in the US, "You're here! In America! You're Black! Speak English. This ain't Africa! You're taking our jobs; you think you're better than us." And back and forth, and back and forth we go. We wound, retreat, and reemerge with fresh insults and unfresh trauma. Such is a lingering legacy of combined anti-Blackness and the language of whiteness.

This is a weaponizing of emotions—feelings of belonging, betrayal, and broken brotherhood—wielded like deadly samurai swords. This

The following is an excerpt from *Emotional Justice: A Roadmap for Racial Healing* (2022) by Esther A. Armah, reprinted with permission from Berrett-Koehler Publishers.

weaponizing entrenches historical separation and cultural segregation. What does that look like? Award-winning filmmaker dream hampton's documentary *Let's Get Free: The Black August Hip Hop Project* shows us.

The film is in tribute to incarcerated political prisoners. It focuses on social justice and Black liberation and features African American hip hop artists performing in New York, Cuba, and South Africa. On their South African leg, the artists attended the 2001 World Racism Conference in Durban, South Africa. There was an exchange between African Americans and Black South Africans that reveals this legacy of losses and comparisons.

The hip hop artists sit on a panel behind a desk with mics looking out over an audience that includes young Black South Africans and international media. The artists share messages of oppression, trauma, and loss stemming from being Black in America. Sections of the Black South African audience, arms folded, faces set, stare at them as they speak.

An African American woman, wearing a bright-yellow windbreaker, mic gripped, addresses the audience: "Coming to Africa, we are African Americans—and we don't know the African experience. Apartheid in South Africa—it is 90% Black; it's not comparable to the many abuses that we experience in the United States, which is still a majority white country."

Some of the young Black South Africans roll their eyes. They are becoming agitated. The exchange continues.

Another hip hop artist in shades and a black beanie says, "Us as kidnapped Africans in America, we fully understand our role in Africans' liberation worldwide."

After several more statements about oppression and racism in America from the panel and the international media, the Black South Africans grow even more agitated. The mic is finally passed to a Black South African high school student. Hand raised, with pushed-back natural hair and a white T-shirt with a map of South Africa around her neck, she starts to speak. She is angry. She stares directly at each of the artists and sweeps her arm to indicate that her comments are to all the hip hop artists on the panel: "For next time—or any other time—you come, *we're here*! And we deserve to be *heard*! The past injustices that happened to us are *still* happening to us and are still going on! It may seem that under the banner of this conference everything is fine! Everything is not so well! I am a student—I still suffer to go to school. My parents still need to struggle! How far can *you* empathize with *us*? *Never*. Because what *we* feel, *you* don't feel."

She hands the mic over, turns her back, turns back around, and crosses her arms facing the artists, face stony. Spotty applause breaks out; it comes from other Black South Africans.

Uneasiness, hurt, anger, and contempt move between the South Africans in the audience toward the African Americans on the panel. The air changes. Violence hovers. Stares are lengthening between panelists and audience members. Murmuring in South African languages grows, choking, accusing. The artists shift in their bodies; they exchange glances, the kind that say, "Shit's about to go down."

One of the hip hop artists responds, gesturing constantly with his hands, his voice emotional, passionate: "Listen! I understand what you're sayin' 'bout tryna empathize or whateva! But at least *you* guys still had *your* language! *We* don't even know who *we* are! Imagine if you didn't even know who you are? Imagine! *You* know who *you* are—who's your mother, who's your grandfather, who's your grandmother! So you have some sense of who you are! We don't even know who we are!"

In this exchange, shared trauma becomes a litigated history of loss versus loss, of mine is worse than yours, of what do you know about what it is to be my kind of Black. In this case, this emotional litigation is between South Africans and African Americans.

In the documentary, the exchange doesn't end in a peaceful coming together. There is a drifting apart between the two groups, but the unease, the hurt words, the resentment remain.

This chasm that divides us as global Black people is a supremacy of Black traumas and unheard hurt. Prosecuting loss buries already buried trauma even deeper into global Black bodies—it becomes a coffin that buries us all.

This pain becomes accusation and moves from the personal to the political, from the individual to the institutional. It then travels into our movements that philosophize about a pan-Africanism but don't recognize how untreated traumas feed an emotional relationship to our Blackness, not an ideological or philosophical one. What that means is that the division, the misunderstanding, the hurt, the anger, the resentment emerge to influence how we work, lead, and build with one another. It becomes a back-and-forth about who belongs where and who doesn't, what is owed and to whom, and on and on and on. What it does, fundamentally, is divide, and entrench division. It causes us to implode; it causes our movements to implode.

Scars from the Language of Whiteness

These scars are not only between Black folk in America and Africa. A segregated Blackness narrative dominates across parts of Africa too. During my first trip to South Africa, I remember the open hostility, dismissal, and judgment from Black South Africans toward me. I was judged as an African who wasn't specifically South African. This too has a term, *amankwerekwere*, meaning "people from Africa." Sounds strange, right? Especially since I was from Africa, just as they were. The language of whiteness flourished in South Africa, too, creating an Africa that was wretched, corrupt, and criminal, and specifically separating South Africa from this "other Africa." That is why unlearning the language of whiteness is for all of us—global Black folks, too. South African writer Sisonke Msimang writes about this in her visionary memoir, *Always Another Country*.

From Southern Africa to West Africa. In Senegal, a friend shares a story of an incident in Dakar, where a man told her that her Blackness is not his. They have a name for those like her: *nnack*—when you hear it said, it sounds like someone hawking up phlegm from their throat, ready to spit—it feels as it sounds.

Pause. Breathe. Close your eyes. It is here we so need revolutionary Black grace. What cannot win in our fight for full liberation is a divided, segregated Blackness. We are global Black family. We cannot heal with one another like this. We simply cannot.

Between Us . . . Black Women and Men

It is between us as Black women and men that these scars show up as generational inheritance. They are wounds soaked in blood, bone, burden, and brutality. Revolutionary Black grace between us is tender territory that must be carefully navigated. For Black women, there is—and has been—an emotional labor engaged in for Black men that is historical, transformative, and traumatic. That labor is how we love one another; it is how we hurt one another—it cannot be how we heal one another.

Emotional Justice requires emotional labor—from all of us. Our freedom movements were the result of the efforts of women and men; that is our history. The erasure train has traveled from Africa to America across continents, cities, and communities, removing Black women from seats at tables of resistance, disappearing our stories, reducing our sacrifice, and diminishing our struggle. Erasure is the language of trauma; it feeds the emotional economy. It does nothing for our healing. Doing this emotional labor is not a question about whether or not we love one another as Black people; it is about how we love one another, and how that love must reimagine emotional labor as part of our collective healing process.

We did not get free alone, we do not survive alone, we cannot heal alone—we thrive together. That togetherness requires a revolutionary

Black grace in which emotional labor is recognized, respected, and equally divided. There can be no Emotional Justice among us as global Black people without the equal division of emotional labor.

Honoring Our Journey, Finding Our Connection

We can recognize distinct Black experience without creating Black supremacies. We can honor the specificity and the distinction of a Blackness shaped by America, shaped by Africa and the Caribbean, and shaped by Europe—and how that Blackness shows up in Britain, in France, and in Africa. Each matters. We must recognize how historical oppressive systems had an expansive hand in reimagining our Blackness.

In other words, we can honor our unique and specific Blackness, but frame it in connection with a global Blackness. That globality goes back to Africa, a continent of beginnings and of re-makings, but also one of an enduring land, with myriad stories. Our road to healing as global Black people honors, revels in, and acknowledges—it doesn't diminish. That is how global Black people unlearn the language of whiteness, develop emotional connections to one another, and replace the emotional economy with revolutionary Black grace.

Global Black people fought for our freedom across Africa, in America, across Europe. We inspired one another. The independence movement of Ghana in the 1950s and 1960s parallels the rise of the civil rights movement in America. In the UK, there were freedom and resistance movements rising up to fight oppression. Courage was all of ours. Leaders such as Kwame Nkrumah, Ghana's first post-Independence Black president, and the Ghanaian women who funded the independence movement; Winnie Mandela of South Africa; Malcolm X; and Martin Luther King Jr. were all moved and shaped by a global Blackness. Martin Luther King Jr. came to Nkrumah's inauguration and spoke of the connection between Blackness in America and what was happening in Ghana, as did Fannie Lou Hamer when she went to Senegal. All of it speaks to the freedoms we fought for and the systems we navigated to survive.

Because of these journeys, revolutionary Black grace honors a Blackness that, yes, has been commodified, criminalized, demonized, deified, desired—but one we must make our own without diminishing one another. This is careful, challenging work. It is a path that covers millions of miles. And it is a practice of healing that evicts a centering of whiteness.

Our Blackness is interconnected, evolving, and changing, while the language of whiteness stays the same and has the same objective. This language always seeks to bury your you-ness and create a striving to be more somebody else. In being somebody else, you step away from an interconnected Blackness. No healing, no grace, no freedom comes from that.

Black Privilege Is Not the Answer

The contemporary story of Blackness centers America. That centering has consequences. It leads to a privileging of your Blackness, not connecting it to that of other Black folk in other parts of the world. There is a parallel narrative in places such as the UK, the "You have it better than the Blacks in the USA" narrative. This is a nurtured story, a fiction designed to hold up your Britishness with an exhale of "Thank God, we're not them." It's a deadly lie.

We cannot get to healing by walking a path of privilege.[1] We cannot replace white privilege with African privilege or African American privilege and expect to clearly hear one another as Africans and Black peoples of African descent around the world. Refusing to adopt privilege doesn't mean that our healing journeys don't include colliding traumas and conflict. They do. They will. There is centuries' worth of untreated trauma to unpack and heal. But we can't do that as we have been.

Revolutionary Black grace makes space to shape the conversation, honor the foundation, recognize the tradition, and reimagine our union. That starts by rebuking as lies these narratives of deficit and notions of supremacy—white and Black.

The Emotional, Not the Political

This work is about our emotional connection to our Blackness and to the Blackness of one another. An emotional connection to Blackness is not the same as a political one. Blackness is absolutely personal and political—that is a centuries-long marriage. That's not what I mean.

You can be philosophically pan-African, but your emotional connection to Blackness is not necessarily about those politics—a politics of possibility

[1] https://nonprofitquarterly.org/putting-privilege-in-perspective/

and connectivity that unifies Black people from around the world and centers global Blackness. That is a neat, clear philosophy. But your emotionality is not neat; it is messy—how can it not be, given the history and its legacy of untreated trauma? Your emotional connection may have been nurtured by deficiency; by how you've been loved; by how you've not been loved; by how you've been hurt; by how you've been treated, rejected, and discriminated against and how you have witnessed that toward family—that, too, is a generational inheritance. All these things shape your sense of self. So you may politically understand, but emotionally respond. That is emotionality masquerading as ideology. And it can fuck shit up. It does. And it has.

We see this in movements whose political ideology aligns, but that still implode. The reparations movement in the US highlights this phenomenon. There are multiple intersecting issues that we mischaracterize as political when they are in fact about the emotional. One of those issues is an ongoing fight to disconnect an American blackness from a global Blackness.[2] That hurts the healing of us as a global Black people. Those advocating that disconnect use tactics of attack, lambasting, and vicious critique—all weapons designed to entrench division. If our aim is to repair what has been broken, lost, and stolen, but our approach is to separate one Blackness from another, then we are engaging the weapons of whiteness while claiming that this is healing. That shit doesn't work. Not for healing.

There is a trauma among us that goes beyond language. There are connections among us that break down beyond legacy. What also lies between us as global Black people—across North America, in Europe, and in Africa—is a range of emotions: betrayal, resentment, a yearning, an anger, a sadness, a mourning, a magic, a beauty, a belonging, a desire for belonging, the pain of rupture. There is all of this between all of us.

History stripped millions of an identity, but not of a cultural memory. The DNA of the drum creates a global Black drumline, and in it we can find one another, and honor one another's journey. That is revolutionary Black grace.

The badassness of Blackness is universally understood, from culture, to art, to fashion, to food, to emulated beauty. We are swagger and flava, and all the things. What still connects us is Africa. Our first home. That doesn't mean we as global Black people all feel connected to Africa. We may not. We do not.

Our Blackness may be connected to our roots in the Southern states or to the history of Chicago or Detroit. It may flex its cultural muscles to

---

[2]https://nonprofitquarterly.org/californias-plan-for-lineage-based-reparations-for-slavery-is-it-enough/

soundtracks of London or Nottingham or Birmingham. All of these are part of our Blackness; all must be acknowledged. So this is not about the denial of the geographical spaces and places that shaped you, that you call home.

Home sits uneasy on tongues trained by the West's particular love language of violence toward Black bodies. America is a superpower—one that understands itself in superlatives: first this, biggest that, big, bigger, biggest, biggerlicious. To be Black in America is to be the descendant of those who built it, and to be simultaneously rejected by it. This does not mean that Black folks in America are not American, or that America is not their home. Absolutely not. They are, and it is. It simply means there is an uneasiness in this relationship to this history within this nation. Poet Hafiyah Geter reminds us that this is "a nation that doesn't love someone who looks like me." America's better self is rooted in Blackness, resistance, movement building, and a refusal to capitulate to the whiteness narrative of beasts and burdens.

Britain was an empire. It's relationship of superiority wreaked havoc with Black and Brown people. That superiority was a delusion. It manifests in two ways: a constant erasure of Britain's violence in her former colonies, and a romanticizing of that time as one of a manufactured greatness. This doesn't mean that Black folks in Britain don't love where they live, haven't built homes and family and community. They absolutely do and have. So much of Europe's wealth and Britain's power is rooted in Blackness from the Caribbean and Africa.

Finding home within one another means staying when it gets hard and when your soul connects to conflict, not comfort. But making a home takes time and action. It means engaging in an ongoing practice of empathy toward those who look like you—even when they don't feel you, and you don't feel them. Revolutionary Black grace means finding homes in and with one another by going on journeys of decentering whiteness and of honoring the full expanse of our Blackness across regions, countries, and continents. Doing that is a practice, not just a philosophy.

What Is Healing Justice?

Nineequa Blanding

In public health, we often talk about closing the gap in health inequities in order to create conditions for optimal health for all. These discussions reflect a growing consensus that health is a human right, which sets the stage for a shared vision of health justice. They also mirror ongoing efforts to achieve racial equity by addressing structural racism and its attendant injustices, and, in the process, expanding the health focus from the individual to the collective and society. These conversations and the work they inspire position the field of public health as a major actor in helping to protect, promote, and preserve our wellness.

"Health is a state of complete physical, mental, and social well-being and not merely the absence of disease or infirmity."[1] It is "a dynamic state of wellbeing emergent from conducive interactions between individuals' potentials, life's demands, and social and environmental determinants."[2] Although our collective health and well-being depend on mutuality and our ability to heal, these critical concepts are often missing from public health discussions centered on addressing health inequities.

Focusing on mutualism and healing builds a shared understanding of our interdependence and our inherent capacity to heal. As we strive to create conditions in which everyone can thrive, we must all collectively heal from the trauma caused by structural racism and understand that our connections with one another are inextricable from our ability to improve our health. These efforts lead to new approaches that draw on our shared strengths and shift us away from focusing on perceived deficits. As Sara Horowitz, founder and former executive director of the Freelancers

---

[1] "Constitution," World Health Organization, accessed November 8, 2022, who.int/about/governance/constitution.

[2] "Meikirch Model: A New Concept of Health Based on Science," accessed November 8, 2022, meikirch-modell.ch/en/.

[3] "Reclaiming Our History of Mutualism: A Conversation with Steve Dubb, Rithika Ramamurthy, and Sara Horowitz," *NPQ* 29 no. 2 (Summer 2022): 98–107.

Union, notes, "mutualism is not about charity, it's about human beings' strengths—our powers, our magic . . . mutualism calls on these to be in reciprocal relationship."[3]

What strategies will enable us to understand our interconnectedness, leverage our shared power, and heal from the trauma caused by structural racism?

A movement is under way to create spaces that allow for an exploration of practices to transform oppression—within our bodies, our communities, and the systems that perpetuate it. Longtime freedom activist and scholar Angela Davis—who has more than 50 years of experience leading social justice movements—highlights such healing-based transformation in her work. Davis says, "Self-care and healing and attention to the body and the spiritual dimension—all of this is now a part of radical social justice struggles."[4]

In part, this shift in the social justice struggles that Davis references is the emergence of healing justice, launched in 2007 by the Kindred Southern Healing Justice Collective.[5] Cara Page, one of the leading architects of healing justice, defines this work as one that "identifies how we can holistically respond to and intervene [in] intergenerational trauma and violence."[6] This movement, which is quickly gaining momentum, draws on the historic ways that communities have resisted systemic oppression and thrived.

The Kindred Collective states, "We do not seek to promote single healers as one model, nor models of healing as singular, nor to build individualized care, but to build mechanisms and systems that build collective wellness; transform generational trauma and violence; and build quality care that is accessible to all."[7]

Thus, healing justice work honors ancestral and Indigenous wisdom in an effort to respond to generational trauma, facilitate collective healing, and transform systemic oppression. It proposes that healing and joy are essential elements of liberation.

----

[4]Sarah Van Gelder, "The Radical Work of Healing: Fania and Angela Davis on a New Kind of Civil Rights Activism," *YES!*, February 19, 2016, yesmagazine.org/issue/life-after-oil/2016/02/19/the-radical-work-of-healing-fania-and-angela-davis-on-a-new-kind-of-civil-rights-activism.
[5]"What Is Healing Justice?," Kindred: Southern Healing Justice Collective, accessed November 8, 2022, kindredsouthernhjcollective.org/what-is-healing-justice/#values.
[6]See "Healing Justice," Move to End Violence, accessed November 8, 2022, www.movetoend violence.org/elements/healing-justice.
[7]"Health and Healing Justice and Liberation Values," Kindred: Southern Healing Justice Collective, accessed November 8, 2022, kindredsouthernhjcollective.org/values/.
(This quote was lightly edited for clarity.)

Although healing justice initially developed in the Southeast region of the United States, healing justice–centered approaches are evolving, led by a growing network of global healers and changemakers who seek to forge an accessible path to our collective well-being—both within communities of color and across cultures.

In that spirit, The Kindred Collective outlines a framework for healing justice that centers on four main values[8]—some of which are absent from both traditional public health frameworks and approaches to advancing equity:

Our Collective Wisdom and Memory Enable Well-Being

We value our collective wisdom and memory towards our collective well-being.

—*The Kindred Collective*[9]

A major aspect of healing justice involves naming the historic and present-day violence and oppression imposed on communities of color by government and healthcare, the criminal legal system, education systems, and more. According to the Kindred Collective, healing justice work acknowledges that our collective well-being is "integrally connected to . . . abusive experiences as based on a legacy of trauma, control and genocide of communities."[10] This view uplifts the notion that individual and collective trauma are, in fact, linked.

Current research provides evidence that supports the understanding that healing justice draws on cultural wisdom that understands that our individual health is dependent on our collective well-being. Recent developments in epigenetic studies are now confirming that trauma is passed down through generations, which can shape quality of life and, ultimately, life expectancy.[11]

....

[8] Ibid.
[9] Ibid.
[10] Ibid.
[11] Martha Henriques, "Can the Legacy of Trauma Be Passed Down the Generations?," *BBC Future*, March 26, 2019, bbc.com/future/article/20190326-what-is-epigenetics.

The long-standing history of oppression—in the form of anti-Blackness and structural racism—and its impact on our health are made visible through modalities such as community storytelling, accounts of visceral experiences, and decades of social and biomedical research. In *Medical Apartheid*, for example, author and medical ethicist Harriet Washington documents—in over 400 pages—stories of the multitude of traumas imposed on Black people in the name of science.[12] One of these harrowing stories is that of Saartjie (pronounced *SART-kay*, which means "little Sara" in Afrikaans) Baartman—famously known as Sarah Baartman.

As Washington recounts, at the age of 21, under the guise of promised prosperity, Baartman was forced to "enter an arena where she would become an object of unbridled medical curiosity and physical lust."[13] She was taken from her home by British surgeon Dr. William Dunlop and subjected to years of anatomical scrutiny. "Men of science made pilgrimages to London's academic and medical settings to sketch, measure, and endlessly analyze" her body.[14] After years of suffering rape and countless supposed medical examinations—actions justified, in the name of science, by racist ideology that permeates our medical system today[15]—Baartman "died from an infectious illness at the age of twenty-seven."[16]

After Baartman's death, her body was held captive by scientists and placed on public display in Paris's Musée de l'Homme until 1985.[17] Baartman's story is one of many examples of the "medically exploitative display of black peoples."[18] Widespread systemic trauma such as this creates intergenerational ripple effects that are further compounded by present-day oppression.

Racial inequities persist across all social systems, not just in healthcare, and they are driven by historic and present-day oppression and violence that rely on their continued justification and normalization of ideologies similar to those that normalized Baartman's subjugation. In response, healing justice "honor[s] individual agency, and therefore honor[s] people's right to make decisions about their own bodies."[19]

---

[12] Harriet A. Washington, *Medical Apartheid: The Dark History of Experimentation on Black Americans from Colonial Times to the Present* (New York: Harlem Moon, 2006).
[13] Ibid., 83.
[14] Ibid.
[15] Mathieu Rees, "Racism in Healthcare: What You Need to Know," *Medical News Today*, September 16, 2020, medicalnewstoday.com/articles/racism-in-healthcare#pain-treatment.
[16] Washington, *Medical Apartheid*, 85.
[17] Ibid.
[18] Ibid., 84.
[19] "Health and Healing Justice and Liberation Values."

Healing justice sheds light on oppression and simultaneously uplifts the power of community to heal. "We see that health and healing can be achieved by returning to ancient & traditional healing and earth & nature-based modalities and creating new practices to respond to our political and social context."[20] In our time, when so many systems are working to remove the autonomy and agency we have over our bodies as individuals, these practices are needed.

Wellness Is Liberation

We value wellness as a tool of liberation.
—The Kindred Collective[21]

Healing justice values wellness as a path to liberation. The Kindred Collective notes that these efforts work to "sustain our individual and collective wellness as a response to transform generational violence and trauma."[22] Healing justice addresses "racism and oppression as a public health issue and social illness that informs our physical, emotional, environmental, spiritual, and psychic well-being."[23] It uplifts the strength and inherent capacity of communities to harness our own power and transform oppression through healing.

In this way, healing justice pushes the existing health justice and health equity frameworks beyond what is currently considered to fall within the rubric of health. It brings attention to the inequities—the systemic injustices—that shape social determinants of health; but it also goes deeper by focusing on the traumas that have resulted from historic, intergenerational oppressive social relationships that affect individual and community health today.

Healing is restorative and essential to our well-being. When we create the conditions for healing to occur—an intrinsic process—and actively engage in our own healing, we harness our individual and collective strength to move beyond trauma. This work creates a path for the healing

....
[20] Ibid.
[21] Ibid.
[22] Ibid.
[23] Ibid.

of both people and systems, fostering new ways of being. Healing justice offers a way for us to reimagine how we show up for each other and how current systems dictate communities' trajectories.

Artist and healer Londrelle notes, "The thoughts we feel create our reality. If our minds are rooted in fear, our vision becomes clouded, and it becomes difficult to see the abundance that surrounds us."[24] When we allow ourselves to heal from fear caused by systemic oppression, we operate from a place of power and can shift our thinking from a scarcity mindset toward abundance, creating new possibilities for ourselves and our future generations.

Our Interdependence Is Essential

We value our interdependence.

—*The Kindred Collective*[25]

As noted by the Kindred Collective, healing justice values "dignity for all life" across all races and identities.[26] This framework centers on an understanding "that the ways we live with and treat each other ha[ve] direct impact on our wellness and collective well-being towards . . . transforming our conditions."[27] Our wellness is reliant on our relationships with individuals, our communities, society, and all life within the earth's ecosystem.

In a recent article on healing-centered leadership, Shawn Ginwright, professor of education in Africana Studies at San Francisco State University and CEO of Flourish Agenda, speaks to the need for this work:

> *The only path to reimagining the future is through healing our collective trauma and restoring a sense of possibility in our work. This can only happen when we foster a collective imagination that restores communal wisdom and sets a path toward more humane ways to show up in life.*[28]

---

[24] "Hello, I'm Londrelle," Chopra, accessed November 8, 2022, chopra.com/bio/londrelle.
[25] "Health and Healing Justice and Liberation Values."
[26] Ibid.
[27] Ibid.
[28] Shawn A. Ginwright, "Healing-Centered Leadership: A Path to Transformation," *NPQ* 28, no. 4 (Winter 2021).

Ginwright highlights a key aspect of healing justice—that our individual healing enables a shift in how we relate to one another, cocreate community, and transform systems.

The healing justice framework also values and is "conscious of the connection of our health . . . to the environment and the . . . healing of the earth."[29] As climate change affects every country across the globe, keen attention to and a shared understanding of our interdependence are needed.[30] In *Design as Politics*, Tony Fry notes, "No matter the differences of our circumstances as individuals, cultures, or nations, we now share a time that is new. We all share a continual moment of the diminishment of time. The actual finite time of our life on the planet (and the life of much else) is being reduced by our own destructive actions as a species."[31]

Our Wellness Requires Honoring All Bodies

We value all bodies and the conditions that we live in.

—The Kindred Collective[32]

The healing justice framework provides an opportunity to expand the ways that public health examines inequities. This country's systems are entrenched in structural racism and white supremacy, and this ideology shows up in how population health data are collected, analyzed, and used to develop interventions. Without an intentional effort, public health data approaches can perpetuate long-standing inequities rather than addressing them.

The Robert Wood Johnson Foundation speaks to this issue by noting, "We use the category of race as a means of identifying and measuring disparities. However, race has no biological meaning; it is a social construct designed intentionally to relegate people and communities of color to second-class status and to privilege white people. It is the racism that

---

[29] "Health and Healing Justice and Liberation Values."
[30] Cyndi Suarez, "Designing for Climate Change—in Time, for Equity," *NPQ*, November 10, 2021, nonprofitquarterly.org/designing-for-climate-change-in-time-for-equity/.
[31] Tony Fry, *Design as Politics* (Oxford, UK: Berg, 2011, first published 2010), 49–50.
[32] "Health and Healing Justice and Liberation Values."

accompanies [unfounded] racial hierarchy that has profound health consequences. The gaps and failures in our public health data systems today, in fact, stigmatize entire communities instead of doing what data can and should do: provide the roadmap and path toward systemic change."[33]

At present, there is a tendency to compare outcomes for Black people, Indigenous people, and people of color to their white counterparts. Yet, in the absence of efforts to counter unfounded racial hierarchies, this approach can unintentionally uplift white supremacist ideology. The health outcomes of white people cannot serve as the gold standard that people of color strive to attain. Our ideal should be grounded in a vision of collective liberation, healing, and well-being.

Indeed, healing justice requires expansive thinking beyond limited notions of good versus bad health, and honors all bodies. As noted by Adaku Utah of Harriet's Apothecary, this framework is "informed and grounded by economic, racial, disability, and reproductive justice movements."[34]

Further, tracking and analyzing data through a demographic lens places the onus of health inequities on individuals and communities rather than addressing the social ills and systemic oppression that create these injustices in the first place.

A New Vision for Addressing Structural Racism

The United States is residentially segregated by race. Public health studies show that life expectancy rates vary dramatically by neighborhood, and therefore by/in conjunction with race. The Robert Wood Johnson Foundation has mapped life expectancy rates by neighborhood across the United States.[35] In some areas, there is a 30-year gap in life expectancy between neighborhoods that are positioned just a few short miles apart but have different racial makeups. Structural racism, not race, drives these stark differences.

---

[33] Richard E. Besser, "To Transform Public Health, We Must Reimagine Our Data Systems," Centers for Disease Control and Prevention, last modified November 22, 2021, cdc.gov/minori tyhealth/racism-disparities/expert-perspectives/besser/index.html.

[34] Harriet's Apothecary, accessed November 8, 2022, harrietsapothecary.com/.

[35] "Mapping Life Expectancy," Robert Wood Johnson Foundation, September 11, 2015, www.rwjf.org/en/library/articles-and-news/2015/09/city-maps.html

Racism affects everyone, inhibiting our ability to attain optimal health as a whole. Although structural racism traumatizes people of color most, studies show racial trauma also affects white people. Structural racism structures opportunity in a way that "saps the strength of the whole society" by wasting human resources.[36] It is also arguably the most significant barrier to racial and health equity.

Recognizing the debilitating impacts of structural racism across systems, local jurisdictions across the country have galvanized to formally acknowledge racism as a public health crisis[37] and create policies and practices that aim to transform the social determinants of health, which influence how communities live, grow, work, and play.[38] These determinants include housing,[39] education, economic stability, neighborhood environments, social cohesion, healthcare,[40] food security,[41] water access,[42] civic engagement,[43] incarceration,[44] and more.

In an October 2021 report, the American Public Health Association (APHA) revealed its analysis of 198 declarations and 38 accompanying strategic actions to promote health equity.[45] The report details the growing

---

[36] "How Racism Makes People Sick: A Conversation with Camara Phyllis Jones, MD, MPH, PhD," Kaiser Permanente Institute for Health Policy, August 2, 2016, kpihp.org/blog/how-racism-makes-people-sick-a-conversation-with-camara-phyllis-jones-md-mph-phd/.

[37] "Racism Is a Public Health Crisis," American Public Health Association, accessed November 9, 2022, apha.org/topics-and-issues/health-equity/racism-and-health/racism-declarations.

[38] Steve Dubb, "Social Determinants of Health Can Lose Meaning in For-Profit Translation," *NPQ*, February 19, 2018, nonprofit quarterly.org/social-determinants-health-can-lose-meaning-profit-translation/.

[39] Steve Dubb, "Kaiser Makes First Investments from $200 Million Affordable Housing Fund," *NPQ*, January 18, 2019, nonprofit quarterly.org/kaiser-makes-first-investments-from-200-million-affordable-housing-fund/.

[40] Sonia Sarkar, "Control in Healthcare: History and Reclamation of Bodily Autonomy," *NPQ*, July 18, 2022, nonprofitquarterly.org/control-in-healthcare-history-and-reclamation-of-bodily-autonomy/.

[41] Eileen Cunniffe, "During Pandemic, Healthy Food 'Prescriptions' Matter More Than Ever," *NPQ*, August 21, 2020, nonprofit quarterly.org/during-pandemic-healthy-food-prescriptions-matter-more-than-ever/.

[42] Jazmyn Blackburn and Vanessa Barrios, "To Bridge Health Equity and Infrastructure, We Must Harness Grassroots Power and Creativity," *NPQ*, July 18, 2022, nonprofitquarterly.org/to-bridge-health-equity-and-infrastructure-we-must-harness-grassroots-power-and-creativity/.

[43] Steve Dubb, "Health Funders Call on Philanthropy to Support Power Building," *NPQ*, September 19, 2022, nonprofitquarterly.org/health-funders-call-on-philanthropy-to-support-power-building/.

[44] Chelsea Dennis, "Report Calls for Systemic Change to Drive Down Women's Incarceration Rates," *NPQ*, November 4, 2021, nonprofitquarterly.org/report-calls-for-systemic-change-to-drive-down-womens-incarceration-rates/.

[45] *Analysis: Declarations of Racism as a Public Health Crisis* (Washington, DC: American Public Health Association, October 2021).

movement within local government to finally acknowledge that structural racism is a threat to public health.[46] Since 2018, APHA has tracked 250 declarations issued by high-ranking government officials and adopted by entities such as city/town councils, county boards, governors and mayors, education boards, public health associations, and public health departments. The number of these declarations increased at the height of the pandemic, as COVID shed light on long-standing injustices faced by Black and Indigenous people and people of color.

APHA's analysis revealed that nearly all the declarations include a commitment to some level of data collection, analysis, and reporting, with varied commitments to creating a task force to ensure accountability. More than a third of the declarations outline an obligation of forming and strengthening partnerships with community groups and organizations that are addressing racism—and almost half of those declarations include strategic action to promote an "equity in all policies" approach to future policy development, along with a commitment to reviewing existing policies and programs through a racial equity lens.[47] Leading with a racial equity lens enables examination of how policies affect people's experiences along racial lines—shaping opportunities, outcomes, and power.

Although significant efforts are under way in local jurisdictions to address systemic racism as a public health crisis, strategies that foster community healing to address the harms caused by structural racism are not at the forefront of these efforts' strategic plans. This prompts the question: what if healing justice efforts served as a guidepost, as the foundation of a collective vision, for all government strategies to address structural racism?

What would our future look like if we all operated from a place of healing? It would be a world where we value wellness as liberation, appreciate our interdependence, are in tune with our inherent capacity to heal, honor the wisdom of all cultures and bodies, and are guided by a shared understanding that our collective health is inextricable from our relationship with the earth. Healing justice is critical for catalyzing the type of systems transformation that enables such a vision to become reality.

---

[46] Michele Late, "Racism Declarations Pass New Milestone," Public Health Newswire, *The Nation's Health*, July 25, 2022, publichealthnewswire.org/Articles/2022/07/25/Racism-Public-Health.

[47] *Analysis: Declarations of Racism as a Public Health Crisis*, 2.

The US "Healthcare System" Is a Misnomer— We Don't Have a System

Amira Barger

Healthcare in the United States is a social contract—and an out-dated one. I learned this firsthand while working in community clinics across Dallas, Texas. There, I sought to address patient needs holistically by helping patients navigate social services, including access to food, shelter, jobs, education, healthcare, and more. After years of navigating the murky waters of state-sponsored health insurance and social services, I realized that the current system not only doesn't work for everyone—it doesn't even work as a system. States collect and share data in disparate ways.[1] Our medical billing is a mess,[2] and public, corporate, and nonprofit health entities operate in silos.[3] In fact, anyone who has worked in the so-called system will tell you that these various entities work against one another, rather than together to meet communities' needs.

Equitable Care

The solution is a system that takes into account the totality of our linked human experience and treats us all as whole persons.

Holistic-minded health solutions seek to address health literacy, food insecurity, transportation, housing, and other factors known as the social

---

[1] https://www.hhs.gov/sites/default/files/HHS_StateofDataSharing_0915.pdf
[2] https://public3.pagefreezer.com/browse/HHS.gov/30-12-2021T15:27/https://www.hhs.gov/about/news/index.html
[3] https://news.weill.cornell.edu/news/2019/02/most-causes-of-healthcare-fragmentation-not-related-to-medical-need

determinants of health. According to one report, "Positively affecting one or more social determinants of health generally requires the participation of multiple stakeholders to produce complementary sets of strategies, activities, and interventions, including strategies for monitoring social determinants of health with non-health data."[4] The CDC emphasizes that addressing these factors is vital to improving health and reducing health disparities.[5] Doing so requires integrating several elements into healthcare infrastructure:

- **Programs.** Implementing successful health equity strategies
- **Measurement.** Instituting data practices to advance health equity
- **Policy.** Passing and enforcing laws, regulations, and rules to improve population health
- **Infrastructure.** Investing in organizational functions that support health equity

Our institutions have done little to consistently provide equal access to health. Historically, hospitals were built on public trust—by, for, and in the community. Today, we find our collective health in a fragmented ecosystem. This disorganization serves only the privileged few, while the most vulnerable—and Black patients, in particular—pay the highest price. Profits and policy[6] stand in the way of treating patients' whole person needs, which include the biological, behavioral, social, and environmental.[7]

Driven by Profit

Understanding what's wrong with US healthcare begins with understanding the motivations of its main stakeholders, the 4Ps—patients, providers (professionals and institutions), payors, and policy makers.[8] In the United States, most healthcare providers work for companies that serve at the

[4] https://journals.lww.com/jphmp/Abstract/2016/01001/Toward_Achieving_Health_Equity_Emerging_Evidence.8.aspx
[5] https://www.cdc.gov/minorityhealth/publications/health_equity/index.html
[6] https://stanmed.stanford.edu/how-health-insurance-changed-from-protecting-patients-to-seeking-profit/
[7] https://www.nccih.nih.gov/health/whole-person-health-what-you-need-to-know
[8] https://www.ncbi.nlm.nih.gov/pmc/articles/PMC6549107/#:~:text=In%20healthcare%20the%20main%20stakeholders,four%20Ps'%20in%20healthcare).&text=Moreover%2C%20industry%20(e.g.%20medical%20device,and%20media%20are%20also%20important

pleasure of their investors, payors, and boards—whose primary interest, following shareholder theory, is making a profit.[9] Preventative measures keep people healthy and out of hospitals, but hospitals make money by treating the unwell. US healthcare operates within this contradiction.

Healthcare entities often talk about putting people first, but in practice, patients are viewed as numbers on a spreadsheet and come in at a distant second to the almighty dollar. As a result, health plans and systems are often barriers to care. Health providers vet our worthiness for care before we gain access to the services that, in most cases, we pay for out of our own pockets.[10] In doing so, those who have taken an oath to "do no harm" do harm every day, even if unintentionally. The industry's drive for profit ails us—and it is driving millions of us to an early death.

The Racial Divide

As Jeneen Interlandi notes in *The New York Times Magazine*, "the United States remains the only high-income country in the world where such (health)care is not guaranteed to every citizen."[11] Instead, we operate in a two-tier healthcare system—and as Interlandi's article argues, our lack of universal healthcare is due to the systemic anti-Black racism on which the US was built. In other words, our so-called system is working just as it was designed to. "There has never been any period in American history where the health of Blacks was equal to that of whites," writes Evelynn Hammonds, a historian of science at Harvard University, "Disparity is built into the system."[12] In a nation built on the dehumanization of Black people, it is clear Black people remain collateral damage in the pursuit of profit.

Abenaa Hayes, founder and CEO of Elysee Consulting, is a health equity and DEI expert who says, "Profit-driven motives need to take a backseat to the larger societal good. And I don't think we've all gotten there yet, but that seems to be one of the most obvious things to advance equity."[13]

---

[9] https://www.forbes.com/sites/stevedenning/2017/07/17/making-sense-of-shareholder-value-the-worlds-dumbest-idea/?sh=29d0d9a42a7e
[10] https://patientengagementhit.com/news/implicit-bias-in-primary-care-yields-racial-health-disparities
[11] https://www.nytimes.com/interactive/2019/08/14/magazine/universal-health-care-racism.html?mtrref=undefined&assetType=PAYWALL
[12] https://www.nytimes.com/2020/01/13/upshot/bad-medicine-the-harm-that-comes-from-racism.html
[13] https://www.elyseeconsulting.co/

Black Distrust

According to the Robert Wood Johnson Foundation's "Discrimination in America Report," 22% of Black Americans reported avoiding medical care due to concerns about discrimination or poor treatment.[14] Available data validate these concerns.[15] "A significant and longstanding body of research suggests that discrimination by providers and institutional bias are drivers of racial disparities in health, contributing to racial differences in diagnosis, prognosis, and treatment decisions," according to Kaiser Family Foundation.[16] Delivering care based on sociopolitical constructs is ill-advised and harmful—and it's the basis of our current "system." A series of focus groups conducted in 2001 asked patients whether discrimination affected their access to quality healthcare. One participant's response sums up the collective sentiment: "The medical world just reflects the real world."[17]

The Black community's understandable reluctance to engage with racialized medicine is an ongoing public health concern. To allay community concerns, we must examine interpersonal and institutional communication exchanges. One study noted that patients who perceived that their providers treated them with dignity reported higher satisfaction with care, more adherence to treatment plans, and greater satisfaction with preventive care—one of our most effective public health tools.[18] However, as reported by NPR, Black patients report that many clinicians are dismissive, condescending, or impatient, which does little to engender trust.[19] Whether it be misinformation, ignoring patient preferences, a lack of cultural humility, a barrage of complicated insurance choices, unclear instructions from providers, or a language barrier—all are rooted in poor communication. Some Black patients say they'd prefer to work with Black doctors if they could find one.[20] Addressing health disparities requires culturally and linguistically appropriate care, as well as increasing representation within the healthcare workforce.

---

[14] https://www.rwjf.org/en/insights/our-research/2017/10/discrimination-in-america-experiences-and-views.html
[15] https://www.urban.org/sites/default/files/publication/104568/black-and-african-american-adults-perspectives-on-discrimination-and-unfair-judgment-in-health-care_0.pdf
[16] https://www.kff.org/racial-equity-and-health-policy/issue-brief/use-of-race-in-clinical-diagnosis-and-decision-making-overview-and-implications/
[17] https://www.ncbi.nlm.nih.gov/books/NBK220347/
[18] https://www.ncbi.nlm.nih.gov/pmc/articles/PMC1466898/
[19] https://www.npr.org/sections/health-shots/2021/05/28/996603360/trying-to-avoid-racist-health-care-black-women-seek-out-black-obstetricians
[20] https://www.webmd.com/story/where-are-all-the-black-doctors

Health Equity

In a system so obviously compromised, achieving health equity begins with mitigating the moral injuries experienced in healthcare settings. The term *moral injury* was first used to describe soldiers' responses to their actions during times of war. With regards to healthcare, a 2018 STAT article defined moral injury as "being unable to provide high-quality care and healing."[21] Taking steps to make visible these injuries creates space for exploring solutions.

Moving toward health equity also requires reframing our regulatory landscape. Though the Affordable Care Act (ACA) and the Health Insurance Portability and Accountability Act (HIPAA) advanced protections and accountability, both are insufficient. By using veiled processes and strategic positioning, healthcare stakeholders are still able to shape narratives and act with little accountability from regulatory bodies, such as the FDA or attorney general. This systemic failure compounds the moral injury experienced by well-meaning healthcare providers and advocates as they navigate, and reluctantly become complicit in, a compromised system.

Many healthcare providers across the United States are, in fact, part of nonprofit hospital systems[22] whose missions are, ostensibly, to serve patients who reflect the demographics of the surrounding communities.[23] These hospitals are paramount to advancing equity as they serve as entry points to social services for millions, including society's most vulnerable.[24] After all, healthcare begins at the local level, with trusted neighbors and partners.[25] COVID-19 brought to light the shortcomings of our healthcare industry, devastating people in communities where limited access to healthcare is most acute.[26] Still, even amid the pandemic, we saw glimmers of progress, however brief, as hospitals worked diligently to reach out to people who, for a host of systemic reasons, have been historically hard to reach.

[21] https://www.statnews.com/2018/07/26/physicians-not-burning-out-they-are-suffering-moral-injury/
[22] https://www.aha.org/statistics/fast-facts-us-hospitals
[23] https://lownhospitalsindex.org/2022-winning-hospitals-racial-inclusivity/
[24] https://www.chestercountyhospital.org/news/health-eliving-blog/2019/november/8-surprising-ways-hospital-social-workers-can-help-you
[25] https://www.ncbi.nlm.nih.gov/books/NBK218224/
[26] https://www.mayoclinic.org/diseases-conditions/coronavirus/expert-answers/coronavirus-infection-by-race/faq-20488802

Data-Driven Solutions

Decade after decade, mounting attention is paid to the individual behaviors of patients and healthcare providers or relationships between the two. These relationships are important to address, but changing them means taking intersectional and structural approaches to analyzing and dismantling unjust systems. In 2021, the Association of American Medical Colleges argued that medical education must include curriculum on the social drivers of health to aid medical practitioners in understanding the systemic causes of their patients' experiences.[27] For this to occur, the collection and regulation of healthcare data are paramount.

Data-driven metrics are vital in closing knowledge gaps and advocating for comprehensive patient care. Consider that 16% of residents living in the mainland United States live 30 or more miles from the nearest hospital.[28] Fewer than 10% of physicians practice in rural areas, though 20% of the population inhabits those areas.[29] These numbers suggest that nearly 80% of patients in rural America are medically underserved.[30] Collective efforts by public health departments, state, county, and local governments, community-based organizations, and corporations are necessary to track, measure, and analyze existing inequities. Such collaboration would allow us to formulate a baseline, understand disparities, and work to eliminate them.

Systemic Alignment

By using data to understand racial and other social disparities in healthcare, nonprofit systems can be redesigned for equity. Cone Health, CommonSpirit Health, and Parkland Center for Clinical Innovation/Parkland Health are examples of nonprofit health systems that have rethought their policies, practices, and the services they provide in order to holistically address patient health needs in their communities. They are designing and implementing scalable, data-driven solutions with the understanding that the most effective models of care link clinical and social care. Their

[27] https://www.aamc.org/news-insights/medical-schools-overhaul-curricula-fight-inequities
[28] https://www.cnn.com/2017/08/03/health/hospital-deserts/index.html
[29] https://www.aha.org/system/files/2019-02/rural-report-2019.pdf
[30] https://www.healthstatus.com/health_blog/wellness/health-care-deserts-what-they-are-and-what-to-do-if-you-live-in-one/

solutions include integrated care teams, preventive care models, whole-person care, coordinated care, wellness offerings, and more.

Our collective inaction is the greatest impediment to equitable healthcare. Our misguided insistence on treating the symptoms of illness—rather than root causes—relegates patients to the sidelines as subjects to be studied instead of humans to be cared for. We need to act. We know that what is currently in place does not work. The only way forward is to use the tools at our disposal to create a functional health-care system—an interconnected network, each doing its part in concert for the good of all.

Pro-Black Actions That Health Justice Organizations Can Model

Amira Barger

Racial disparities in healthcare are killing Black people across the United States. People of color and other underserved groups have higher rates of illness and death across a range of health conditions. Before COVID-19, 70,000 Black people died every year because of these compounded disparities. The pandemic exacerbated[1] this excess of Black mortality.[2] In 2020, Black people in the United States had a death rate that was one-third higher than that of Latinx people and more than double that of White and Asian/Pacific Islander people.

If Black lives matter to the nonprofit sector, it must acknowledge and address these disparities and the preventable deaths that result from them. Marginal responses will not do, as these issues are not marginal, and communities are in crisis. Using available data,[3] we can poignantly describe the problem, put it in context to expose and fix health inequities,[4] and design actions to create a pro-Black healthcare system.

[1] https://www.ncbi.nlm.nih.gov/pmc/articles/PMC7762908/#:~:text=Approximately%2097.9%20 out%20of%20every,Asians%20(40.4%20per%20100%2C000)

[2] https://jamanetwork.com/journals/jamanetworkopen/fullarticle/2775299

[3] https://www.kff.org/coronavirus-covid-19/issue-brief/tracking-social-determinants-of-health-during-the-covid-19-pandemic/

[4] https://www.ama-assn.org/delivering-care/health-equity/put-context-data-can-help-expose-and-fix-health-inequities

Acknowledgment: A Vital Antiracism Tool

As examples in the next section will show, nonprofit healthcare institutions have ignored racial injustice for far too long and, consequently, have remained complicit in its continuation. Although the nonprofit sector is entrusted with walking alongside the "most vulnerable" communities, it remains capable of perpetuating harm thanks in large part to the sector's origins in saviorism, patriarchy, and white guilt and the dehumanization of the very people we seek to serve—a legacy that continues to the present day.[5]

One of the first steps in practicing antiracism is sincere acknowledgment.[6] A potentially powerful catalyst for advancing change, acknowledgment makes a thing known, and it communicates the importance of knowing that thing. One might have assumed that, given their general proximity to populations most affected by inequity, nonprofit organizations would be ahead of the curve on racial justice issues.

Unfortunately, this has not been the case.[7] Although the sector purports to care about Black, Latinx, Indigenous, and Asian/Pacific Islander communities, its leaders are often disconnected from the experiences of the communities they serve. Despite recent attempts to diversify the sector's leadership, nonprofit management remains overwhelmingly white.[8] Nonprofit boards are often whiter, and much of the donor base is, too. Distanced from the needs of low-income people of color, these leaders struggle to recognize and acknowledge racial and economic injustice, let alone respond to it.

Who holds the power to shape what justice looks like matters. If white supremacy is at the root of the injustices the sector seeks to solve, and white people who are privileged in this system are formulating solutions to these injustices, how can justice be achieved? "You cannot be the poison and the antidote," as podcaster and antiracism guide Louiza "Weeze" Doran puts it.[9] We must address the exclusion of historically marginalized people from decision-making to fully address healthcare's racial disparities.

---

[5] https://ssir.org/articles/entry/todays_charitable_sector_and_its_roots_and_challenges
[6] https://www.facebook.com/moveon/videos/414267779201099/
[7] https://www.urban.org/urban-wire/nonprofit-leadership-out-step-americas-changing-demographics
[8] https://racetolead.org/nonprofits-so-white-new-report-on-lack-of-inclusion-offers-strategies/
[9] https://www.accordingtoweeze.com/

Acknowledging Racial Health Disparities to Address Them

On the 2021 National Day of Racial Healing, Dr. Gail C. Christopher of the National Collaborative for Health Equity delivered a powerful message about embracing truth. She spoke of the need to understand what racism is—a false hierarchy of human value embedded in our nation's history—to be able to address it:

> *If we're ever really going to end racism in this country, we have to understand that what we have to do is change our fundamental conceptual framework about relationship, about how we relate to one another as human beings. And as long as we allow this backdrop of disparity and inequity in the dignity, and the respect, and the value that human beings are to be accorded and afforded, we will continue to have racial injustice.*[10]

Healthcare disparities signal a growing crisis of racial injustice. This crisis is not simply a matter of racialized identity, but of white supremacy's insistent denial of Black people's very humanity and right to live. Racism, the health injustices it has engendered, and our failure to address these injustices are barriers to achieving health equity—particularly for Black and Indigenous people and communities. As a starting point, nonprofit healthcare organizations must measure and acknowledge existing health disparities and take accountability for the disparities they perpetuate. Over the last few years, some healthcare organizations have taken that important first step.

Harvard University publicly acknowledged its deep ties to colonial-era slavery.[11] It released a 100+ page report outlining the Harvard Medical School's history and impact on public health today. This exploration eventually led to a $100 million fund for slavery reparations.[12]

The American Medical Association acknowledged the 1910 Flexner Report, a document that established new standards for medical education and its effect on Black medical schools and physicians, as well as the

[10]https://www.nationalcollaborative.org/dr-gail-christophers-americacanheal-on-the-national-day-of-racial-healing/
[11]https://apnews.com/article/6b25d83deacd4133ba6a723442958916
[12]https://www.reuters.com/world/us/harvard-sets-up-100-million-endowment-fund-slavery-reparations-2022-04-26/

report's far-reaching impacts on Black Americans and their health outcomes.[13] This acknowledgment created a basis for shared understanding, leading the association to take further action—specifically, creating a racial justice strategic plan that outlines a three-year road map for advancing health equity and reconciliation.

Seattle Children's Hospital acknowledged its institutional racism, leading to an action report by an external investigator.[14] The hospital added a chief equity, diversity, and inclusion officer, but mishandling of the release of the report's findings led to staff resignations, employee strikes, and petitions for the removal of hospital administration. In other words, acknowledgment, although important, also requires sincere and consistent follow-through for real change.

Understanding Health Equity

Health equity is achieved, according to the Centers for Disease Control and Prevention, when every person has the opportunity to attain their full health potential regardless of their social circumstances.[15] Each one of us requires food, housing, income, education, a stable environment, sustainable natural resources, and peace of mind. These requisites are often referred to as the social determinants of health—the non-medical factors that affect our well-being. When these requisites are missing, people struggle to thrive. As C-E. A. Winslow states in "The Untilled Fields of Public Health," "Health is not merely the absence of disease. It is obtaining one's highest standard of health through organized efforts and informed choices of society, communities, and individuals."[16]

To address issues, a holistic approach is needed. Mainstream media narratives that portray marginalized communities as hesitant to access care fail to discuss structural barriers to healthcare access, including distance to care, language challenges, and lack of information on how to get proper care to communities. Appreciation of such structural barriers requires not simply working to address a symptom but working in partnership with

---

[13] https://www.ama-assn.org/press-center/press-releases/ama-adopts-new-policy-increase-diversity-physician-workforce

[14] https://www.seattletimes.com/seattle-news/seattle-childrens-staff-call-for-full-report-from-probe-into-racism-at-hospital-system/

[15] https://www.cdc.gov/nchhstp/healthequity/index.html

[16] https://www.science.org/doi/10.1126/science.51.1306.23?cookieSet=1

the community to solve the root causes of a given issue. Such partnerships can be achieved by starting with a series of questions that examine the nonprofit sector's proximity to the people and the problem.

Some nonprofit organizations have begun to do just that. In 2019, the Collective Impact Forum, New Profit, and FSG hosted a virtual gathering to discuss a paper titled "The Water of Systems Change," a paper that presented six "systems change" criteria as prompts for social justice leaders to consider:

1. Do we have proximity to the people and the problem we are addressing?
2. Are we engaging with individuals most affected by the problem as assets—meaning possessing talents, skills, and expertise—in developing solutions?
3. Do we view and embody collective leadership as a critical component in achieving systems change?
4. Are we focused on shifting multiple interrelated systemic conditions?
5. Are we systems aware—understanding relationships and power dynamics between players in the system?
6. Are we addressing the deeper, transformative levers of systems change (power dynamics, relationships, and narratives) in addition to structural levers (practices, policies, and resource flows)?

Given that up to 70% of health disparities are driven by non-medical social factors such as housing, education, and food security, gatherings like the one just cited are paramount for curating holistic approaches to healthcare.[17] Such events invite leaders from across sectors and encourage them to engage questions (like those mentioned) in an intersectional analysis of the non-medical factors affecting health outcomes. Organizations can use these prompts as a framework for considering how they function in community and pursue holistic change.

Next Steps, Sustained Actions

Moving the needle toward health and racial justice requires a robust strategy that typically begins with an institutional equity audit. This tool establishes a baseline for progress on racial equity and provides an

---

[17] https://www.healthaffairs.org/doi/10.1377/hlthaff.21.2.78

organizational road map for transforming systems for long-term gain, moving beyond responses rooted in crisis. The audit considers stakeholders' lived experiences and uses quantitative and qualitative methods—including surveys, focus groups, demographic data, stakeholder life cycle data, policy, and practice insights—to obtain the information and feedback needed to develop a strategy for change toward equity. Each strategy element is backed with data tied to proposed actions.

Conducting such an analysis is key if healthcare organizations are to address the country's disparities and their impact on "the overall health of the nation" and its prosperity, as a 2021 Kaiser Family Foundation issue brief observed.[18] According to a report by Deloitte, unaddressed health inequities could cost $1 trillion by 2040, and, more specifically, could cost each individual citizen $3,000 annually.[19]

Moving past acknowledgment, healthcare entities must advance actions that aim to help Black people thrive. Black Americans are asked to trust the healthcare system and heed recommendations to improve health outcomes. But how can we expect Black communities to trust a system that has historically oppressed them?

Taking data-driven actions to address the most acute problems for Black people most affected by health disparities will improve the system for all.[20] Because the United States was built on a foundation of anti-Black racism,[21] our actions must follow racial equity principles, like those outlined by the Dismantling Racism Works collaborative.[22] A core principle of this framework—"honor and build power on the margins"—underlies the following suggestions for pro-Black actions that health justice organizations can model.

1. **Attribute accountability and responsibility.** The Frameworks Institute workshops speak to the importance of attributing responsibility for a challenge or solution carefully.[23] In the field of health justice, we attribute responsibility for illness to systemic, structural, policy, or

[18]https://www.kff.org/racial-equity-and-health-policy/issue-brief/disparities-in-health-and-health-care-5-key-question-and-answers/
[19]https://www2.deloitte.com/us/en/insights/industry/health-care/economic-cost-of-health-disparities.html
[20]https://www.usnews.com/opinion/blogs/policy-dose/articles/2016-04-14/theres-a-huge-health-equity-gap-between-whites-and-minorities
[21]https://news.harvard.edu/gazette/story/2020/06/orlando-patterson-explains-why-america-cant-escape-its-racist-roots/
[22]https://www.whitesupremacyculture.info/racial-equity-principles.html
[23]https://www.frameworksinstitute.org/presentations/

individual factors. Rather than focusing on individual behaviors and factors alone, we must examine and hold accountable social systems as they are the producers of unjust and inequitable conditions.

2. **Prioritize participatory design.** Codesigning opportunities for prevention, intervention, and treatment is the most equitable path forward. In their recent guide, "Rejecting Racism and Embracing Anti-Racism in Public Health + Healthcare," the Equitist proposed a useful framework to approach decision-making.[24] The 5 Ps of equitable collaboration (people, priorities, policies, proof, and pay) provide a framework that uses inquiry as a strategy and seeks to enhance collective participation, trust, and transparency between nonprofit staff members and affected community members.

3. **Tie public health and social movements together.** We must make the injustices that perpetuate health disparities visible. As the Open Society Foundations' landmark 2019 report, "Building Narrative Power for Racial Justice and Health Equity," states:

Closer ties between public health and social movements promoting racial, economic, and social justice are critical for nurturing a narrative of health directed toward addressing social and political inequalities, not individual behavior or perceived cultural differences. Racial justice and health equity require action on a structural level. A solution cannot be individually based, because the root causes of inequity do not lie within the control of individuals. Success depends on developing narratives that move and motivate both constituents and colleagues.[25]

Highlighting gaps in care while developing scalable programs to address them is one way to make visible systemic injustices. For example, in 2020, the Kaiser Permanente Bernard J. Tyson School of Medicine opened its doors with an aim to matriculate more physicians from historically excluded communities. Toward this end, they decided that the first five admitted classes will incur no tuition costs, highlighting the need to remove economic barriers to provide racially equitable care.[26]

[24] https://www.endracisminhealth.org/

[25] https://www.opensocietyfoundations.org/publications/building-narrative-power-for-racial-justice-and-health-equity#publications_download

[26] https://www.bizjournals.com/sanfrancisco/news/2019/02/20/kaiser-permanente-medical-school-free-tuition.html

4. Use data to inform efforts at repair. According to KFF,

> *Data are a cornerstone for efforts to address disparities and advance health equity. Data are essential for identifying where disparities exist, directing efforts and resources to address disparities as they are identified, measuring progress toward achieving greater equity, and establishing accountability for achieving progress. Without adequate data, inequities remain unseen and unaddressed.*[27]

In partnership with communities, we must use all available information and tools at our disposal to address the issues that face us.

When it comes to addressing health disparities, to date, no sustainable, systemic effort has been brought to scale. Capable of combining collective impact, scale, and rapid response, nonprofits are uniquely positioned to be on the front lines of dismantling health systems that maintain the status quo and rebuilding new ones. We, the nonprofit sector, must acknowledge systemic racism in healthcare, atone for this violence, and collectively act to build pro-Black healthcare.

---

[27] https://www.kff.org/policy-watch/advancing-health-equity-requires-more-better-data/, last accessed March 09, 2023.

Repairing the Whole

How Reparations Can Address Physical and Mental Health

Trevor Smith

Shortly after the US Constitution was ratified, Benjamin Franklin penned a letter to French scientist Jean-Baptiste Le Roy, in which he said that "in this world, nothing is certain except death and taxes."[1] Although certain, death can come in myriad ways, and if we peel back behind some of the leading causes of death, we find that chronic stress is linked to six of them.

Stress, like most health issues, is not equally distributed across racial groups. Black adults are 20% more likely to report serious psychological distress compared to white adults.[2] Those who live in poverty and face daily struggles of overpoliced neighborhoods, underfunded schools, and lower-paid jobs are two to three times more likely to report serious psychological distress.

The psychological effects of these economic disadvantages don't only affect parents, but they also heavily affect children, even before they are born. Studies have shown that prenatal stress can have significant effects beginning in the womb and spanning across a lifetime.

This stress, according to experts,[3] can arise from traumatic experiences, life-changing events, or daily microaggressions. And it has negative influences not only on the outcome of the pregnancy but also on the behavioral and physiological development of the child. Threatening situations, no matter how big or small, increase the body's heart rate, blood pressure, and the pace of breathing.

---

[1] https://constitutioncenter.org/blog/benjamin-franklins-last-great-quote-and-the-constitution
[2] https://www.apa.org/pi/oema/resources/ethnicity-health/african-american/stress
[3] https://www.ncbi.nlm.nih.gov/pmc/articles/PMC5052760/

For Black families, particularly those dealing with the weight of poverty, threatening situations are plentiful. According to the Economic Policy Institute,[4] 64% of Black children have been exposed to one or more frightening or threatening experiences, while only 48% of white children have.

TABLE 1

Low-income and African American children are more likely to have stressful childhoods

Share of kindergartners exposed to frightening or threatening childhood experiences, by family income and by race

Number of frightening or threatening experiences:	0	1	2	≥ 3
By family income				
≥ $20,000	50%	26%	15%	10%
< $20,000	36%	30%	17%	17%
% more/less likely	-28%	18%	15%	74%
By race				
White	52%	22%	14%	12%
Black	36%	32%	18%	14%
% more/less likely	-31%	45%	29%	21%

Notes: Data are based on a study sample of 1,007 children who were born between 1998 and 2000 and were age 5 at the time these data were collected (2003–2005). ⬛

Source: Manuel E. Jimenez et al., "Adverse Experiences in Early Childhood and Kindergarten Outcomes," *Pediatrics* 137, no. 2 (2016), 1–10, https://doi.org/10.1542/peds.2015-1839, Supplemental Table 6

Economic Policy Institute

Source: Adapted from Manuel et al., 2016.

When accumulated, trauma—which is the emotional, psychological, physical, and neurological response to stress—can lead to adverse effects. From daily racial microaggressions to lethal encounters, when children are frequently exposed to sustained traumatic events, they are more likely to have adverse behavioral effects and/or suffer from depression.

....

[4] https://www.epi.org/publication/toxic-stress-and-childrens-outcomes-african-american-children-growing-up-poor-are-at-greater-risk-of-disrupted-physiological-functioning-and-depressed-academic-achievement/

A study launched by Dr. Monnica Williams,[5] a psychologist based at the University of Ottawa, found that Black students who reported higher rates of perceived discrimination had higher rates of alienation, anxiety, and stress about future negative events.[6]

Each generation of Black Americans has faced horrific forms of racial discrimination whose scars they still carry today. The vestiges of slavery can be seen through our mass incarceration policies. Police officers, stationed around the clock in Black neighborhoods, evolved from plantation overseers. Even our economy, as detailed in the *New York Times*' 1619 Project,[7] has the fingerprints of slavery all over it. This history, and our current experiences, does not simply affect people in one single moment in time.

As a report from the National Coalition of Blacks for Reparations in America (N'COBRA) published last year—titled *The Harm Is in Our Genes: Transgenerational Epigenetic Inheritance & Systemic Racism in the United States*—details the trauma stemming from enslavement, Jim Crow, mass incarceration, the war on drugs, and police terror, which can be passed down across generations through epigenetic change.[8]

The idea that trauma can be inherited and therefore alter how a person's genes function (epigenetic change) is not new. It was first introduced in 1967 by Dr. Vivian Morris Rakoff, a Canadian psychiatrist who recorded elevated rates of psychological distress among the children of Holocaust survivors.

His initial research, which has been supported by subsequent studies, has found that the children and descendants of Holocaust survivors had higher levels of childhood trauma, increased vulnerability to post-traumatic stress disorder, and other psychiatric disorders. In one of his earlier papers, Rakoff wrote that "the parents are not broken conspicuously, yet their children, all of whom were born after the Holocaust, display severe psychiatric symptomatology. It would almost be easier to believe that they, rather than their parents, had suffered the corrupting, searing hell." [9]

Other studies have examined the intergenerational effects on First Nations, Inuit, and Métis peoples in residential schools[10] run by the

....

[5] http://www.monnicawilliams.com/
[6] https://www.apa.org/monitor/2019/02/legacy-trauma
[7] https://www.nytimes.com/interactive/2019/08/14/magazine/slavery-capitalism.html
[8] https://www.ncobraonline.org/wp-content/uploads/2020/06/NCOBRA-2021-The-Harm-Is-To-Our-Genes-Full-Report-11.15-compressed.pdf
[9] https://www.theglobeandmail.com/canada/article-psychiatrist-vivian-rakoff-believed-there-was-no-divide-between-the/
[10] https://www.scientificamerican.com/article/canadas-residential-schools-were-a-horror/

Canadian government for over a century. They found that children, and in some cases grandchildren, of those who attended these schools were more likely to report psychological distress, suicide attempts, and learning difficulties.

Can Reparations Heal?

Just as educators cooperated in carrying out genocidal policies through their participation in residential schools (in the United States,[11] as well as in Canada), the medical industry has its own sorry history. For a long time, many in that field justified racial health disparities through racist and mythical biological arguments that claimed Black people were inherently inferior to white people. This US mental model was thoroughly used throughout the antebellum period and beyond. It is the root of the early 20th-century eugenics movement[12] that led to the sterilization of thousands of Black people and was a source of inspiration for Adolf Hitler's *Mein Kampf* and South African apartheid.

The notion that the medical industry has played a role in strengthening white supremacist theories and fortifying a racial caste system is one that I don't believe many can argue with. The question at hand remains: what do reparations look like within a health context?

Reparations and Trauma

Large-scale trauma affects people in multiple ways, explains Dr. Yael Daniel,[13] a prominent researcher in the field of intergenerational trauma and founder of the International Center for the Study, Prevention, and Treatment of Multigenerational Legacies of Trauma.[14] It only makes sense then that our solutions are also multifaceted.

A trauma-informed framework must be applied to any reparations effort to ensure that we are creating a sustainable social policy that uproots

---

[11] https://nonprofitquarterly.org/recalling-the-violence-of-the-indian-school-200-years-after-its-founding/
[12] https://nonprofitquarterly.org/recalling-the-violence-of-the-indian-school-200-years-after-its-founding/
[13] https://www.apa.org/monitor/2019/02/legacy-trauma
[14] https://icmglt.org/about-us/

the tenets of white supremacy. This approach, according to experts,[15] should seek to go beyond broad notions of trauma and address specific sociopolitical and economic drivers. Trauma-informed care within a context of reparations means employing a holistic focus not only on the economic impact of the legacy of slavery but also its psychological and health impact.

Acknowledgment of Harm

An admission that harm was done is one of the first needed steps on the road to racial repair. Although it has had its critics, acknowledgment of past wrongs to those who were harmed by them was a core component of South Africa's Truth and Reconciliation Commission.[16] Accepting responsibility for harm that was caused is a necessary step in a reparation process by creating the space for the responsible party to admit wrongdoing, and the harmed party to have the choice to start a healing process.

Last year, the American Psychological Association apologized for its role in perpetuating systemic racism. "The American Psychological Association failed in its role leading the discipline of psychology, was complicit in contributing to systemic inequities, and hurt many through racism, racial discrimination, and denigration of people of color, thereby falling short on its mission to benefit society and improve lives," the statement read.[17]

A powerful acknowledgment not only addresses the historical ways in which harm was caused by the perpetrator but also offers an apology and accepts responsibility for the ways in which both the action and inaction of the perpetrator caused harm, which the APA statement goes on to do.

Although apologies such as these from medical associations and other institutions within the medical industry are important, without deep structural action in the form of redress, reckoning, and acknowledgment, these are just more empty words.

---

[15] https://www.ncbi.nlm.nih.gov/pmc/articles/PMC4815621/
[16] https://www.sahistory.org.za/article/truth-and-reconciliation-commission-trc
[17] https://www.apa.org/about/policy/racism-apology

Increasing Black Wealth to Improve Black Health

In 2016, the typical white family had nearly 10 times the amount of wealth of the average Black family.[18] "Power, money, and access to resources—good housing, better education, fair wages, safe workplaces, clean air, drinkable water, and healthier food—translate into good health," according to Harvard researchers.

Those who live in poverty have less access to healthcare, lack healthy nutritional options, are more likely to be uninsured, face higher threats of eviction and homelessness, and are concentrated in jobs that since the onset of the pandemic have put them in positions more likely to contract COVID-19.

Because health outcomes are so inextricably linked to income and wealth, increased economic power by means of a reparations package that seeks to close the racial wealth gap would target the structural health issues that Black people face. Increased wealth for Black Americans would mean more discretionary income to devote resources to healthier food options, preventive health screenings, and mental wellness programs.

As noted by the Harvard researchers, efforts to provide better healthcare in a "population that lacks access to essential resources for health are bound to fall short." Therefore, to address the structural inequity within the healthcare system, we must take an explicit racially conscious approach rather than a racially blind one.

Decolonization of the Medical Industry

From both a mental and physical health perspective, we must invest in and restructure the medical workforce. Studies have shown that sharing a racial identity with your doctor is associated with improved health outcomes. For example, a study in Florida that examined the racial relationship between doctors and the infants they cared for found that when Black doctors delivered Black babies, the infant mortality rate fell by 50%.[19]

---

[18] https://www.brookings.edu/blog/up-front/2020/02/27/examining-the-black-white-wealth-gap/
[19] https://www.pnas.org/content/117/35/21194

The prevalence of implicit bias, particularly in the medical field, has been well documented. Studies have shown that Black people, particularly men, are four to nine times more likely to be misdiagnosed with schizophrenia than white Americans,[20] while also less likely to be diagnosed with post-traumatic stress disorder.

Although Black Americans make up 13% of the US working-age population, they comprise only 5% of the healthcare workforce, even as surveys have shown that patients develop more trust and feel better understood by providers who look like them. Nonetheless, simply focusing on racially diversifying the medical industry alone will not address the deep inequities Black communities face.

Education experts, such as Gloria Ladson Billings,[21] have long called for large-scale investments to create more culturally competent K–12 pedagogy that seeks to affirm, appreciate, and correctly contextualize Black history and culture. This same framework must also be applied to the medical industry. There must be a deeper investment and commitment to address the various educational barriers at play to address these pipeline problems.

Turning Research into Action

Similar to wealth, trauma is not equally inherited in this country. In every historical period, Black Americans have faced racial violence and discrimination within every single US institution.

Research on this subject is plentiful. (I have included a list of resources at the bottom of this article.) And there is more research that could be done to explore the intergenerational effects of trauma, particularly within the Black American community.

No single entity within the medical industry alone can repair the racial trauma that Black people carry today. A comprehensive national effort that reaches deep into states and cities across the country must be launched to address the multitude of economic, social, and psychological harm done to Black people. Considerable organizing will be required for the nation to take on this work. But while the task ahead remains challenging, the effort is essential to heal the trauma of our nation.

---

[20] https://pubmed.ncbi.nlm.nih.gov/30526340/
[21] https://naeducation.org/our-members/gloria-ladson-billings/

Currently, a bill in Congress would establish a commission to study what reparations might look like across the country and within different contexts. This is important, but research is not enough. Research without real commitment and sustained action would only kick the can down the road.

Even in our sector, though, particularly among ivory-towered academic and philanthropic institutions, too often this research is devoid of real action and power building. As we continue our learning journey around reparations, it's important that we use community-engaged methods to include the input and participation of those at the forefront of the issue. This will not only foster greater trust between grassroots organizations and those conducting research but also ensure that the programs and services are effectively empowering the community that researchers seek to serve.

Addressing Inequities in Health Technology

Sonia Sarkar

Recently, the Techquity for Health Coalition, a group of healthcare companies, policy experts, and researchers, launched an effort to highlight and address inequities in the health technology industry.[1] In theory, tech solutions such as disease management apps and wearable devices make users' and care providers' lives easier. In practice, these technologies can worsen inequities—and introduce new ones—particularly for marginalized communities already subject to harmful practices such as data surveillance.[2]

The announcement follows a report published last spring by Ipsos and the HLTH Foundation, the coalition's backbone organization.[3] The report includes insights from interviews with industry stakeholders and outlines opportunities and risks inherent to the growing health technology industry, which received nearly $40 billion in investment in 2021.[4] In it, the authors note technology's increasing influence on health outcomes, sharing that an individual's access to education, employment, or even food—all key determinants of health—is significantly reliant on their ability to use and access technology.

In the past decade, due to changing health policies and financial incentives, health systems are increasingly acknowledging patients' social needs and implementing technology platforms to address them. For example, when a patient comes into the doctor's office, they are screened

[1] https://www.viveevent.com/2023event/techquity#resources
[2] https://www.newamerica.org/oti/reports/centering-civil-rights-privacy-debate/for-marginalized-communities-the-stakes-are-high/
[3] https://a.storyblok.com/f/112494/x/81389f48d9/ipsos_hlth_techquity-whitepaper.pdf
[4] https://www2.deloitte.com/us/en/insights/industry/health-care/health-tech-private-equity-venture-capital.html

for social needs such as food and housing insecurity and employment needs. If a need is found, the patient's care team integrates this information into their care plan. They might discuss the issue with the patient then use the technology platform to refer the patient to a food pantry or housing services, in the same way a referral to a specialist doctor takes place. Community-based organizations providing these services receive these referrals, becoming part of a patient's care.

These new workflows, and the technologies to support them, represent an exciting advancement in healthcare. However, as healthcare institutions invest billions of dollars in those technologies, we have to look at the challenges presented by this shift. At the patient level, there are access and use barriers. A patient expected to view their community referral on a phone app might have limited internet or receive confusing guidance on how to use the app. Patients I've worked with have experienced unclear user interfaces, culturally insensitive information, or a lack of accessibility accommodations. Furthermore, having to interact with an app can create a sense of distrust and distance for patients, who may fear stigma or discrimination from their healthcare provider as they share sensitive information.

The Techquity for Health Coalition aims to address such barriers, particularly with regards to technology access and use and industry engagement. On the access front, for example, healthcare stakeholders could advocate for or directly finance broadband services and health technology devices. In terms of use, the report emphasizes human-centric product development, including bringing members of underserved communities directly into product design and deployment. Ideas for industry engagement include diversifying the technology workforce, effective and transparent communication with patients and communities, and dedication of long-term healthcare and technology dollars to achieving equity.

Systemic Risks Associated with Healthcare Technology

While improving technology adoption and workforce diversity are desired outcomes, there are three key ways that health technology can deepen inequities.

1. **Data ethics.** Healthcare institutions and private technology companies now store, own, and use sensitive individual data. What rights

does a patient have to their own data and to understanding how it is being used or affecting their care?

In the aftermath of the Supreme Court's decision to overturn *Roe v. Wade*, many advocates and patients I've worked with fear that data collected by cycle-tracking apps, disease management platforms, and other healthcare data collection methods could be used to surveil and criminalize those seeking an abortion.

Community leaders also point out the risk of technology companies aggregating and sharing data with their healthcare clients without any place-based context or relationships. In previous roles where I've evaluated these companies and considered using them for local health initiatives, I've heard pitches promising population-level data analytics that will supposedly enable healthcare stakeholders to figure out where to focus their community efforts. Most of the time, though, these programs do not consider that the variables that affect a community's health are complex and specific—in ways that numbers rarely capture. Beholden to business models that emphasize scale and fast quantitative analysis, health technology companies can end up reinforcing biases about marginalized communities.[5]

2. **Algorithm bias.** Related to data ownership is the concern that data will be used to inform automated workflows and "flag" systems that profile patients with certain demographic characteristics.[6] Taking the example of a patient getting screened for food or housing needs, a health technology algorithm could automatically flag a low-income BIPOC patient as a "high-risk" patient, independent of the patient's specific situation. This alert might trigger several actions in the system, such as the development of treatment recommendations.

Indeed, racial bias is prolific across algorithms, with particular implications in healthcare: a 2019 study found a biased hospital algorithm that recommended specific treatments for Black patients only if they were significantly sicker than White people with the same health issue.[7] For communities of color, women, LGTBQ+ communities, people with disabilities, and many more, algorithmic discrimination creates further layers of harm.

---

[5] https://blog.petrieflom.law.harvard.edu/2022/09/02/harms-and-biases-associated-with-the-social-determinants-of-health-technology-movement/https://blog.petrieflom.law.harvard.edu/2022/09/02/harms-and-biases-associated-with-the-social-determinants-of-health-technology-movement/

[6] https://www.healthaffairs.org/do/10.1377/forefront.20210903.976632/

[7] https://www.science.org/doi/10.1126/science.aax2342

3. **Investment and ownership.** Health technology companies typically aren't reflective of the patient populations they hope will use their products. A 2020 report by Rock Health found that, as with technology as a whole, white and Asian founders are overrepresented in the health technology industry, while Black and Latinx founders were underrepresented.[8] This is true on both the investor and entrepreneur sides of the equation, with significant impacts on financing: 57% of the surveyed Black women who had founded health technology firms reported bootstrapping their businesses, compared to 10% of surveyed white men.

Financing inequity can also be seen in the introduction of new private-sector companies into a publicly and privately funded health system, raising questions about how investments and profits are distributed. For example, community organizations that provide food and housing services are often asked to invest time and training capacity in order to participate in social-needs platforms. This can be a burden on entities with limited capacity and funding, particularly in under-resourced communities. Although these organizations are a crucial part of the advertised solution, they may not be a part of product design and development, nor are they entitled to any profits generated.

Activism to Address the Harms of Health Technology

As industry leaders turn their attention to the double-edged sword of health technology, it remains to be seen how they will interact with activists' efforts to address these issues at the global and local levels.

One of those efforts, the 2019 conference, "Political Origins of Health Inequities: Technology in the Digital Age," brought together policy makers and practitioners from across the globe to look at the impact of digital technology on health inequities. A special issue of *Global Policy* authored by conference attendees highlighted the need for "better transparency and public deliberation about digital health technologies as part of the broader

---

[8] https://rockhealth.docsend.com/view/hg56jbhaeaeanh6k?mc_cid=71d6138522&mc_eid=532ab528b3

political determinants of health . . . these spaces for debate and governance are key to ensuring that we do not blindly enter into social contracts regarding new technologies."[9]

Community leaders are stepping into conversations on technology governance, pushing healthcare institutions to share power by incorporating individuals with lived experience of healthcare inequity into technology and data decision-making. In San Diego, an effort is under way to develop a community-driven, antiracist community information exchange model.[10] The group involved, composed of community organizations, healthcare stakeholders, the local county health department, and United Way's 211 program, defines a community information exchange as a "community-led ecosystem" of partners who take a shared and integrated approach to delivering community care. Unlike the process of screening a patient for social needs and referring them to a service, which reactively addresses patients' social needs, the CIE is intended to be proactive, identifying such needs ahead of time and centering patients' proposed ideas for addressing them. To achieve this, the organization is engaging and collaborating with community members in system design, as well as proposing accountability mechanisms for technology vendors that participate in the model.

Models such as this point to a crucial element of any industry effort to address inequities in health technology. Individuals and communities who have long experienced health inequities should have a seat at the table and should shape not only technology design and development but also sector-wide standards surrounding those processes.

---

[9]https://onlinelibrary.wiley.com/doi/full/10.1111/1758-5899.13001
[10]https://ciesandiego.org/wp-content/uploads/2021/12/A-Vision-for-the-Future-FINAL.pdf

V

Implementing Reparations: Work and Ownership

Resurrecting the Promise of 40 Acres*

The Imperative of Reparations for Black Americans

William A. Darity Jr. and A. Kirsten Mullen

In the final chapter of our new book, *From Here to Equality: Reparations for Black Americans in the Twenty-First Century*,[1] we include the following epigraph from a quote by Malcolm X:

> *If you stick a knife in my back nine inches and pull it out six inches, that's not progress. If you pull it all the way out, that's not progress. The progress comes from healing the wound that the blow made. They haven't even begun to pull the knife out . . . they won't even admit the knife is there.*[2]

In the context of an ongoing social injustice, "pulling the knife out" ends the harmful act. It is a desirable and essential step, but it is only an act of suspension. Insofar as it does not "heal the wound," it is not an act

---

*This is an excerpt from: Resurrecting the Promise of 40 Acres: The Imperative of Reparations for Black Americans. It will explain the bracketed ellipses. https://rooseveltinstitute.org/publications/resurrecting-the-promise-of-40-acres-the-imperative-of-reparations-for-black-*americans*/
[1]William A. Darity Jr. and A. Kirsten Mullen, *From Here to Equality: Reparations for Black Americans in the Twenty-First Century* (Chapel Hill: University of North Carolina Press, 2020).
[2]Malcolm X, television interview, March 1964, Malcolm X & Dr. Betty Shabazz Memorial and Educational Center.

of restitution, remediation;[3] therefore, "pulling the knife out" is not reparations. Reparations require the culpable party to make amends for the harm inflicted on the victim, which demands remediation.

In *From Here to Equality*, we advance a general definition of reparations as a program of acknowledgment, redress, and closure. **Acknowledgment** constitutes the culpable party's admission of responsibility for the atrocity. **Admission** should include an enumeration of the damages inflicted on the victims and the advantages appropriated by the culpable party. **Redress** constitutes the acts of restitution, steps taken to "heal the wound." **Closure** constitutes an agreement by both the victims and the perpetrators that the account is settled. Representatives chosen by members of the aggrieved community can communicate with the culpable party to establish the point at which restitution is adequate for the debt to be paid.[4] Thereafter, the victims will make no further claims for compensation, unless a new atrocity occurs or an old atrocity recurs.

Eligibility: Black American Descendants of Persons Enslaved in the United States

The case we make for Black reparations in the United States centers on the provision of compensation for a specific community that consists, today, of approximately 40 million Americans. In *From Here to Equality*, we advance two criteria for Black reparations eligibility. First, an individual must establish that they have at least one ancestor who was enslaved in the United States.[5] Second, an individual must demonstrate that they have

---

[3] Jacqueline Bhabha, "Addressing the Legacy of Slavery," in *Time for Reparations: A Global Perspective*, Jacqueline Bhabha, Margareta Matache, and Caroline Elkins, eds. (Philadelphia: University of Pennsylvania Press, September 2021).

[4] We further outline the proposal for an elected Reparations Supervisory Board that would determine when closure is achieved, while also fulfilling other ongoing tasks; see Darity and Mullen, *From Here to Equality*, 267.

[5] This standard, of course, will create substantial business for genealogists, but the agency administering the reparations program can facilitate the process by subsidizing genealogical research support for applicants.

self-identified as Black, Negro, or African American on an official document—perhaps making public the self-report of their race on the US Census—for at least 12 years before the enactment of a reparations program or a study commission for reparations, whichever comes first.[6] In short, the reparations plan we put forward designates Black American descendants of US slavery as the target community.

This community's claim for restitution anchors on the US government's failure to deliver the promised 40-acre land grants to their newly emancipated ancestors in the aftermath of the Civil War.[7] That failure laid the foundation for the enormous contemporary gap in wealth between Black and white people in the US. If the land allocation had been made to the freedmen and freedwomen, and had that ownership been protected, we speculate that there would be no need to consider the case for Black reparations today.[8]

Though the government's decision to deny Black Americans this equity stake has led some contemporary pundits to refer to "slavery reparations," the case we make does not center exclusively on the horrors of American chattel slavery. Instead, we argue that three historical phases of atrocities merit incorporation into the criteria for Black reparations. First, of course, is slavery itself, the crucible that produced white supremacy in the United States. Second is the near century-long epoch of legal segregation in America—or American apartheid—that we refer to colloquially as the "Jim Crow" era. Finally, there are the ongoing atrocities associated with the period following the Civil Rights Act of 1964: mass incarceration; police executions of unarmed Black people; sustained credit, housing, and employment discrimination; and the immense Black-white wealth disparity. Black American descendants of US slavery have borne and continue to bear the undue burden of the cumulative effects of all three of these phases of the nation's trajectory of racial injustice.

---

[6] Parental eligibility can dictate qualification for minors who are at least 12 years of age. Proof of paternity or maternity at least 12 years before the enactment of a reparations program or a reparations study commission—again, whichever comes first—would have to be established. Children will be able to receive reparations payments when they reach legal adulthood; in the meantime, funds would go into a federally secured trust account for them.

[7] Walter L. Fleming, "Forty Acres and a Mule," *North American Review* 182, no. 594 (May 1906): 721–37.

[8] Protection of Black property would have required the Union Army to maintain its presence in the former secessionist states for at least a generation and/or directly arming the freedmen. Under General Sherman's Special Field Order No. 15, 400,000 formerly enslaved persons settled on 40,000 acres of land. Even that allocation, a mere fraction of the full 5.3 million acres specified in Sherman's order, was restored to the former slave holders at the direction of President Andrew Johnson. See Darity and Mullen, *From Here to Equality*, 158–59.

Calculating What Is Owed

We view the Black-white wealth gap as a blight on the nation. While the 40 million eligible recipients of Black reparations constitute about 13% of the American population, they possess less than 3% of the nation's wealth. This translates into an average (or mean) differential, per household, of about $800,000 in net worth.[9]

Prioritizing the Mean of the Racial Wealth Gap

To eliminate the racial wealth gap in its entirety, it is essential that the *mean* gap be erased, rather than setting a far less ambitious goal such as closing the gap at the Black-white *median* differential.

Although, the usual discussion of wealth gaps focuses on median differences because the median captures the typical condition for American households, targeting the median will leave the racial wealth gap largely untouched. The fact that 97% of white wealth is held by households with a net worth above the white median ($171,000) makes any policy that seeks to close the racial gap at the median a policy that discounts, overwhelmingly, the largest proportion of racial wealth inequality.[10]

Indeed, the magnitude of the Black-white wealth gap that requires erasure should not be constrained by the fact that there is a highly unequal distribution of wealth among white Americans. In fact, there is a similarly highly unequal distribution of wealth among Black people over a disproportionately, far smaller total.[11]

Ultimately, a well-designed reparations program could have a powerful impact on producing greater wealth equality among Black Americans. Consider the median-to-mean ratio.[12] Suppose all Black households

---

[9] Lisa J. Dettling et al., "Recent Trends in Wealth-Holding by Race and Ethnicity: Evidence from the Survey of Consumer Finances," *FEDS Notes*, September 27, 2017.

[10] William Darity Jr., Fenaba R. Addo, and Imari Z. Smith, "A Subaltern Middle Class: The Case of the Missing 'Black Bourgeoisie' in America," *Contemporary Economic Policy* (May 2020), 6.

[11] Ibid., 3–5.

[12] A measure like the variance is not useful in this context; the variance as a measure of inequality is insensitive to the effects of an equal allocation of funds, regardless of the size of the allocation. We use the median-to-mean ratio instead. When that ratio reaches 1:1, there is perfect equality.

received an additional $800,000 to make up for the mean deficit. As of 2016, the Black median-to-mean ratio was $17,600/$138,000 or approximately 13%. If the Black mean rises to the same level as the white mean through the provision of an additional $800,000 to each Black household, the intra-group Black median-to-mean ratio would change dramatically to $817,600/$938,000, or approximately 87%.[13]

Eliminating the Black-white (pretax) wealth differential should be a core objective of the redress component of a plan for reparations. We estimate that this will require an allocation of between $10 and $12 trillion in 2016 dollars to eligible Black Americans. That allocation should serve as the *baseline* for Black reparations in the 21st century.

The Cost of Slavery

Another approach to calculating a formal bill entails measuring the costs of slavery to the immediate victims. As a basis for measuring the damages of slavery, some estimates have focused on what was, de facto, unpaid labor under the coercion of enslavement. Professor Thomas Craemer, however, has argued that slavery involved the theft of the full 24 hours of each day in the lives of the enslaved. In today's dollars, he arrives at an estimate of $14 trillion for the cost of American slavery to the enslaved.[14]

However, this may be an *underestimate* of the total costs, as Craemer's assessment does not account for the psychological trauma inflicted on the enslaved, nor does it account for the accelerated mortality and morbidity consequent on the system. A potential justification for treating the $14 trillion sum as transferrable to today's descendants of the victims of chattel slavery is the argument that there has been an intergenerational transmission of the harms, uninterrupted because of the neglect of the provision of the promised 40 acres.

---

[13] We offer a possible alternative to the equal allocation approach in *From Here to Equality* as a method for generating a more equitable distribution of wealth among Black people. There is the option of combining a uniform payment to all eligible recipients with the "designat[ion of] a portion of the funds for competitive application, with priority given to the applicants with lower current wealth or income positions" (p. 267). However, if the concern is the highly unequal distribution of wealth among white Americans, or across all Americans generally, this should be addressed by a separate set of policies distinct from a Black reparations project.

[14] Thomas Craemer, "Estimating Slavery Reparations: Present Value Comparisons of Historical Multigenerational Reparations Policies," *Social Science Quarterly* 96, no. 2 (June 2015): 639–55.

The Promise of 40 Acres

The 40-acre land grants themselves afford another route for calculating the size of a potential Black reparations bill. The conventional interpretation has it that the promised allocations were to have gone to households composed of those newly emancipated. If a typical household consisted of four persons, the allocation would have amounted to 10 acres per person. With four million emancipated persons at the close of the Civil War, the overall distribution of land to the formerly enslaved would have come to at least 40 million acres. With an average value of an acre of land set at $10 in 1865,[15] the overall value of the allocation would have been $400 million. The present value compounded at a 6% interest rate (the average rate of return plus an inflation adjustment) amounts to $3.1 trillion. Financial expert John Talbott has suggested computing a present value predicated on a 9% interest rate, consistent with the average return on an investment in the US stock market from 1870 to 2020. This results in an estimated reparations bill of $16.5 trillion.[16]

Though we are open-minded about a variety of strategies for *calculating* the size of social debt that is owed, our central argument here is that the elimination of the Black-white wealth gap should provide the foundation for the magnitude of redress that this stark American racial injustice demands. After all, the racial wealth gap is the economic measure that best captures the cumulative effects of the full trajectory of American white supremacy from slavery to the present.[17] Given that the disparity

---

[15] For the $10 per acre of land in 1865 estimate, see Anuradha Mittal and Joan Powell, "The Last Plantation," *Food First Backgrounder* 6, no. 1 (Winter 2000): 1–8.

[16] John Talbott suggested 9% interest in personal correspondence with one of the coauthors, January 7, 2020.

[17] The COVID-19 crisis hardly obviates the need to institute a reparations plan, at least after the worst of the crisis has, hopefully, passed. The adverse effects of extreme Black-asset poverty become more apparent in emergency conditions such as the crisis produced by the pandemic. Racial wealth differentials impose a correspondingly high degree of danger and harm on Black Americans (see Danyelle Solomon and Darrick Hamilton, "The Coronavirus Pandemic and the Racial Wealth Gap," Center for American Progress, March 19, 2020). The lack of wealth increases Black vulnerability because Black people have been disproportionately concentrated in the personal service/contact jobs that have been destroyed by the pandemic, or they are disproportionately concentrated in health service jobs that place them at the greatest risk of exposure to the virus. One message to be taken from the pandemic is that the racialized dangers of the current situation might have been moderated had the racial wealth gap been eliminated already. A second message, evidenced by the federal government's capacity to mobilize resources without taxing first, is that the nation is capable of financing Black reparations. See William A. Darity Jr. and A. Kirsten Mullen, "The Racial Disparities of Coronavirus Point Yet Again to the Need for Reparations," *Philadelphia Inquirer*, April 20, 2020; and William A. Darity Jr. and A. Kirsten Mullen, "Coronavirus Is Making the Case for Black Reparations Clearer Than Ever," *Newsweek*, May 5, 2020.

began with the wealth that white people accumulated through extraction from enslaved Black people, which grew exponentially with each generation, closing the gap requires direct redistribution.[18]

Culpability: A Matter of National Responsibility

So, who should pay the bill? In *From Here to Equality*, we argue that the culpable party is the United States government. "Authority is constructed and contextual," and all three phases of the atrocities cataloged here were products of the legal and authority framework established by the federal government.[19] Often, the federal government further sanctioned racial atrocities by silence and inaction.

In turn, this means that local or piecemeal—little by little—attempts at racial atonement do not constitute reparations proper. In the past several years, many states, localities, and individual institutions have begun to consider "reparations."

But these are insufficient for a several reasons. First, many of these "reparations" efforts do not involve restitution. Second, most states, localities, and individual institutions do not have the resources to repay on anything like the scale we are suggesting. Finally, and most importantly, Black reparations are not a matter of personal or individual institutional guilt; Black reparations are a matter of national responsibility.

In many instances, local initiatives labeled "reparations" are not that at all. Whether at the state or municipal level, many efforts frequently constitute acknowledgment, admitting that atrocities were committed. These measures are often followed by inadequate attempts at redress—the allocation of funds for research or the construction of memorials,

---

[18] Laura Feiveson and John Sabelhaus, "How Does Intergenerational Wealth Transmission Affect Wealth Concentration?" *FEDS Notes* 182, no. 594 (June 1, 2018); William Darity Jr. et al., *What We Get Wrong About Closing the Racial Wealth Gap,* Samuel DuBois Cook Center on Social Equity, Duke University, April 2018; Jermaine Toney, "Is There Wealth Stability Across Generations in the U.S.? Evidence from Panel Study, 1984–2013," Challenging Racial Disparities Conference: Race and Justice in America Today, held at Rutgers University, June 4, 2019; and Andreas Fagereng et al., "Heterogeneity and Persistence in Returns to Wealth," *Econometrica* 88, no. 1 (January 2020): 115–70.

[19] "Framework for Information Literacy for Higher Education," Association of College and Research Libraries, January 11, 2016.

for example—rather than substantial compensatory payments to Black Americans. While these scattered steps to take some type of action may begin to pull the knife out, they do not heal the wound produced by the harm; typically, they fail to provide any compensatory payment.

Even if they do afford a compensatory payment, a series of local initiatives is highly unlikely to match the minimum bill for Black reparations. As noted, this debt will require at least $10 trillion to eliminate the Black-white wealth disparity. Taken separately or collectively, there is no evidence that local "reparations" will come close to addressing the full scope of the measured harm or achieving an appropriate level of restitution.

[. . .]

Learning from Other Cases: Precedents for Reparations

Valuable insights for how to best execute a national program of reparations can be gained from previous experiences with plans of restitution. Here, we focus on five precedents, two overseas (German reparations for victims of the Nazi Holocaust and reparations in post-apartheid South Africa) and three in the United States (Japanese American reparations after World War II, post-9/11 reparations for victims' families, and post–Sandy Hook reparations after the 2012 school shooting).

These cases are disparate. The German, South African, and Japanese American cases are all instances of state actions against an ethnic, racial, or religious minority. The 9/11 and Sandy Hook cases stem from external crimes. Three groups—victims of the Holocaust, the 9/11 attacks, and Sandy Hook—received redistributive justice soon after the period of victimization. Reparations for Japanese American people required many years of debate on and pressure for payment and justice. The South African case is one in which the goal, as stated by the Truth and Reconciliation Commission, was insufficiently ambitious. *All of them* demonstrate how, in the aftermath of unfathomable incidents, people—both government officials as well as those leading private charitable efforts—attempt to come to terms with placing a value on and compensating for lost lives and lost livelihoods, ultimately reaching closure for all concerned.

Key lessons include the following:

- Leadership from within the communities most affected is essential to ignite action and ensure that restitution is comprehensive and sufficient.

- Movement pressure outside of the political system is effective when it is combined with consenting formal political leadership (e.g., prime ministers, members of Congress) and high-profile bipartisan or multi-party commissions.
- Political commissions must have the proper mandate, focused not on repayment for demonstrable individual atrocities but on the comprehensive costs of social systems of oppression.
- Significant payment and restitution can be achieved even when reparations are politically unpopular.
- An enumeration of contingencies must be made to ensure the payments are made under challenging circumstances.
- Work performed by a study commission for reparations must be completed in a timely manner, within a maximum horizon of 18 months.
- Financial goals of a reparations project should be met within a decade.
- Valuing human life and coming to agreement on "sufficient" payment is difficult, but, within limits, identical payments are ultimately preferable.
- Financial outlays should be combined with educational, historical, and narrative efforts to ensure that the case for reparations is well understood in the public ethos.

[. . .]

Precedents for HR 40: Lessons Learned

Some specific recommendations for an African American reparations commission follow. [. . .] The Commission to Study and Develop Proposals for Reparations for African Americans, designated in HR 40, could perform such a function.

However, given the unique aspects of the Black American case, HR 40 is not adequate in its current form and requires revision. Unlike the original text that uses 1619 as the starting point, we designate 1776 as the point of origin for the case for Black reparations. The culpable party is the US government, and it did not exist in 1619. Although the current version of HR 40 distributes appointment of the commissioners between the executive and legislative branches and unspecified "grassroots organizations," the commission should be appointed by

Congress as well—because, ultimately, legislation for Black reparations must be enacted by Congress.

The core charge for the commission must be providing Congress with a detailed template for legislation that will activate a comprehensive plan for Black reparations. This will include specifying criteria for eligibility for Black reparations consistent with the standards described at the start of this report and specifying precisely how the amount and deployment of a reparations fund will raise Black net worth sufficiently to eliminate the (pre-tax) Black-white wealth gap within a decade.

To mitigate conflicts of interest or any appearance of wrongdoing, the commissioners should not receive a salary, although they should receive reimbursement for reasonable expenses associated with the fulfillment of their responsibilities. Nor should any organization to which they belong receive any funds from the budget assigned to the commission. However, there must be salaried professional staff members of sufficient size and skill to support the commissioners' efforts. Additionally, the commission should be directed to produce its report within 18 months of its inception.

And although closure is one of the imperatives of any reparations program, arriving at closure does not mean forgetting the record of atrocities. Thus, a key dimension of a Black reparations program must be the development and application of a rigorous and accurate curriculum, fully integrated into public school instruction across at least three generations at all grade levels, telling the story of America's racial history. Germany's efforts to maintain an authentic memory of the Holocaust is instructive and should serve as a model for this initiative.

To prepare its report, the commission must also hold public hearings and maintain a variety of mechanisms to ensure that eligible recipients' voices are heard, including having regional offices across the country. The commission should draw on specialists in American history, economics, sociology, politics, psychology, medicine and public health, and law and litigation, particularly those who are knowledgeable about constitutional law. Ideally, the commissioners themselves will possess such expert knowledge. Notably, these appointees should be well versed in the history of slavery and Jim Crow, employment discrimination, wealth inequality, health disparities, unequal educational opportunities, criminal justice and mass incarceration, media practices, political participation and exclusion, and housing inequities.

[. . .]

Conclusion

As we have previously stated in other works, monetary restitution has been a centerpiece of virtually all other cases of reparations, both at home and abroad.[20] Some reparations commentators are concerned that money is not enough, but we believe that money is exactly what is required to eliminate the Black-white wealth gap—the most glaring indicator of racial injustice in America. Ultimately, respect for Black Americans as people and as citizens—and acknowledgment, redress, and closure for the history and financial hardship they have endured—requires monetary compensation.

Moreover, an emphatic message that "the murderers cannot inherit" will be delivered. This message reminds us of the American government's promise of land to the formerly enslaved. In 1865, under the authority of President Abraham Lincoln, the process of allocating 40-acre parcels to each Black family of four on affordable terms—land that had been abandoned by and confiscated from the Confederate rebels—had begun. Lincoln's successor, President Andrew Johnson—and in our estimation, the country's most villainous president—asserted his authority and reversed Lincoln's orders, ultimately allowing the murderers to become the heirs. Reparations for living Black Americans would enable the descendants of the enslaved to receive the inheritance that was properly theirs all along. Today's Black-white wealth gap originated with that unfulfilled promise of 40 acres. The payment of this debt is feasible and at least 155 years overdue.

*****

The authors would like to express their gratitude to Mehrsa Baradaran, Kendra Bozarth, Hasan Jeffries, Spencer Overton, Anna Smith, and Felicia Wong for their thoughtful comments and valuable insights throughout the development of this report.

---

[20]William Darity Jr. and A. Kirsten Mullen, "How Reparations for American Descendants of Slavery Could Narrow the Racial Wealth Divide," *Think: NBCNews*, June 20, 2019.

Solutions Centering Black Women in Housing

Natasha Hicks, Anne Price, Rakeen Mabud,
and Aisha Nyandoro

There are myriad ways that our housing markets fail Black women. From current discriminatory practices in the private lending market to historic exclusion from public home-buying programs, the effects of these inequitable practices and policies on Black women include a lack of wealth and an incalculable loss of mental and physical health.

The harms that Black women face in our housing market are the result of decisions made by the government and real estate industry to segregate housing markets, setting the stage for corporations to profit off Black women's pain. Without understanding the decisions that got us here, we cannot build a housing system that is just and equitable.

A History of Racist Policies

Modern-day inequities in the housing market are rooted in exclusionary policies that embedded racism into the very bedrock of the US housing system. Shortly after the turn of the 20th century, real estate developers required prospective white home buyers to sign racist covenants that prevented these buyers from selling or renting housing to Black people. At the same time, real estate agents "steered" Black buyers and renters to areas that were designated—formally or informally—as Black neighborhoods.

In the 1930s, the federal government refused to insure mortgages in Black neighborhoods, a practice known as "redlining."[1] Simultaneously,

---

[1] https://www.npr.org/2017/05/03/526655831/a-forgotten-history-of-how-the-u-s-government-segregated-america

the Federal Housing Administration subsidized[2] new residential suburbs while stipulating that none of these new homes be sold to Black families. Private banks also redlined Black neighborhoods, denying loans to Black homeowners seeking to maintain their properties and causing building stock in many Black neighborhoods to deteriorate. The government's new Public Works Administration (PWA) Housing Division then "routinely razed"[3] these neighborhoods to build public housing projects that denied Black applicants. Even after passage of the 1968 Fair Housing Act,[4] which prohibits discrimination in housing based on race, color, national origin, religion, sex, familial status, and disability, exclusionary zoning laws continued to offer "a loophole for discrimination,"[5] keeping low-income people out of neighborhoods with more amenities and opportunity.

By locking Black homeowners out of such neighborhoods, US housing policies contributed significantly to the racial wealth gap[6] and reduced economic opportunity[7] for Black Americans while subsidizing[8] wealth-building opportunities for white people. They also excluded Black families from access to high-quality public education. But the harms of these policy choices go deeper; they set up Black families for extraction.

From Racist Exclusion to "Predatory Inclusion"

Policies in the 1970s that purportedly encouraged Black homeownership[9] resulted in what Dr. Keeanga-Yamahtta Taylor describes as "racist exclusion [giving] way to predatory inclusion." When homes went into foreclosure, the government paid mortgage lenders in full, incentivizing real estate brokers and mortgage bankers to target poor Black families because poverty would likely drive such borrowers to fall behind on their mortgage payments. And because Black people were being sold overvalued homes—another strategy

[2]https://www.npr.org/2017/05/03/526655831/a-forgotten-history-of-how-the-u-s-government-segregated-america
[3]https://www.banking.senate.gov/imo/media/doc/Rothstein Testimony 4-13-21.pdf
[4]https://www.hud.gov/program_offices/fair_housing_equal_opp/fair_housing_act_overview
[5]https://tcf.org/content/facts/understanding-exclusionary-zoning-impact-concentrated-poverty/?agreed=1
[6]https://www.brookings.edu/essay/homeownership-racial-segregation-and-policies-for-racial-wealth-equity/
[7]https://tcf.org/content/report/attacking-black-white-opportunity-gap-comes-residential-segregation/?agreed=1
[8]https://www.brookings.edu/essay/trend-1-separate-and-unequal-neighborhoods-are-sustaining-racial-and-economic-injustice-in-the-us/
[9]https://www.nytimes.com/2019/10/19/opinion/sunday/blacks-hud-real-estate.html

to squeeze as much profit out of Black borrowers as possible—lenders knew that they would profit from repayment until the borrowers could no longer bear the financial burden. They could then move on to extracting from the next poor Black family eligible for federal mortgage lending programs.

Given this sordid history, it is no surprise that during the 2000s housing bubble, lenders and Wall Street investors disproportionately targeted Black homebuyers[10]—and especially Black women[11]—for predatory subprime mortgages.[12] Black women lost their homes[13] and wealth[14] while the banks that issued manipulative subprime loans made billions of dollars. In short, banks profited from racism while also, as it so happens, triggering a years-long economic recession.

While unscrupulous lenders siphoned off Black wealth, Black women paid[15] the biggest price, and today, bankers continue targeting Black women for exploitative high-cost loans. They form part of system that fails to recognize Black women's humanity and need for stability. As Black women have expressed, stable housing is essential to economic and personal security. Carol, a low-income Black woman in Clay County, Georgia, said having a home of her own after a lifetime of renting is her biggest dream: "Even if I don't have lights, I have a roof over my head. I can lay my head in peace and not have to worry about someone telling me I have to get out." Tiyonda, a Black mother who currently lives in subsidized housing in Jackson, Mississippi, agrees: "It would mean peace for me. It's something I really want to experience."

Toward Repair: Addressing Black Women's Exclusion from Housing

We cannot expect a housing system that was built on predatory practices and anti-Blackness to work for Black women today. Small tweaks cannot tackle the vast inequities baked into the US housing market, nor can they make our society see that Black women's housing security affects Black

[10]https://www.npr.org/sections/thetwo-way/2012/07/12/156680278/wells-fargo-agrees-to-175-million-settlement-over-lending-discrimination

[11]https://journals.sagepub.com/doi/pdf/10.1007/s12114-011-9107-1

[12]https://publicintegrity.org/inequality-poverty-opportunity/predatory-lending-a-decade-of-warnings/

[13]https://medium.com/the-establishment/how-the-foreclosure-crisis-targeted-women-1625af58bb90

[14]https://prospect.org/justice/staggering-loss-black-wealth-due-subprime-scandal-continues-unabated/

[15]https://journals.sagepub.com/doi/abs/10.1007/s12114-011-9107-1?journalCode=rbpa

people's collective economic security. As a first step toward repairing the US housing system's entrenched inequalities, we must address Black women's exclusion from access to housing and reimagine our housing system to center Black women and their needs.

Confronting and rectifying these historic wrongs requires leading with two core principles: (1) reducing the outsized power of bankers and other lenders, which allowed them to get away with extractive practices such as predatory lending, and (2) demanding governments acknowledge that the system is broken and fix it. Regulating housing finance, curbing predatory lending, increasing public investment in housing, and ensuring that the country's fair housing laws are fully enforced are just a few of the ways policy makers can hold the private sector to account. Policy makers should also pursue rent stabilization policies[16] to stop skyrocketing housing costs and take on profiteering landlords who use inflation as an excuse to drive[17] rents to unsustainable levels. Only by using all the policy tools at our disposal will we build a housing system that does not extract wealth from Black women.

Policy makers must also advance policies designed to empower Black women. For too long, Black women have been funneled into low-quality, low-wage jobs, denying them the security and stability that wealth accumulation brings. Policy solutions must use a "both/and" approach, focusing on programs that combine ways to build *both* income and wealth. Insight Center has laid out a framework, Generations Ahead,[18] for creating such a policy. Similar efforts are being undertaken locally, such as Saint Paul's CollegeBound Boost program,[19] which combines a guaranteed income with college savings account investments.

A New Vision: Centering Black Women in Housing

Still, better policy choices will only get us so far. Ultimately, creating a just housing system must start with collectively creating a new vision, policies, and programs for housing that center Black women's thoughts and

[16]https://www.marketwatch.com/story/an-inflation-crisis-on-steroids-advocates-urge-congress-and-biden-administration-to-help-tenants-facing-rising-rents-11659517471
[17]https://groundworkcollaborative.org/wp-content/uploads/2022/10/Rent-Inflation-Memo_10-13_final.pdf
[18]https://insightcced.medium.com/63dcc5caf1f9
[19]https://www.stpaul.gov/news/mayor-carter-announces-collegebound-boost-expanding-city-saint-pauls-guaranteed-income-and

experience. That means refining current policies to better target and uplift Black women. It also means treating housing as more than a commodity by listening to the experiences of Black women who describe a home as a place of safety, privacy, community, family, and joy.

What would our homes, neighborhoods, and cities look like if we centered Black women's joy, dreams, and notions of safety? Efforts such as the Black Thought Project,[20] codesigned by Alicia Walters and the Insight Center,[21] offer a window into how grounding our policy solutions in Black women's experiences can help us envision solutions. The Black Thought Project transforms public and private walls in Oakland, California, into interactive art installations, providing Black people with community chalkboards to share and reflect on their perspectives. Black women's responses to these walls touched on the importance of kinship networks and family, the harm caused by and distrust in government programs and policies, the pain of changing neighborhoods and gentrification, and the desire for financial and emotional safety.

Centering Blackness could also mean building a housing system[22] that is structured around the village, reenvisioning the single-family house and city grids to better support kinship networks, which are integral to Black culture. Such a system would reflect the legacy of generations of Black families who make up the lifeblood of many American cities but are currently facing gentrification-induced displacement. Scholar Mehrsa Baradaran's proposed 21st-Century Homestead Act[23] provides a framework for just this; it would combat racially discriminatory housing policy by transferring land to residents of small and medium-sized cities with high housing vacancies.

We see examples of such a holistic approach in the work of Moms 4 Housing,[24] a grassroots group in Oakland, California, composed of unhoused and housing-insecure mothers. Moms 4 Housing describes its goal as "reclaiming housing for the community from speculators and profiteers." In late 2019, several Black women affiliated with the organization took over a vacant home in the city for nearly two months before being evicted. Their direct action[25] highlighted the unfairness of letting houses sit empty while families—particularly those headed by Black

---

[20] https://www.blackthoughtproject.com/
[21] https://insightcced.org/people/alicia-walters/
[22] https://nextcity.org/urbanist-news/hear-us-we-must-center-blackness-in-housing
[23] https://digitalcommons.law.uga.edu/cgi/viewcontent.cgi?article=2288&context=fac_artchop
[24] https://nonprofitquarterly.org/tenant-opportunity-to-purchase-bills-advance-in-san-francisco-bay-area/
[25] https://www.vice.com/en/article/bvgnmm/moms-4-housing-occupied-a-vacant-house-in-oakland-eviction

women—are denied homes, and it drew the support of several politicians and community advocates.

The group's assertion that housing is a human right is part of a long history of organizing that places shelter at the center of fights for economic and gender justice. Sixty years ago, the National Welfare Rights Organization's Johnnie Tillmon called for a guaranteed income as one way to provide Black women with the resources needed to survive. She pulled no punches with her assessment of the massive inadequacies[26] of the existing social safety net: "The man, the welfare system, controls your money. He tells you what to buy, what not to buy, where to buy it, and how much things cost. If things—rent, for instance—really cost more than he says they do, it's just too bad for you. He's always right."

For too long, Black women have been navigating a racist housing system that was designed to extract their wealth. Policy makers have failed to recognize housing as a right and confront the underlying racism and sexism in our housing system. Building a housing system that works for Black women can start with policy changes—whether regulations that safeguard people from exploitation or large-scale investments in housing—but cannot stop there. Rather, we need a new vision that brings Black women to the table and lets them shape an alternate future of housing that works for all.

[26] https://msmagazine.com/2021/03/25/welfare-is-a-womens-issue-ms-magazine-spring-1972/

Linking Racial and Economic Justice

The Struggle of Our Time

Steve Dubb

The legacy of the civil rights movement to provide economic equality is not lost or forgotten.

—*Gary Cunningham, CEO, Prosperity Now*

Last month, Prosperity Now,[1] a national economic and racial justice nonprofit, hosted its first national in-person conference since 2018. Held in Atlanta, Georgia, the conference attracted over 1,200 people, making it one of the largest gatherings of racial and economic justice advocates since the start of the pandemic.

Historically, Prosperity Now, formerly called the Corporation for Enterprise Development, had focused on promoting tax incentive policies that support individual savings and wealth building[2] by low-income Americans. This is still part of its agenda. However, Cunningham noted, the nonprofit now takes a much broader approach than seeking to "change a little program here and there." A principal goal of the gathering in Atlanta, Cunningham insisted, was "to reimagine economic justice for all." This reflects an organization-wide decision "to go bold and big to focus our work exclusively on racial and economic justice."

---

[1] https://prosperitynow.org/ (published in October 12, 2022).
[2] https://community-wealth.org/sites/clone.community-wealth.org/files/downloads/article-dubb-cfed10.pdf

The opening plenary—titled "Where Do We Go from Here?"—was an explicit callback to the last book published by Dr. Martin Luther King Jr., in 1967—namely, *Where Do We Go from Here: Chaos or Community?*[3] In the book, King called for the "total, direct, and immediate abolition of poverty."[4] King, of course, began his organizing and preaching career in Atlanta, so the callback was appropriate.

Earlier in 1967, at Riverside Church[5] in Harlem, King made explicit the link between racism and economic injustice, noting, "When machines and computers, profit motives and property rights, are considered more important than people, the giant triplets of racism, extreme materialism, and militarism are incapable of being conquered."

The extraordinary victories of the civil rights movement in the political sphere are rightly celebrated. Passage of the Voting Rights Act in 1965, for example, marked the first time that the United States approached universal adult suffrage, a "minimum threshold"[6] that, according to political scientists, must be crossed for a country to be considered a "democracy."

Yet, when it comes to the civil rights movement's economic agenda, the record of achievement is far less pronounced. Today, for example, the racial wealth and wage gaps[7] remain largely unchanged, and are indeed worse, than they were in King's time.

So, where does the movement go from here? This question, posed at the conference's opening session, served as a common thread that helped to connect the conference sessions. Following are some key themes that were raised over the course of the gathering.

The Long March of Institutions

One suggested strategy, offered by Glenn Harris, president of Race Forward,[8] was to gain ownership of institutions. As Harris put it, "We have to own the institutions in our lives." He particularly emphasized the need to own and control institutions at the local level. "There is so much national noise, and it matters," Harris noted. "But the real change we are

---

[3] https://newsroom.ucla.edu/stories/chaos-or-community-ucla-professors-on-Martin-Luther-King

[4] https://inthesetimes.com/article/martin-luther-king-jr-day-socialism-capitalism

[5] https://www.americanrhetoric.com/speeches/mlkatimetobreaksilence.htm

[6] https://www.ncbi.nlm.nih.gov/pmc/articles/PMC3003825/

[7] https://nonprofitquarterly.org/a-most-dangerous-intersection-revisiting-race-and-class-in-2020/

[8] https://www.raceforward.org/about/staff/glenn-harris

looking for is happening in our neighborhoods, our local communities. You can't lose sight of that."

Dr. Manuel Pastor,[9] a longtime advisor of labor and social movement activists based at the University of Southern California, concurred. "How do you become impatient about injustice but patient about strategy?" Pastor asked. Transformation, he contended, will occur through "the long march of institutions."

Challenging Harmful Narratives Through Data Linked to Activism

A second plenary session was titled "Our Lives, Our Stories, Our Solutions." On that panel, Eva Matos,[10] an associate managing director for Ideas 42,[11] a nonprofit consulting group, identified five false narratives[12] that her group aimed to challenge. One is the false notion that poverty is a personal moral failing. The second is the myth that the United States is a meritocracy. A third myth is that welfare cheating is normal. The fourth is fatalism—the myth that poverty is inevitable. And the fifth is the paternalist myth—that is, the pernicious notion that people with low incomes need decisions to be made for them. In short, media discourse reduces poverty to individual behavior, ignoring systemic drivers of poverty that are rooted in structural racism and capitalism.

At a later plenary session on "Using Data to Advance Racial Wealth Equity," Ibram X. Kendi, author of *How to Be an Antiracist*[13] and founding director of the Boston University Center for Antiracist Research,[14] argued that research could help challenge the false narratives that Matos referenced. As Kendi emphasized, while some may like to attribute the racial wealth gap in whole or part to Black Americans' alleged deficiencies, data from the field roundly refute such claims.

For example, Kendi noted that a common refrain is, "If only Black people would save more," the racial wealth gap would be less. But Kendi

---

9 https://dornsife.usc.edu/eri/manuel-pastor/
10 https://www.ideas42.org/about-us/people/#33433
11 https://www.ideas42.org/about-us/
12 https://twitter.com/dodsonadvocate/status/1571951467539431424
13 https://www.ibramxkendi.com/how-to-be-an-antiracist
14 https://www.bu.edu/antiracism-center/

pointed out that the "data have shown that if you control for income, there are no differences in savings patterns. Studies show when you control for income and wealth, there aren't disparities in financial education."

During the conference, two large data projects on racial justice were highlighted. One is the Black Wealth Data Center,[15] which aims to be a one-stop shop for racial impact data. The effort is funded by Bloomberg Philanthropies and is being incubated by Prosperity Now.

A second project, led by Alicia Garza, cofounder of Black Lives Matter and a principal of Black Future Labs, is called the Black Census.[16] As Garza notes, this is the project's second iteration; in 2018, an estimated 30,000 Black Americans were surveyed. This iteration aims to conduct 250,000 interviews. The census is finding that "economic issues across the board are what are keeping people up overnight. Not having the safety net supports you need. Along with student debt being a huge concern. Unaffordable housing. Quality of affordable healthcare."

Both Kendi and Garza were clear that data alone is insufficient. It needs to be embedded in larger movement strategies. Kendi called for a four-pronged approach that combines research with policy work, narrative change, and advocacy. For Garza, too, policy and advocacy are critical. As Garza put it, the objective of the census is to build "a legislative agenda we are fighting for. We are providing an opportunity for people to win locally and change federal policy." She added that she envisioned the census as a "vehicle for collaboration and a vehicle for power building."

The Importance of Historical Analysis

At a plenary session on "Big Ideas for Economic Equity," Darrick Hamilton,[17] a New School economist and founding director of the Institute on Race, Power, and Political Economy,[18] emphasized the need for historically grounded understanding. "The racial wealth gap is an implicit measure of our racist past," Hamilton emphasized. "We focus on poor financial choices. That framing is wrong. The directional emphasis is wrong. Meager economic circumstance constrains choice itself and leaves poor borrowers with little or no options other than to use predatory services."

----

[15]https://www.bloomberg.org/founders-projects/the-greenwood-initiative/black-wealth-data-center/
[16]https://blackcensus.org/
[17]https://www.newschool.edu/milano/faculty/darrick-hamilton/
[18]https://www.newschool.edu/institute-race-power-political-economy/

In another plenary session on "Radical Collaborations: Centering Children and Families on the Path to Justice," Hamilton's historical point was driven home by *Washington Post* reporter Robert Samuels. Along with fellow *Post* reporter Toluse Olorunnipa, Samuels is the coauthor of the book, *His Name Was George Floyd: One Man's Life and the Struggle for Racial Justice*,[19] a biography based on 400 interviews conducted after Floyd's murder.

Samuels noted that in researching the book, he and Olorunnipa went back seven generations. They learned that after emancipation, Floyd's great-great-grandfather "amassed over 500 acres of land," making him one of the wealthiest landowners in North America. "If George Floyd were white, he would have been born into wealth," Samuels observed. "But before a single generation, all that land was stolen." As a result, the Floyd family enjoyed no intergenerational wealth, instead growing up in segregated communities with inadequate schools. Samuels added, "What George Floyd went through has happened to untold numbers of Black people. . . . The history of your family and what they went through has an impact [o]n how you live your life."

The Struggle for Economic Democracy

The closing plenary, titled "Until We All Prosper: The Road to Economic Justice for All," focused on the intersection of democracy and economic justice. Not surprisingly given current voter suppression[20] efforts, much of the discussion focused on defending the right to vote. Miles Rapaport,[21] who, with E. J. Dionne Jr. coauthored *100% Democracy: The Case for Universal Voting*,[22] laid out the struggle's different dimensions—including campaigns to enable same-day registration, restore voting rights for the formerly incarcerated, expand mechanisms for voting (such as mail-in voting and ballot drop boxes)—as well as defensive struggles against voter suppression laws and the influence of wealthy donors.

In her remarks, though, Taifa Smith Butler,[23] president of Demos,[24] made explicit the deep connections between political and economic

---

[19] https://www.penguinrandomhouse.com/books/703358/his-name-is-george-floyd-by-robert-samuels-and-toluse-olorunnipa/
[20] https://nonprofitquarterly.org/whats-at-stake-in-the-wave-of-voter-suppression-bills/
[21] https://ash.harvard.edu/people/miles-rapoport
[22] https://thenewpress.com/books/100-democracy
[23] https://www.demos.org/bio/taifa-smith-butler
[24] https://www.demos.org/

democracy. "Economic and political power are inextricably linked," Butler observed. She added, "This system was designed to create winners and losers. We have valued the landowner or the land thief. We have valued white skin or the capitalist or the wealthy. We have undervalued folks like Indigenous people from day one. . . . We have undervalued agriculture, domestic workers, care givers."

"Unless and until we make sure we center people of color," Butler continued, "we will continue to perpetuate exploitation and oppression in our economy."

Early in the conference, Cunningham had challenged attendees to reimagine economic justice for all. What does this entail? For Butler, the answer to this question was clear: "Democracy is everything. It is the ability for us to influence the economic forces that shape our lives. . . . We want people to have agency and control over the economy." That, Butler added, "is the work we want to dig into in this next generation."

What If We Owned It?

Darnell Adams

T he story of Black co-ops and alternative economics in the United States is one of violence and persecution—but it is also a story of hope and determination. The history of Black cooperative economics and its leaders has remained largely—and intentionally—hidden from view, but that knowledge has been brought back into mainstream awareness with the 2014 publication of *Collective Courage: A History of African American Cooperative Economic Thought and Practice*, Dr. Jessica Gordon Nembhard's gargantuan work of gathering and remembering the histories of Black communities that, despite the ongoing threat of violence, practiced economic cooperation throughout the 19th and 20th centuries.[1] Bolstered by this renewed understanding, many BIPOC communities are creating their own paths for liberation and healing by focusing on the solidarity economy in its many forms. And Black co-op leaders across the country are playing a key role in innovating new solutions to address the old systemic challenges. One space in which this is happening—the space of food co-ops—is experiencing something of a renaissance.

Organizing for Sovereignty

I want to know safety and joy more than I know about pain and anxiety. I want wholeness, Black love, held equity based on a membership model, infrastructure that builds an economic base; resources that are not moved into hierarchy but into the streets.

—*Erin Dale Byrd, Fertile Ground Food Cooperative, Southeast Raleigh, North Carolina (first published in NPQ magazine Spring 2022)*

[1] Jessica Gordon Nembhard, *Collective Courage: A History of African American Cooperative Economic Thought and Practice* (University Park, PA: Penn State University Press, 2014).

Wanting to take a closer look at the emergent Black leadership in the food cooperative movement, I spoke with nine colleagues, representing six co-ops from around the country. I posed the question "What does organizing for sovereignty look like?" This led to deep reflections about the underlying nature of the communities they are working to support.

Black Americans have always relied on cooperative economics for their survival. Cooperative economics in Black communities has demonstrated the potential not only to provide for individual needs of food and shelter but also to play an important role in the development of political agency within the community. In his book *Economic Co-Operation Among Negro Americans*, W.E.B. Du Bois described how groups of enslaved people would work together to save enough money to buy individuals out of slavery.[2] Citing Du Bois and Frederick Douglass, Nembhard writes, "For two centuries they did not earn a regular wage or even own their own bodies, but they often saved what money they could and pooled their savings to help buy their own and one another's freedom (especially among family members and spouses)." In addition, Nembhard writes:

> *Du Bois notes that the African American "spirit of revolt" used cooperation in the form of insurrection to establish "widespread organization for the rescue of fugitive slaves." This in turn developed, in both the North and the South, into "various co-operative efforts toward economic emancipation and land buying," and those efforts led to cooperative businesses, building-and-loan associations, and trade unions.[3]*

More recently, the Freedom Quilting Bee project offers a beautiful example of how cooperative economics works.[4] In 1966, a collective of Black women in rural Alabama—under the leadership of Estelle

---

[2] W. E. B. Du Bois, *Economic Co-operation Among Negro Americans. Report of a Social Study Made by Atlanta University, Under the Patronage of the Carnegie Institution of Washington, D.C., Together with the Proceedings of the 12th Conference for the Study of the Negro Problems, Held at Atlanta University, on Tuesday, May the 28th, 1907* (Atlanta: The Atlanta University Press, 1907).

[3] Nembhard, *Collective Courage*, 31, 34.

[4] "Freedom Quilting Bee," Rural Development Leadership Network, accessed February 15, 2022, ruraldevelopment.org/FQBhistory.html. See also "Freedom Quilting Bee: History, Activities, Plans," Rural Development Leadership Network, accessed February 15, 2022, ruraldevelopment.org/FQBhistory.html; and Stella Hendricks, "A Timeline of the Freedom Quilting Bee," *BMA/Stories*, Baltimore Museum of Art, March 8, 2021, stories.artbma.org/timeline-the-freedom-quilting-bee/.

Witherspoon—founded the Bee to support local people who lost their income and/or home after registering to vote.[5] These quilts, made during the winters, were sold in stores like Bloomingdale's and Sears and exhibited at the Smithsonian Institute. With the money raised from the sale of the quilts, the collective was able to buy 23 acres of land in 1968 to build a sewing factory where it could produce more quilts. The collective sold eight lots to farming families who had been evicted from land they rented from white landowners, it leased part of its building from 1970 to 1996 to a day care center, and it became a member of the Artisans Cooperative. In Syracuse, New York, a group of women opened a store called the Bear Paw specifically to sell the Bee's quilts and other products the Bee had expanded to making, such as place mats, aprons, and pot holders. Until 2012, when it closed after the passing of the last original board member, Nettie Young, the collective continued to develop products and explore new enterprises.[6]

For over a century, Black people have organized and run food cooperatives, farm cooperatives, cooperative schools, insurance mutual groups, and credit unions.[7] Why has this history been lost? In an interview with Laura Flanders, Dr. Nembhard offered the following insight:

> *It was dangerous, especially in the South. Your stuff could get burned, you could get lynched. Why? Because you're being either too uppity by trying to do something on your own, or because you're actually challenging the white economic structure. And you weren't supposed to do that. The white economic structure actually depended on all these Blacks having to buy from the white store, having to rent from the white landowner. So they were going to lose out if you went and did something alternatively.*[8]

The Emergence of Black Food Co-ops

Throughout the 20th and 21st centuries, the sabotage of Black cooperative practices has shape-shifted from acts of overt violence to less visible forms of obstruction. In terms of Black food cooperatives, the latter takes

---

[5] "Freedom Quilting Bee."
[6] "Freedom Quilting Bee: History, Activities, Plans"; Hendricks, "A Timeline of the Freedom Quilting Bee."
[7] Nembhard, *Collective Courage*, 61–77.
[8] Laura Flanders, *Jessica Gordon Nembhard: Cooperative Economics and Civil Rights*, The Laura Flanders Show, April 8, 2014, video, 15:28, youtu.be/_TVIghQMkBg.

the form of an industry development model that uses data to exclude the communities that are most in need of access to healthy and nutritious food. Meanwhile, food cooperatives and community-supported food systems become ever more necessary. Grocery stores have either pulled up stakes or altogether avoided Black and Brown communities, creating a long-standing issue regarding access to fresh food.

This is not a new phenomenon. As with many other lack-of-access issues—employment, healthcare, transportation, clean water—lack of access to fresh food is a racialized and well-documented problem that has been decades if not centuries in the making. According to a 2014 Johns Hopkins University study, "[at] equal poverty levels, Black neighborhoods have the fewest supermarkets."[9] This problem has pushed neighborhoods to address the root causes and create businesses owned by the communities and designed for the benefit of the communities.

Mikaela Randolph, board chair of SoLA Food Co-op in South Los Angeles, reflects on this point:

> We are the recipients in our community of not having an adequate amount of grocery stores. So, when you're talking about food access and sovereignty, it's like freeing ourselves from limitations. Because we are limited in our immediate community of South L.A.—which is actually really large—with respect to having adequate access to, adequate quality of, foods—and we also have high incidence of comorbidities: high blood pressure, diabetes. We see dialysis centers popping up in our communities, and not grocery stores—right?

The standard development model currently used to determine the viability of a food co-op relies heavily on data regarding household income and, inevitably, skews the outcome toward more affluent communities. A common (not publicly shared) calculation included in these market studies is aptly titled the "Natural Foods Propensity Score." The calculation highlights who is likely to purchase natural foods, and where those people live. Based on census data, this score has reinforced an assumption that for a co-op to be successful, it needs to be situated in middle- to upper-middle-class communities. Why this assumption? The models

---

[9] Kelly M. Bower et al., "The Intersection of Neighborhood Racial Segregation, Poverty, and Urbanicity and Its Impact on Food Store Availability in the United States," *Preventive Medicine* 58 (January 2014): 33–39.

and business development frameworks for co-ops have largely focused on predominantly white, middle- to upper-middle-class college-educated communities.[10]

As recently as five years ago, developers were saying that they didn't have the data to support development of food co-ops in areas like South L.A.; Dayton, Ohio; Detroit, Michigan; Cleveland, Ohio; and Southwest Raleigh, North Carolina. To this assertion, Black co-op leaders across the country have been responding: "If you don't have the data, we'll figure it out ourselves."

Exploring ways to solve for the specific needs of their communities, Black co-op leaders have asked, "Does the majority of food in a co-op need to be natural—in other words, minimally processed—or can there also be selections of conventional foods that are more processed but less expensive?" Five or six years ago it was a radical notion that a co-op could have a large percentage of conventional or "clean conventional" foods—foods that have been processed using minimal chemicals or perhaps none, but which have not undergone the expensive process of being certified "organic." The decision to bring in conventional foods alongside natural and organic foods is one way that Black co-op leaders are innovating the co-op model to address the challenges of their communities.

We are seeing a remarkable shift in a short period of time. This past summer, Gem City Market, founded in 2015 in Dayton, Ohio, opened a 12,000-square-foot full-service grocery store offering everything from fresh produce to a hot food bar.[11] They lean heavily toward local foods but also have a large array of conventional and clean conventional foods.

Reflecting on the increase in the number of food co-ops currently organizing in the United States, Stuart Reid, executive director of the Food Co-op Initiative, says, "We can go back five years, but before that there were relatively few active [Black-led] start-up efforts. We started seeing more inquiries around the time that Renaissance [Community

---

[10] It is largely understood that food co-ops in the 1990s and through the 2000s were being built in wealthy, college-educated communities, and focused on natural/organic foods. Like many assumptions of this sort, this is not written down as a business model, per se, that I'm aware of. I have, for instance, images from a presentation by a co-op market study analyst that hints at the implicit principles/assumptions: "Very few preliminary market studies have been conducted for conventional foods co-ops, therefore there is no track record"; and "A person that has the propensity to purchase natural/organic food" (i.e., a person who has higher education and income levels that give them that level of purchasing power).

[11] "Now Open!," Gem City Market (Community Co-op Grocery Store, Dayton, Ohio), accessed February 15, 2022, gemcitymarket.com/.

Cooperative] was making news, and it has continued to increase, with a major bump after the combined impact of COVID and George Floyd's murder."[12]

Indeed, over the past two years, forces operating within and around us have brought us all to a full stop and opened the space for reevaluation. One thing that's become clear to many Black co-op organizers in the food cooperative movement is that they are ready for this time, *because they have been doing the work all along.*

Healing for Sovereignty

Trauma decontextualized in a person looks like personality.
Trauma decontextualized in a family looks like family traits.
Trauma in a people looks like culture. [13]

In 2017, I was the project manager of a start-up food co-op in Boston and responsible for community organizing and business development. One morning, I was standing in line at a local coffee shop when a Black woman approached me and started yelling, "What are you doing working for a bunch of white people who are just trying to gentrify this community? How dare you even do anything for them?" Everything around us came to a halt.

My first reaction was confusion. I remember thinking, What is she saying? What is happening? My second reaction was curiosity. I thought, I'm just going to listen to her. I knew her anger couldn't be personal, because she didn't know me. I took a breath and let her say the things that she needed to say.

When she was done, I said, "Thank you. But I disagree with you. I'm the one who's managing the project." I explained that the cooperative was

---

[12] Unfortunately, the Renaissance Community Cooperative closed its doors in 2019. For more on this, see Marnie Thompson, Sohnie Black, and Ed Whitfield, "The Ballad of the RCC, or 'Nice Try. Now Try Again.'," *Nonprofit Quarterly*, December 17, 2019, nonprofitquarterly.org/the-ballad-of-the-rcc-or-nice-try-now-try-again/; and Steve Dubb, "Anatomy of a Failed Co-op: Lessons from Greensboro's Renaissance Community Cooperative," January 3, 2020, nonprofit quarterly.org/webinar- anatomy-of-a-failed-co-op-lessons-from-greensboros-renaissance-community-cooperative/.

[13] Krista Tippett, "Resmaa Menakem: 'Notice the Rage, Notice the Silence,'" *On Being with Krista Tippett*, On Being, June 4, 2020, onbeing.org/programs/resmaa-menakem-notice-the-rage-notice-the-silence/.

owned and controlled by the community members for the benefit of the community members, and that the rumor of a "white lady" who owned the co-op was untrue. What *was* true was that there were a few white ladies on the board. However, this was a collective effort emerging from the community that would benefit from it.

Our exchange ended on a note of calm. "I just hope you know what you're doing," she said. I told her that I was glad that we got a chance to talk.

In the two and a half years that I worked to organize this food co-op, I was met with curiosity and enthusiasm but also distrust, frustration, and anger. I heard and felt the mistrust about the project, especially for the idea that it was a white, gentrifying project. At community meetings, members expressed anger that nothing ever seemed to change.

I have been hesitant to write about such experiences, because I do not wish to contribute to the narrative that Black folks are broken. I do not believe that. What I do wish to acknowledge is that the terror that lives within us from generations is both in the past and the present. But it is not our only story. To the degree that there is trauma, there are equal amounts of strength, creativity, and love. If this weren't the case, we would not still be here. If there were only trauma, there would be no hope, no dreaming. I have come to trust that speaking to the trauma that is present is helpful in healing. To acknowledge what is present can be used as a springboard to building a culture that gives people more opportunities to thrive.

In *My Grandmother's Hands: Racialized Trauma and the Pathway to Mending Our Hearts and Bodies*, somatic therapist and trauma expert Resmaa Menakem writes about traumatic retention: "Oppressed people often internalize the trauma-based values and strategies of their oppressors. These values and strategies need to be consciously noticed, called out as traumatic retentions and challenged."[14] Menakem notes, "Another fairly common traumatic retention is a reticence to own a home or a business, or even to be part of a start-up food co-op. It's not hard to see how people whose ancestors were considered property would not be delighted by the concept of ownership."[15]

While organizing in a community that had been historically disinvested, I found myself straddling the vision of the future and the multiple realities of the past and the present. There were indeed many concrete examples that folks shared with me about promises of adequate economic investments that seemed never to come. Community input about

[14]Resmaa Menakem, *My Grandmother's Hands: Racialized Trauma and the Pathway to Mending Our Hearts and Bodies* (Las Vegas, NV: Central Recovery Press, 2017), 79.
[15]Ibid., 80.

predatory practices that led to loss of homes and businesses also didn't appear to be valued or was outright ignored. Based on these truths, it was absolutely rational to be reticent to enter into a community business venture like ours. The traumatic and sometimes violent past was not so long ago as to be disconnected from the present.

Completing the Action That Was Thwarted: Moving Through Trauma

In therapy a traumatic experience is sometimes described as an attempted action that got thwarted and became stuck in the body. A common first step in the mending of trauma is completing the action that was thwarted. This releases the trauma energy stuck in your body. You can then use this energy to metabolize the trauma.[16]

Co-op organizing requires action. It requires the coming together of hundreds of people to not only imagine a new future but also move oneself and marshal all resources over a span of many years—in the form of outreach, networking, community meetings, door knocking, political maneuvering, capital raising, and self-governance. Action is key to mending the trauma. As Menakem writes:

> *In the healing of intergenerational trauma, you may also complete an action that was attempted and thwarted by a traumatized ancestor. The trauma got stuck in their body, and then passed down to you. Even though you may be cognitively unaware of this trauma—or of your ancestor's experience and incomplete action— your own efforts simultaneously heal your trauma and release future generations from its grip.[17]*

Leaders in the Black food co-op movement have been speaking to the different manifestations of intergenerational trauma that are undermining Black communities. These leaders understand that healing in

....

[16] Ibid.
[17] Ibid., 179.

communities is not just about economic opportunities and access to nutritious food but also about providing a sense of safety and dignity to the shopper and worker. It's this experience of sovereignty that leaders in this movement are working to provide.

The food co-op leaders I spoke with, while deeply entrenched in the day-to-day aspects of organizing and opening a cooperative grocery store, also spoke about love of self, love of others, and healing from trauma. I was struck by the complexity of their vision—one that made space not only for economic thriving but also for the physical and mental well-being of their communities, and which often spoke explicitly, if indirectly, to this neurobiological understanding of how integral stuck, interrupted action is to trauma that doesn't get healed, even across generations.

For Kenya Baker, director of Unified Power, Co-op Dayton, a key question is what to do with the trauma. "How do we release it?" she asks. "One of the things our community has started doing is healing circles. We come together with other community members. Not to drink, not to smoke, not to party, not to kick, not to gossip—but to deal with our trauma. To process trauma. To release it."

Unhealed trauma can lead to distrust and resistance when it comes to genuine community development. Baker spoke to the resistance she encountered while building support for their project.

> We're not used to seeing development in our community, so immediately the thought is, it's not for us. But that's part of the self-hate. Because we don't believe we deserve it. We have never done it for ourselves. I had so many naysayers from the community who were Black nationalists, or Black organization leaders. And a lot of them, I'm really proud to say, are now members of the grocery store. But it was a process. I tell people this grocery store is a community-led development. If it is to remain a community-owned and -led development, you must get engaged. Three days after we opened, the president of the NAACP called me and said, "I think I'm ready to get my membership."

As Janet Howard, board member at the Fertile Ground Co-op, noted, "Our experience in America has led us to all of this distrust, and to easily lash out at our own rather than finding the source—which would amount to being in conversation with political leaders about how they disinvested from our community."

Given the context in which Black communities are organizing cooperatives, it is not surprising that healing from trauma is not far from the minds of Black co-op leaders—in particular, the practice of visioning the space, and the processes of group learning and striving. Information gathering—the gaining of new knowledge—is also a route toward healing. Common Share Co-op board president Kinga Walker-McCraven described ways in which to create the space for people's trust and engagement to emerge. She sees it as a process of growing capacity within individuals and community.

> *One thing that I'm working on right now is really diving deeply into each person's personal values, strengths, talents, and natural gifts that we can highlight and affirm, and help them to grow even deeper and find their place. It really does come down to each person being able to really sink into who they are, what they offer, where they're comfortable. I want to develop that in our board and in our community, so that we have a high-functioning community of people.*

Baker adds:

> *You have to have a level of faith, because it makes dreaming safe. COVID slowed things down a lot. It gave people an opportunity to reimagine—because these structures that create obstacles for people to be able to self-determine were dreamed up and put in place by man. This is our opportunity to reimagine and then cocreate, with our brothers and sisters, what we want our future to look like.*

In *My Grandmother's Hands*, Menakem writes about "clean" and "dirty" pain:

> *Experiencing clean pain enables us to engage our integrity and tap into our body's inherent resilience and coherence, in a way that dirty pain does not. Dirty pain is the pain of avoidance, blame and denial. When people respond from their most wounded parts, become cruel or violent, or physically or emotionally run away, they experience dirty pain.[18]*

Menakem offers a process in which a traumatized body can move through pain "cleanly." One step is to "stay present and in your body as you move through the unfolding experience with all its ambiguity and uncertainty, and respond from the best parts of yourself."[19]

Indeed, moving through trauma is not only an emotional and mental journey but also one of activation of the body. In organizing to create a

....

[18] Ibid., 28–29.
[19] Ibid.

cooperative—in the unknown places where there is no one road map—all the community's wisdom, gifts, and skills are needed. In this coming together, this building of relationship, this learning together and making decisions together, comes the opportunity to heal from our collective trauma—to complete the thwarted actions of our parents, our great-grandparents, and beyond.

Building for Sovereignty

Food co-ops focus on addressing the immediate and long-term needs of their communities. This provides the framework for alternative business practices to those of traditional grocery stores. Co-ops place emphasis on job creation, procuring products from local producers, and having proactive policies to minimize environmental impacts of their operations. These business practices have a multiplier effect that filters through the local economy. Indeed, the data tell the story: "For every $1,000 a shopper spends at their local food co-op, $1,604 dollars [sic] in economic activity is generated in their local economy—$239 more than if they had spent that same $1,000 at a conventional grocer in the same community."[20]

Building a community-owned food co-op requires intensive business development—as one might expect with any multimillion-dollar business—but co-ops are unique in that they have international guiding principles that are of great benefit both to start-up co-op business ventures and those that already have their doors open. "Co-operation Among Co-ops"—the sixth principle of the guide "7 Cooperative Principles," decrees that co-ops support one another by providing technical assistance and capital through local, regional, national, and (sometimes) international structures.[21]

Further, there is an ecosystem of food co-op development supports, such as the nonprofit Food Co-op Initiative (FCI)[22] (whose mission is "to increase the number, success, and sustainability of new food cooperatives delivering access to healthy food in diverse communities across this

[20] *Healthy Foods, Healthy Communities: Measuring the Social and Economic Impact of Food Co-ops* (Iowa City, IA: National Cooperative Grocers Association, 2012); and "Cooperative Identity, Values & Principles," International Co-operative Alliance, accessed February 15, 2022, ica.coop/en/cooperatives/cooperative-identity.

[21] *Guidance Notes to the Co-operative Principles* (Brussels, Belgium: International Co-operative Alliance, 2015).

[22] "New Food Co-ops Start Here," Food Co-op Initiative, accessed February 15, 2022, fci.coop/.

country") and the National Co+op Grocers (NCG), which "exists so that member co-ops are successful, and the total cooperative grocery sector grows in size and scope."[23]

Gerardo Espinoza, executive director of the Local Enterprise Assistance Fund (LEAF),[24] a national lender that focuses on cooperative businesses and housing, considers food co-ops to be "the best of both worlds." Food co-ops have "both the kind of support that a major corporation like Star Market has *and* have the autonomy and independence and flexibility of an independent grocer." What he means is that large supermarket chains have corporatewide processes and systems that maximize efficiencies that are out of reach for smaller, independent stores. But for communities starting a food co-op, a whole support system is in place regarding "what point of sales I should buy, what refrigeration equipment [I should] buy, how to do the merchandising, how to do the member campaign, how to negotiate the lease," notes Espinoza. This support, he affirms, reduces risk, which is extremely important for sustaining small businesses.

In addition to this ecosystem of support, there is the strength of the community ownership itself. The sustained volunteer effort and the matrix of cooperative support systems have helped to provide business stability, making food co-ops a viable option for many communities wanting to address food access issues and for providing an economic boost to those communities.

Yet, building a cooperative grocery store is a daunting task that requires years of effort and significant capital to make the dream a reality. This effort includes predevelopment costs that support the following:

- Business planning and market research
- Deep learning of governance systems
- Enormous community-organizing efforts
- Cost of real estate
- Hiring of architects and store planners
- Purchasing of equipment
- Hiring of staff
- Stocking of shelves with food

---

[23] "National Co+op Grocers (Carrboro)," National Co+op Grocers, accessed February 15, 2022, ncg.coop/partners-find/nc /national-coop-grocers-carrboro. And see "Harmony Natural Foods Co-op," National Co+op Grocers, accessed February 15, 2022, ncg.coop/.

[24] "Since Its Founding over 30 Years Ago, LEAF Has Invested and Leveraged over $122 million, Resulting in the Creation or Retention of More Than 10,300 Jobs," Local Enterprise Assistance Fund (LEAF), leaffund.org/.

JQ Hannah, assistant director of the Food Co-op Initiative, reports:

*To compete in these times, start-up food co-ops must not only
do excellent organizing pre-open but also open very professional
grocery stores that are excellent shopping experiences. Because of
this, the full cost of opening as a start-up generally ranges from
$3.5 million to $5.5 million, depending on the size and scope of the
store. These costs are not only showing no sign of coming down but
are rising rapidly.*

So, despite the benefits that communities can derive by owning a food
cooperative, there are many obstacles, especially with regard to funding.
Randolph highlights this tension, pointing out that our system is economically structured so as to discourage and impede small-business ownership.[25] "That can be really disheartening," she says, especially because "if
we were able to go back to a cooperative model" then this would meet "so
many different needs" for so many communities—needs that otherwise
remain unaddressed. Randolph pointedly asks, "Why aren't we funding
that more? Why isn't there more federal funding? Why isn't there more
state funding and local funding?"

Although co-op members put in a certain amount of equity, there
remain sticking points for getting needed capital, especially when it comes
to traditional lenders. A food co-op has hundreds of owners, and no one
person provides a personal guarantee. In addition, in a situation where a
store is having difficulty repaying a loan, in most cases the value of the
collateral, such as the refrigeration and shelves, are not worth enough to
cover the amount of the loan. This can be a full stop for traditional lenders. Espinoza elaborates:

*I think many people are surprised that even the government some-
times is not flexible. For instance, with the SBA [Small Business
Administration], I believe that it's only relatively recently that they
have been willing to consider worker co-ops as a small business.
But even though it's a small business, it's still requiring collateral.
So they made progress, but not the progress that is needed. For me,
it's always fascinating how a government organization—which
should be the first in line to support this type of initiative because of
all the characteristics of wealth distribution, and so on—is not at
the table. So, that would be one instance of flexible capital—or, in
this case, inflexible capital.*

---

[25] "Bringing Fresh, Healthy Food to South LA," SoLA Food Co-op, accessed February 15, 2022,
solafoodcoop.com/.

The vision is not just to open a store but also for that store to grow and thrive—to become an economic engine, create dignified jobs, and, of course, provide access to healthy food. To have all of those things become a reality, the store needs to function well in the first few years until the point of being profitable, and then continue to grow—sustainably. Not having enough cash on hand in those early years can be a fatal blow in an industry that runs on between 1% and 2% margins. A high debt load with immediate repayment is equally detrimental.

Patience and flexible capital are necessary financial conditions for a food co-op's success. Those two concepts must be intertwined to be effective. Impatient investors needing quick returns would tend to siphon off very-much-needed cash from the new store. Flexibility may need to look like seeking other ways of measuring risk and/or willingness to restructure a loan if there are challenging financial conditions. Funders such as LEAF, Cooperative Fund of New England, Shared Capital Cooperative, and The Working World understand the unique nature of cooperatives and strive to support them with patient and flexible financial tools.[26]

Grants are also an important part of the capital equation, particularly in lower-wealth communities. Co-op members in communities already struggling financially may be limited in the amount of equity and loans they can provide.

Grants can fund those hefty predevelopment costs, increasing the chance of a shorter and more successful development process. And, importantly, grants can also be used as part of how capital stacks up to fund the store.

John Guerra, director of retail and store development for National Co+Op Grocers, underscores this point:

> *It's important, in terms of starting up, to have capital to actually bring to the table—to say [to banks and other investors], "This is the money [we have] to spend on this thing [the co-op]." That's important to show, in terms of community support. But also, you have to have 20 to 30 percent just to get banks to come to the table. In terms of equity, I would say grants can often function in that same way.*

---

[26] Cooperative Fund of the Northeast, accessed February 15, 2022, cooperativefund.org/; "Flipping the Script on Who Has Power and Who Benefits in Our Economy," Shared Capital Cooperative, accessed February 15, 2022, sharedcapital.coop/; and "Our System Is in Crisis," The Working World, accessed February 15, 2022, theworkingworld.org/us/.

Grants that support organizations whose mission is to support food cooperatives, such as FCI, are yet another piece of the financial puzzle. They have the line of sight and expertise to assist organizers in the many places across the country where communities have decided to take on this vision of sovereignty by sharing the responsibility, risk, and eventual benefit of a cooperative.

As communities respond to the growing need for more access to food and for spurring economic development, many are turning to the cooperative model as a viable way to bring goods and services to areas abandoned or ignored by traditional grocery stores. For funders whose missions support fundamental shifts in power, the cooperative movement may align with those aims. Malik Yakini—cofounder and executive director of the Detroit Black Community Food Security Network and board member of the Detroit People's Food Co-op—astutely asks:

> *Are the projects that are funded ones that are trying to make this fundamental shift in power, which will ultimately give more autonomy and sovereignty to people? Or are these groups just trying to reform conditions within a system where the people who are in power are still fundamentally in power, and are still making mega-profits, and we just have a kinder and gentler capitalism? And so [funders must have] some kind of clear analysis themselves that this isn't just about, you know, minor reforms, but about a fundamental shift in power: the fundamental shift in how resources are distributed. And then [funders must try] to identify those groups that are striving for those fundamental changes, as opposed to those groups that are doing just the kind of windowdressing reformer things.*

There are many purposes to dreaming, and there are different kinds of dreams. Some dreams hold longing—a vague memory of what once was that can sustain one through hard times. Then there is the kind of dream that leads to action, activated when the conditions are right. Like a seed that sits dormant until the rains finally come.

As food apartheid continues to plague Black and Brown communities, and food cooperatives and community-supported food systems become ever more necessary in communities across the country, Black co-op leaders are engaged in both kinds of dreaming. They are remembering and honoring the dreams of the lineage of organizers on whose shoulders they stand as they move forward in action by learning together and supporting each other—particularly through the National Black Food & Justice Alliance, which holds regular virtual meetings for members.[27]

Back when I was working to organize that food co-op in Boston—sitting in community meetings, door knocking, going to city hall, and talking to economic development people—I had this vision of what we were all working so hard to accomplish together:

> It's a new building, built on the footprint of what had been a business many decades ago. When I walk in, I see a cross-section of the neighborhood, from the folks stocking fresh produce to those ringing up the groceries. The shelves are full. Prices are fair. Bright colors are on the wall, and a large sign greets me: "Everyone Welcome." I recognize these folks, even if we've never met before. They look like me. It's a grocery store envisioned by community members who asked, "What if we owned it ourselves?"

Developing a Food Co-Op: Seven Principles

The consumer-owned food co-op model requires not just business development but also community development. As with many business ventures, coming up with a solid business plan with strong pro forma (financial forecasting), obtaining capital, and assembling a team that can execute the operations are key steps. The development of a food co-op is a process that requires the community to invest its time, energy, and skills for as long as five years to learn about cooperatives, spread the word, create the governance and business structures, and sell equity shares.

It's a complex endeavor, and one that requires communities to marshal their resources to reach their goal. The co-op exists way before the physical store is built: to sell equity shares in the business, it must incorporate. Co-ops begin to organize before the incorporation. How else would you know if people want a co-op? So, those conversations—the sharing

---

[27] "Collectively Creating a Just Food & Land Revolution," National Black Food & Justice Alliance, accessed February 15, 2022, blackfoodjustice.org/.

of ideas, dreams, and possibilities—happen for a long time during the process. The co-op development process itself is a master class in power, relationship building, self-determination, and how to share information. Thankfully, there is guidance—guardrails on how co-ops should conduct their work.

Seven Internationally Recognized Co-op Principles of the ICA (International Co-operative Alliance)

1. Voluntary and Open Membership

Co-operatives are voluntary organizations, open to all persons able to use their services and willing to accept the responsibilities of membership, without gender, social, racial, political, or religious discrimination.

What this means in practice. In adhering to this first principle, food co-ops cast a wide net for those who can join and participate. Importantly, the choice remains in the community members' hands—choice for oneself, as in self-possession: the power to decide one's involvement, level of risk, and reward.

2. Democratic Member Control

Co-operatives are democratic organizations controlled by their members, who actively participate in setting their policies and making decisions. [Individuals] serving as elected representatives are accountable to the membership. In primary co-operatives members have equal voting rights (one member, one vote).

What this means in practice. For consumer cooperatives, boards are elected by membership, and any member in good standing can run for the board. Big decisions that will tangibly affect the co-op and by-law changes are voted on by membership. Can this get messy? Yes. Democracy can be a messy process. However, the board works on behalf of the membership. Members have the power.

3. Member Economic Participation

*Members contribute equitably to, and democratically control, the
capital of their co-operative. At least part of that capital is usually
the common property of the co-operative. Members usually receive
limited compensation, if any, on capital subscribed as a condition of membership. Members allocate surpluses for any or all
of the following purposes: developing their co-operative, possibly
by setting up reserves, part of which at least would be indivis-
ible; benefiting members in proportion to their transactions with
the co-operative; and supporting other activities approved by the
membership.*

What this means in practice. In a nutshell, the money is put to use
for goods, services, and employment that the community needs. But this
principle is not meant to function in isolation from the co-op principles and
values. Indeed, shared social aspirations and needs are just as important.

4. Autonomy and Independence

*Co-operatives are autonomous, self-help organizations controlled
by their members. If they enter into agreements with other organizations, including governments, or raise capital from external
sources, they do so on terms that ensure democratic control by their
members and maintain their co-operative autonomy.*

What this means in practice. The members and the cooperative
are the primary beneficiaries of the cooperative enterprise, both in terms
of the services that are provided and eventual surpluses. The cooperative is a community asset. The shareholders are in the community—not
an outside corporate entity. The co-op members are agents of their own
business venture. They determine what they wish it to accomplish and
how it will be accomplished. The promise of cooperative business is that
a business of scale can be built and run with the community needs at
the center. For many Black and Brown communities, this is often not the
case, with ownership residing elsewhere and profits siphoned off for the
benefit of others.

5. Education, Training, and Information

Co-operatives provide education and training for their members, elected representatives, managers, and employees so they can contribute effectively to the development of their co-operative. They inform the general public, particularly young people and opinion leaders, about the nature and benefits of co-operation.

What this means in practice. Some cooperatives have an open (accounting) book system and extensive training for staff members, so there is not only financial transparency but also the opportunity for broader input, business planning, and problem-solving from the team. In all cooperatives, the business is required to give regular financial reporting to the board and to the co-op members. Board members often need financial training to understand financial statements. For start-ups, extensive cooperative training for organizers takes place for years through organizations such as the Food Co-op Initiative, CooperationWorks!, state-run cooperative development offices, and a variety of cooperative associations such as the National Black Food & Justice Alliance.

6. Cooperation Among Co-operatives

Co-operatives serve their members most effectively and strengthen the co-operative movement by working together through local, national, regional, and international structures.

What this means in practice. This principle guides the behavior and support within the cooperative sector. In this way, although a particular food co-op is a highly autonomous business, it fits into an ecosystem where folks from other communities work in support of one another. One organizer from Raleigh will call another organizer in Detroit to share how they went about acquiring a site for the store or how they capitalized their project. Documents are shared, advice given, ideas copied—so much so, that the sharing has been lovingly referred to as *P6-ing*. This is important. This work is hard, and it is almost impossible to go at it alone. Autonomous, yes; alone, no. For communities healing from years of folks either swooping in with solutions derived from outside the community or from not having access to larger networks with information and resources, Principle 6 is a remarkably different and healing way to do business.

7. Concern for Community

Co-operatives work for the sustainable development of their communities through policies approved by their members.

What this means in practice. The relationship of the co-op to the community beyond the members of the co-op is important. Relationship building goes beyond the point of organizing to grow membership: It also requires care and thoughtfulness regarding what is important to the neighbor next door who chooses not to become a member or shopper, to the business viability of the farmer and fair treatment and appropriate compensation of farm workers, to those who are fighting to keep housing affordable.

The seven principles as laid out here were adapted from Guidance Notes to the Co-operative Principles *(International Co-operative Alliance, 2015). You can find the full, original guide here:* **www .ica.coop/sites/default/files/2021–11/ICA%20Guidance%20Notes%20EN.pdf**.

How Do We Build Black Wealth?

Understanding the Limits of Black Capitalism

Francisco Pérez

In the wake of the mass movement against anti-Black racism that arose in 2020 following the police murders of Breonna Taylor, George Floyd, and countless others, both foundations and corporations have pledged to make amends by investing in Black businesses. According to McKinsey & Company, collectively the nation's leading 1,000 corporations pledged $200 billion.[1] Even if much of that money is simply a relabeling of pre-existing dollars, at least some of it represents new investment.[2]

Hopefully, these investments will have some positive impact, but history encourages us to be cautious. A significant portion of recent investors in Black businesses take Black capitalism as their operating theory—that is, they assume that the path to racial equality is paved with Black business success. If racism has left Black Americans with less capital than white Americans, then the solution is to help Black Americans eventually own businesses as large and profitable as those of white Americans.

Capitalism, in this conception, is "race neutral"—business is business. According to this point of view, to achieve racial justice, the existing economic system does not need to fundamentally change. The problem is simply one of shifting ownership and control of the economic system so

---

[1] https://www.mckinsey.com/featured-insights/diversity-and-inclusion/its-time-for-a-new-approach-to-racial-equity (published in April 2, 2022).
[2] https://nonprofitquarterly.org/can-community-finance-advance-racial-equity-it-takes-an-ecosystem/

that such ownership and control is not enjoyed by predominantly white people but is instead equitably distributed across races.

The appeal of Black faces in high places is undeniable.[3] And certainly no one would argue that representation is unimportant. Nonetheless, such a simple formulation misses a lot, including the fact that such investment practices have been tried before—and failed many times before. The notion of Black capitalism has a long pedigree. It appeared in some of the writings of Booker T. Washington[4] from the 1890s and became US federal policy during President Richard Nixon's administration.[5]

Why did these approaches fail? There are many reasons, but the work of the late Black political scientist Cedric Robinson offers a particularly cogent explanation.[6] In his book, *Black Marxism,* published in the early 1980s, Robinson contended that we should think of the global economic system not merely as "capitalism" but as "racial capitalism,"[7] arguing that racism is not a "bug" of the global capitalist economy. Rather, racism is a core part of capitalism's DNA.

The Enduring Appeal of Black Capitalism

The United States has a long and bloody history of racial terrorism targeting Black-owned businesses. This history includes the racist pogrom that destroyed Tulsa's "Black Wall Street" in 1921, which was widely commemorated last year during its centennial. The implication of these memorials was that, without the ever-present specter of racist violence that characterized Jim Crow, Black Americans would have similar levels of income and wealth to white Americans today.

Promoting Black capitalism has been the preferred approach of both major political parties since Nixon unveiled a program of tax incentives for Black businesses in an effort to head off more militant alternatives. For a nation that venerates entrepreneurship and deifies business leaders, this vision holds great attraction. As Mehrsa Baradaran, author of *The Color of*

---

[3] https://blavity.com/black-faces-in-high-places-why-black-leadership-matters?category1=opinion

[4] https://www.newyorker.com/magazine/2021/02/08/the-plan-to-build-a-capital-for-black-capitalism

[5] https://www.nytimes.com/2019/03/31/opinion/nixon-capitalism-blacks.html

[6] https://bostonreview.net/articles/robin-d-g-kelley-introduction-race-capitalism-justice/

[7] http://racialcapitalism.ucdavis.edu/wp-content/uploads/2017/09/robinson-black-marxism-selections.pdf

Money: Black Banks and the Racial Wealth Gap,[8] outlines in the *New York Times*, "Black capitalism was so politically appealing, every administration since Mr. Nixon's has adopted it in some form. Black capitalism morphed into Ronald Reagan's 'enterprise zone' policy, Bill Clinton's 'new market tax credits,' and Barack Obama's 'promise zones.'"[9] Donald Trump's 2017 Tax Cuts and Jobs Act also included similar "opportunity zones."

Black Capitalism's Shortfalls

Despite repeated promises by US presidential administrations since 1970 to kickstart Black capitalism, it has failed to take off, and racial income and wealth gaps have remained frustratingly persistent. Research by the Washington Center for Equitable Growth,[10] a progressive think tank, shows that racial income inequality has changed little since the civil rights movement. The median income of Black households has hovered at about 55% of that of white households since 1968, while the average income of Black households has been about 60% of white households (see Figure 1).

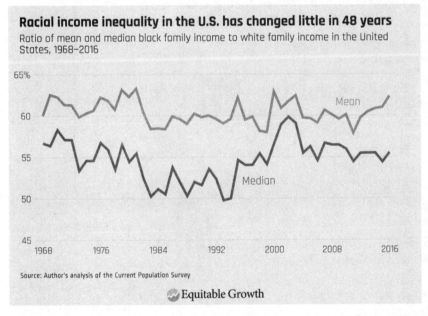

Racial income inequality in the U.S. has changed little in 48 years

Ratio of mean and median black family income to white family income in the United States, 1968–2016

Source: Author's analysis of the Current Population Survey

Equitable Growth

Source: https://equitablegrowth.org/wp-content/uploads/2018/08/maduca-fig-1-1080x762.png/, last accessed March 09, 2023.

---

[8]https://blogs.lse.ac.uk/lsereviewofbooks/2019/01/29/book-review-the-color-of-money-black-banks-and-the-racial-wealth-gap-by-mehrsa-baradaran/

Median Family Wealth by Race/Ethnicity, 1963–2019

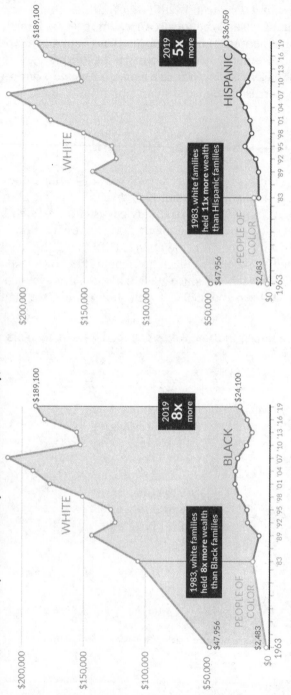

$200,000

$150,000

$100,000

$50,000

WHITE

$189,100

2019
8x
more

1983, white families
held 8x more wealth
than Black families

PEOPLE OF
COLOR

BLACK

$24,100

$47,956

$2,483

$0

1963   '83   '89 '92 '95 '98 '01 '04 '07 '10 '13 '16 '19

$200,000

$150,000

$100,000

$50,000

WHITE

$189,100

2019
5x
more

1983, white families
held 11x more wealth
than Hispanic families

PEOPLE OF
COLOR

HISPANIC

$36,050

$47,956

$2,483

$0

1963   '83   '89 '92 '95 '98 '01 '04 '07 '10 '13 '16 '19

URBAN INSTITUTE

Sources: Urban Institute calculations from the Survey of Financial Characteristics of Consumers 1962 (December 31), Survey of Changes in Family Finances 1963, and Survey of Consumer Finances 1983–2019.

Notes: Amounts are 2019 dollars. No comparable data are available between 1963 and 1983. Disaggregated data for Black and Hispanic are available in 1983 and later. We have used the term "Hispanic" in this chart rather than "Latinx" to match the data source.

Source: https://www.urban.org/sites/default/files/2021–02/wealthbyrace-med.png, last accessed March 09, 2023.

William "Sandy" Darity and Darrick Hamilton—two leading econo-mists studying racial inequality, along with a host of other colleagues—assert in a 2018 paper that the racial wealth gap is the best measure of the burden that historic and ongoing racism has imposed on Black Ameri-cans. The Urban Institute reports that in 1983, the median white family had eight times the wealth of the median Black family. In 2019, the gap was the same (see Figure 2)!

Black Americans make up 13% of the population but own an esti-mated 2.6% of US wealth.[11] Households that fall within the top 1% of wealthiest Americans are 96.1% white[12] and only 1.4% Black. As a research team led by Darity wrote, Federal Reserve data from 2016 indicate that to be in the top 1% of wealthiest white Americans, you need $12 million in net worth, while a measly $1.574 million gets you into the Black 1% club.[13] Why have decades of official support for Black capitalism failed to close the racial wealth gap?

Capitalism and Inequality

One possible explanation is the "Piketty principle," named after the French economist, Thomas Piketty, who documented rising concentrations of wealth in his magnum opus, *Capital in the 21st Century*.[14] Piketty famously argues that the rate of return on capital has been higher than the rate of overall economic growth in most rich countries for most of their history. If capital returns—profits, dividends, interest, and rents—rise faster than overall incomes, then high and rising wealth inequality is inevitable.

Piketty demonstrates that reductions in wealth inequality are excep-tional, the result of political intervention. Wealth inequality in Western Europe fell when the world wars destroyed the fortunes of many rich Euro-peans. Social democratic reform in the wake of World War II—especially progressive taxation and high levels of unionization—also contained wealth inequality. The rise of neoliberalism[15] since the 1980s, however,

[9] https://www.nytimes.com/2019/03/31/opinion/nixon-capitalism-blacks.html
[10] https://equitablegrowth.org/
[11] https://www.huffpost.com/entry/americas-financial-divide_b_7013330
[12] https://images.huffingtonpost.com/2015-04-12-1428856586-2064712-RaceEqualitychart1.jpg
[13] https://socialequity.duke.edu/wp-content/uploads/2019/10/what-we-get-wrong.pdf
[14] https://nonprofitquarterly.org/in-capital-and-ideology-piketty-reminds-us-to-follow-the-money/
[15] https://nonprofitquarterly.org/after-the-next-recession-the-search-for-an-economic-path-forward/

has once again caused income from property to grow much faster than overall income, leading to today's extreme levels of wealth and income inequality.

If large fortunes grow faster than smaller ones and white Americans start with more wealth than Black Americans, it follows that the racial wealth gap will be stagnant at best and, at worst, will increase over time. "Free markets" left to their own devices will never close the racial wealth gap. As Darity et al. explain, "Blacks cannot close the racial wealth gap by changing their individual behavior—i.e., by assuming more 'personal responsibility' or acquiring the portfolio management insights associated with 'financial literacy'—if the structural sources of racial inequality remain unchanged."[16] There are simply "no actions that [B]lack Americans can take unilaterally that will have much of an effect on reducing the racial wealth gap." Black capitalism with its emphasis on individual action is unlikely to succeed. As Baradaran concludes in her *New York Times* op-ed: "If the rollout of the Black capitalism program had demonstrated anything, it was that economic power could not be achieved without government help."

Can Racial Capitalism Be Reformed?

Even if it were possible for Black wealth to grow faster than white wealth despite the headwinds identified by Piketty, it would still take an unbearably long time. Last year, Ellora Derenoncourt, an economist at Princeton University, and three colleagues at German universities released preliminary research that examined the evolution of the racial wealth gap since the end of the US Civil War.[17] The paper's authors estimate that even if Black and white wealth grew at the same rate—that is, with equal capital gains, rates of return, and savings rates, all unlikely outcomes of a system where having money helps generate more money—it would take over 200 years to close the racial wealth gap. Using more realistic assumptions that project forward the economic patterns of the past 50 years, the authors add that the answer to when the racial wealth gap will close, "strikingly, is never."

In response to these dire predictions, Hamilton has proposed that the federal government provide each child who does not already have a trust fund with such a fund on birth.[18] Children born to families with the least

---

[16] https://socialequity.duke.edu/wp-content/uploads/2020/01/what-we-get-wrong.pdf
[17] https://www.russellsage.org/sites/default/files/Derenoncourt.Proposal.pdf

wealth would get the biggest endowments, up to $60,000. When they turn 18, account holders could access the funds for investment—to pay for college, buy a home, or start a business. Although this would certainly make a significant dent in the racial wealth gap, it does not directly address the Piketty principle: so long as white fortunes are growing faster than Black ones, the racial wealth gap will persist.

Darity and his coauthor, A. Kirsten Mullen, have made a more ambitious proposal advocating for reparations[19] for Black Americans for slavery, Jim Crow, and current racial discrimination. This proposal calls for the US federal government to make direct payments, totaling $10 to $12 trillion, to each Black descendant of Africans enslaved in the United States (controversially, the program would exclude Black immigrants). Putting aside whether such a proposal will ever gain majority support in Congress, would it actually close the racial wealth gap for good? Although it would immediately close the wealth gap, such a proposal would not guarantee that the racial wealth inequality would not reemerge. Again, as long as the returns to white wealth remain higher, then white wealth will eventually outpace Black wealth. The problem, as Piketty demonstrates, is that capitalism is an inequality-producing machine.

One of the threads uniting the Black radical tradition is the assertion that it is impossible to achieve racial equality in a capitalist society. For at least a century, Black Marxists such as W.E.B. DuBois,[20] C.L.R. James,[21] and Claudia Jones[22] have argued that capitalism cannot survive without racism, which enables capitalists to "divide and conquer" the working classes. Emphasizing racial divisions hinders workers from organizing stronger unions, lowering the wages of both white and Black workers. Without racist ideas to justify glaring social inequalities, a capitalist social order would be a lot more unstable and susceptible to radical challenges. As historian and prison abolitionist Ruth Wilson Gilmore states bluntly, "capitalism is never not racial."[23]

[18] https://www.bloomberg.com/news/features/2022-03-17/baby-bonds-eyed-as-way-to-close-u-s-racial-wealth-gap

[19] https://nonprofitquarterly.org/resurrecting-the-promise-of-40-acres-the-imperative-of-reparations-for-black-americans/

[20] https://items.ssrc.org/reading-racial-conflict/capitalism-democracy-and-du-boiss-two-proletariats/

[21] https://globalsocialtheory.org/thinkers/james-clr/

[22] https://www.versobooks.com/blogs/5030-the-forgotten-legacy-of-claudia-jones-a-black-communist-radical-feminist

[23] https://monthlyreview.org/2020/07/01/modern-u-s-racial-capitalism/

What Do Racial and Economic Justice Require?

Even if promoting Black capitalism could close the racial wealth gap, is our vision of a just society in the United States simply one where the top 1% is roughly 13% Black, 18% Latinx, 6% Asian, and 1.5% Native American[24]— that is, one where the elite looks more like the mass of workers it exploits? Is massive wealth inequality justified so long as it is not racialized? Are poverty wages less miserable because your boss is Black? Is substandard housing less dangerous because your landlord is Black? Are monopoly prices any more affordable because the company is Black owned?

There is something deeply ahistorical underlying current efforts that ignore and indeed reproduce previous efforts to combat racial inequality by employing the strategies of Black capitalism as the primary path. Even if Black capitalism can ultimately "deliver" racial equality, the data suggest it would take centuries do so. Moreover, our horizon for social justice should be far more profound than simply diversifying the elite.

As long as capitalism remains an "inequality producing machine," it will prevent racial equality. Fred Hampton, the charismatic young leader of the Chicago chapter of the Black Panther Party who was murdered by Chicago police and the FBI in 1969, explained this succinctly: "We're not going to fight capitalism with Black capitalism, but we're going to fight it with socialism."

Black communities have long pursued an alternative approach to racial equality founded on collective ownership and democratic management of businesses and housing. As economist Jessica Gordon Nembhard details in her book, *Collective Courage: A History of African American Thought and Practice*, Black cooperatives are rooted in the mutual aid efforts of the formerly enslaved during Reconstruction. While Booker T. Washington was preaching Black capitalism, W.E.B. DuBois published a book in 1907 titled *Economic Cooperation Among Negro Americans*, advocating for more Black cooperatives.[25] Several prominent leaders of the civil rights movement, such as Ella Baker and Bayard Rustin, were members of the Young Negro Cooperative League in the 1930s.[26] Now grouped under the banner of the "solidarity economy,"[27] these initiatives promised

[24]https://www.census.gov/quickfacts/fact/table/US/PST045221
[25]https://repository.wellesley.edu/object/wellesley30436
[26]https://www.youtube.com/watch?v=ycn6dzwfMEw&ab_channel=KheprwInstitute
[27]https://nonprofitquarterly.org/imaginal-cells-of-the-solidarity-economy/

a more egalitarian society by directly challenging capital's concentrated ownership.

A movement that seeks economic justice without addressing race and other forms of inequality would surely fall grossly short of the mark. But that very same observation, I contend, also applies in reverse: employing Black capitalism as the primary path for achieving racial justice is certain to disappoint. Liberation will only come if we are expansive enough in our vision to address inequality in all its forms.

VI

Organizing for the Future: Community and Politics

Making Black Communities Powerful in Politics—and in Our Lives

Alicia Garza

Despite rigged rules[1] and relentless attacks on our right to vote,[2] Black communities have shown up, shown out, and changed the trajectory of this country for the better. In the last decade, we have transformed the national landscape in ways that bend toward freedom. The global social movement for Black lives has hastened our victories over the last decade. We have shifted the balance of power in Congress, ushered in a new president to replace one pushing us toward fascism, and won important victories in cities and states across the nation. Our legacy is one of resistance, resilience, and change; from slave rebellions to the civil rights movement of the 1960s to the Black Lives Matter movement of today, Black communities have always been at the forefront of significant and meaningful change.

What's good for Black communities is what's good for the country, as Black communities are a bellwether of our society. What Black people need and the issues they experience—such as low wages, expensive healthcare, and unaffordable housing—are what most Americans are experiencing now, even as Black communities have been affected by these issues for decades. By addressing the needs of Black people and securing the things we deserve—including livable wages to raise and support our families; affordable, quality healthcare; physical, social, and emotional safety; and the power to make and change the rules that

---

[1] https://www.vox.com/policy-and-politics/2022/10/2/23377432/supreme-court-alabama-merrill-milligan-racial-gerrymandering-voting-rights-act (first published in October 27, 2022).
[2] https://www.brennancenter.org/our-work/analysis-opinion/5-egregious-voter-suppression-laws-2021

affect our lives—the needs of everyone in this country will also be met. As the saying goes: A rising tide lifts all boats. If you want a pulse on what's happening in the country at-large, listen to Black communities.

However, despite our proven political power and influence, elected officials, political campaigns, and political parties have made little to no meaningful investment in our communities. They are comfortable with talking *at* Black people, but few talk *with* us, limiting our ability to have a say in the decisions and policies that affect us. Hollow gestures, photo ops at the barbershop and chicken spots ahead of an election, and officials who talk without listening—this is what our communities have come to expect from those in power. It's not good enough. We deserve better.

Black people need more than a seat at the table to activate our power—we need to set the menu. When Black voters aren't engaged, the consequences are severe: we are left out of shaping policies that affect us directly and, often, disproportionately. That's why I formed Black Futures Lab[3] and Black to the Future Action Fund,[4] two groups that work to make Black communities powerful in politics so that we can be powerful in the rest of our lives. We do this in five ways.

First, we listen to what Black people are concerned about and want, something political leaders and parties rarely do. The Black to the Future Action Fund's Temperature Check polls[5] and the Black Futures Lab's Black Census Project[6] are two tools we use to share the perspectives and insights of Black people with legislators and other political decision-makers.

Our recently concluded Temperature Check polls, a series of six bimonthly surveys of 1,000 Black adults, offers a one-of-a-kind look at Black communities' top priorities. We found that, overwhelmingly, economic recovery is our top priority. The top two policy priorities of Black adults were consistent in every poll over the entire series: $2,000 monthly relief checks until the economy recovers and increasing the minimum wage to $15 an hour. Nearly twice as many respondents said that their finances worsened during the pandemic (33%) compared to people whose finances improved during the same period (18%). When we asked Black people with an annual household income under $20,000 how they would use monthly relief checks, the majority responded that they would pay for basic needs. Nearly two-thirds said they would pay for utilities and food, and about half would pay their rent and mortgage. Clearly, the pandemic

---

[3] https://blackfutureslab.org/
[4] https://black2thefuture.org/
[5] https://black2thefuture.org/year-in-review/
[6] http://blackcensus.org/

exacerbated generations-old conditions, structures, and policies that have left our communities back and behind.

The poll results also show, in no uncertain terms, how starkly Black people feel unprotected by our government. On average, almost half (48%) of Black people—a core constituency that led Democrats to victory in 2020—are dissatisfied with the direction the country is headed.

The Black Census Project 2022 aims to reach 200,000 Black people from across all 50 states. Translated from English into five languages—Amharic, Spanish, Yoruba, French Kreyol, and Portuguese—the census asks our communities about their experiences, concerns, and dreams for the future. When completed, it will be the largest survey of Black people conducted in American history. The results gleaned from the census will inform a Black legislative agenda that we will organize around in cities and states across the nation. This valuable resource will also provide the Biden-Harris administration, elected officials, cabinets, and campaigns irrefutable insights that they can use to address Black communities' needs. By encouraging our communities to stay engaged, and by informing, influencing, and affecting all the institutions and decision-makers that should be engaging Black people, we will ensure Black voters are not left high and dry until the next Election Day.

Second, we educate, activate, and motivate Black voters and support the leaders who champion their needs and solutions. Black to the Future Action Fund field organizers are knocking on hundreds of thousands of doors in our five priority states—Georgia, North Carolina, California, Louisiana, and Wisconsin—to mobilize Black voters for the upcoming midterm elections. We chose to invest in these states for the next five years because each one offers a tremendous opportunity to shift the balance of power in favor of Black communities and advance progressive policies that reflect our priorities. In North Carolina, we could send to the US Senate a Black woman who's worked to reform the criminal legal system. In Georgia, we could send to the governor's office and the secretary of state's office, respectively, a Black woman and a Vietnamese American woman who want to protect and expand voting rights. In Wisconsin, we could send to the US Senate a Black man who was a community organizer and who worked for years on policies that improve the lives of our communities.

To hone our political power, this fall [2022], we're educating our communities on the role of governors and secretaries of states, the impact of redistricting, how misinformation is being used to dilute our power, and how local and state governments misspent COVID-19 relief and recovery dollars. We designed a comic book to reach our communities about the issues we care most about—and we are working on a report card so that we know who is standing up for us and what we care about.

Third, we train Black leaders to rewrite the rules that hold our communities back. The Black to the Future Public Policy Institute[7] trains future Black policy makers to create and implement policies that will transform our communities and secure our futures. To date, 63 fellows from more than 20 Black-led, Black-serving organizations from across the country have participated in the institute, learning and receiving key insights from local and national leaders like Ebony Meeks, deputy chief of staff to the New York Council Speaker; Alicia Netterville, deputy director for the ACLU Mississippi; journalist Joy Reid; civil rights leader Bryan Stevenson; and Congresswoman Ayanna Pressley.

These fellows have gone on to secure big policy wins in their communities, including the Justice for Survivors Act (AB 124)[8] in California—a policy that was designed inside our institute and became state law in 2020.

Fourth, we also build capacity by investing in Black organizing infrastructure. The Black Futures Lab and the Black to the Future Action Fund launched the Black Organizing Innovations Project,[9] which grants Black-led, Black-serving organizations up to $250,000 to supercharge innovative ideas that best engage Black communities—and ensure they stay engaged. In addition, we are partnering with The Management Center[10] on a unique capacity-building program for executive directors and organizing staff members at Black-led, Black-serving organizations.

Fifth, we practice what we preach. Our all-Black staff represents the diversity found in our communities. We are multigenerational and live all over the country. Some of us are US-born, others immigrants. Some of us are multilingual. We have diverse education and work experiences and are LGBTQ, parents, and more. The organization creates space where staff members can show up as our full selves, and it prioritizes self-care and rest by calendaring time off for all staff members. This is important because if our movements and organizations for change perpetuate the same dynamics that we aim to disrupt, we are not creating change—we are merely rebranding the same set of practices and the same dysfunctions.[11]

We operate in an increasingly tumultuous political environment where the progress that Black communities have led is under vicious attack. Now, it is more important than ever that we keep building Black political power by centering Black people's experiences, needs, and solutions. It's the only way we can win a robust democracy that works for everyone.

....

[7] https://blackfutureslab.org/black-to-the-future-policy-institute/
[8] https://leginfo.legislature.ca.gov/faces/billNavClient.xhtml?bill_id=202120220AB124
[9] https://blackfutureslab.org/organizing-innovations/
[10] https://www.managementcenter.org/
[11] https://nonprofitquarterly.org/leading-restoratively-the-role-of-leadership-in-a-pro-black-sector/

Justice Beyond the Polls

Investing in Black Youth Organizers

Carmel Pryor

C asting a ballot, although important, is the floor, or the bare minimum, when it comes to creating real social change. Electoral engagement is key, without a doubt. But voting is only one part of what it takes to ensure that Black communities are seen and Black people are treated as full human beings who can thrive in this country.

Black youth and their collective power go beyond their strength as a voting bloc, and no one knows that better than Black youth organizers—young leaders who need sustained investment from all levels of government and philanthropy to continue unlocking Black youth power.

Black Youth Fighting Voter Suppression

Black youth are part of the largest voting bloc in America—Generation Z and millennials. And record numbers of young people voted in 2020, with Black youth voting in battleground states in numbers that propelled Biden and the Democrats to victory.[1] Although white youth voted for Biden by a slim margin (with 51% voting for Biden compared to 45% for his opponent), youth of color gave him overwhelming support, ranging from 73% among Latinx youth to 87% among Black youth. This massive turnout happened in the middle of a pandemic and after years of unchecked voter suppression. Nearly 10 years ago, the Supreme Court gutted the Voting

---

[1] https://circle.tufts.edu/latest-research/election-week-2020#young-voters-and-youth-of-color-powered-biden-victory

Rights Act.[2] Ever since, voter suppression and discriminatory voter laws have been designed to block communities of color from the ballot box. Between 2012 and 2018, 1,688 polling places were closed in states that were previously covered by Section 5 of the act, which required preclearance from the federal government for any changes to voting policies and procedures.[3]

Black youth organizers are fighting voter disinformation and suppression targeted at Black voters to ensure access to the ballot box. From the Second City[4] to the Magnolia State,[5] youth organizers are advancing policies to re-enfranchise Americans, an issue that disproportionately affects Black people. Chicago Votes has led some of the most revolutionary voting rights efforts through its Unlock Civics program. In 2019, the organization wrote and passed landmark legislation—the Voting in Jails bill—that expanded voting access for incarcerated citizens who are eligible to vote. This made Cook County Jail the first jail in the country to become an official polling location. Due to the tenacity of Chicago Votes youth organizers, Cook County Jail detainees had a higher voter turnout in the June 2022 primary than the city as a whole.[6] Now, the youth are organizing to pass legislation that would restore voting rights to people in prison. Meanwhile, Mississippi is one of only three states to impose lifelong voting bans on people convicted of certain felonies.[7] Mississippi Votes (MS Votes) worked to fight over 70 voter suppression bills and supported 52 voter suffrage applications through the 2021 Mississippi legislative session. Today, MS Votes continues to lead voting rights restoration efforts.

Investing in Black Youth: Beyond Electoral Engagement

Even as Black youth organizers fight for voting rights, they must be seen and invested in as more than electoral engagement machines. Dakota Hall, executive director of the Alliance for Youth Action,[8] described in a piece

[2] https://civilrights.org/blog/weve-entered-our-10th-year-without-the-full-protections-of-the-voting-rights-act/
[3] https://civilrights.org/democracy-diverted/
[4] https://blockclubchicago.org/2022/07/12/cook-county-jail-voter-turnout/
[5] https://scalawagmagazine.org/2022/10/as-the-south-votes-lessons-from-2020/?utm_campaign=scal-social&utm_source=twitter&utm_medium=social&utm_content=1665499356
[6] https://blockclubchicago.org/2022/07/12/cook-county-jail-voter-turnout/
[7] https://www.splcenter.org/our-issues/voting-rights/voting-rights-ms
[8] https://allianceforyouthaction.org/

for the National Committee for Responsive Philanthropy why philanthropy must make bold investments in movement change.[9] As Hall writes,

> *For local youth-led organizations in the Alliance Network, partisan political funding enables organizations to deepen their impact, be innovative in building power for their communities, and allows youth organizers to have the conversations that need to be had in our communities year-round. These dollars are critical for accountability work, growing a pipeline of strong political champions, and how we win elections and policy change.*

The policies that Black youth are fighting for include student debt relief, college affordability, divesting from the police to reinvest in social services, voter re-enfranchisement, decriminalizing marijuana, promoting healthy babies and mothers through affordable healthcare, ending medical discrimination, and realizing racial equity through economic investments in Black communities, which can be achieved through reparations.

Look to Black youth organizers for the answers. In the Midwest, for example, Black-led youth organizations that care for communities facing police violence have enacted real change. The Minnesota Youth Collective (MNYC) set up mutual aid in their communities after the killing of George Floyd in 2020.[10] Currently, MNYC is a part of the Minneapolis United for Rent Control coalition, building a movement for strong rent control, mobilizing youth to attend council meetings, and organizing community events to demand policies that reflect the needs of the majority renter population in a city where the homeownership gap between white people and people of color is the largest in the nation.[11] In November 2021, the Ohio Student Association (OSA) worked with a coalition of organizations, activists, and individuals—led by families who lost loved ones to police violence—to canvass local residents, host educational events, and collect signatures. Together, they passed the Citizens for a Safer Cleveland ballot initiative, which focused on reforming police accountability and oversight processes by asking for increased authority for the Civilian Police Review Board.[12]

Black youth organizers have also been at the forefront of the fight to cancel student debt and make higher education affordable for all. Their

[9] https://www.ncrp.org/publication/transformative-power-supporting-civic-engagement-responsive-philanthropy-summer-2022/the-case-for-bold-c4-funding

[10] https://www.startribune.com/st-paul-mutual-aid-group-raises-30000-dollars-for-people-experiencing-homeless/600129617/

[11] https://www.minnpost.com/cityscape/2021/06/widening-homeownership-gap-in-twin-cities-is-focus-of-new-report/

[12] https://www.wkyc.com/article/news/local/cleveland/issue-24-cleveland-police-reform-initiative-passes/95-dee2f979-06a1-4b14-b1b0-8185545e18ba

pressure led President Biden to eliminate a significant amount of student debt: up to $20,000 for Pell Grant recipients and up to $10,000 for non-Pell Grant recipients whose individual annual incomes are less than $125,000 (or $250,000 for married couples and heads of households).[13] For nearly a decade, OSA has been dedicated to changing the policy landscape for higher education in Ohio. OSA youth organizers are working to get debt navigation programs passed in state legislatures and to end "transcript traps," where colleges withhold transcripts from students over unpaid bills. The Black women-led Virginia Student Power Network (VSPN)[14] passed legislation to provide in-state tuition and state financial aid for undocumented students in Virginia. VSPN organizers at the University of Virginia also won a tuition freeze at their university, which means that tuition rates are guaranteed to stay the same until the 2024–2025 academic year.

Black Youth Organizing for a Better Future—For Everyone

According to the most recent Alliance for Youth Action poll of people ages 17–39 in 11 battleground states nationwide, 86% of this demographic age group plan to vote in the midterms.[15] These young people don't fit the stereotype once attributed to millennials: spoiled brats eating avocado toast. They are fighting for better futures for us all, and they are ready to make their voices heard.

Given the high percentage of youth who already plan to vote, the conversation about Black youth voters needs to change. Instead of asking if Black youth will show up at the polls, we must ask, Who will they vote for when they show up? Have midterm election candidates shown up for Black youth and the issues they care about most?

Gen Z-ers and millennials live in an era of constant crisis. Amid a nationwide rise in school shootings and gun violence, Black and Brown youth must also deal with neighborhood vigilantes and police killing their

---

[13] https://www.brookings.edu/blog/the-avenue/2022/08/25/bidens-student-debt-cancellation-doesnt-solve-the-root-problems-facing-borrowers-but-its-a-start/
[14] https://www.vastudentpower.org/
[15] https://allianceforyouthaction.org/young-voters-in-battleground-states-on-the-midterm-elections/

peers such as Trayvon Martin and Breonna Taylor.[16] They are trying to survive a global pandemic and the everyday effects of environmental racism—such as unsafe water in predominantly Black cities—while preparing for their futures under a global climate emergency. After seeing their parents suffer through multiple economic recessions, they find themselves earning wages that are not adjusted for inflation. And they have seen how a resurgence of white supremacism and the rise of authoritarianism that led to an attempted coup on January 6, 2021.

It is almost a broken record now: every election year, we are told, is the "most important election of our lifetimes," but the issues that affect Black youth seem to receive attention only when it is time for them to vote again. The singular focus on getting out the Black youth vote during an election year—followed by years of ignoring the issues and policies that would help Black youth thrive—reminds me, an elder millennial, of a Wyclef Jean song. "Gone Till November"[17] tells the story of a man who leaves his girlfriend for long periods of time to take care of "other business," neglecting their relationship. Elected officials take a similar approach to Black communities, putting on the backburner the policy priorities of Black voters—and Black youth specifically—until it is time to seek their votes again. Young people see through this facade. Although Black youth will vote this November, youth-led civic organizations should not be seen as get-out-the-vote machines.

For Black youth organizers, democracy is about more than voter participation. Voting must be combined with other actions to protect our democracy. This means voting *and* taking direct action, voting *and* organizing, voting *and* engaging in civic education. Democracy is about the work that takes place in the street, at city and school council meetings, and at local political homes like Chicago Votes, Mississippi Votes, Minnesota Youth Collective, Ohio Student Association, and Virginia Student Power Network—and it even looks like running for office themselves. Black youth organizers are building power beyond the voting booth right now. It is time for us to invest in Black youth organizing beyond election years.

---

[16] https://slate.com/news-and-politics/2022/02/black-lives-matter-trayvon-martin-and-the-rise-of-vigilante-violence.html
[17] https://www.youtube.com/watch?v=kI6MWZrl8v8

The Liberatory World We Want to Create

Loving Accountability and the Limitations of Cancel Culture

Aja Couchois Duncan and Kad Smith

There is no end to this love
It has formed your bodies
Feeds your bright spirits
And no matter what happens in these times of breaking—
No matter dictators, the heartless, and liars
No matter—you are born of those
Who kept ceremonial embers burning in their hands
All through the miles of relentless exile
Those who sang the path through massacre
All the way to sunrise
You will make it through—

—Joy Harjo, from "For Earth's Grandsons," An American Sunrise
(NPQ magazine Spring 2022)

Love, a Forgotten Tongue

In *Measuring Love in the Journey for Justice*, Shiree Teng and Sammy Nuñez "call upon love as an antidote to injustice."[1] But too often in our equity-based systems-change work, love is a forgotten tongue. Even in contexts where Black, Indigenous, and people of color (BIPOC) are leading organizations, networks, and change efforts, our engagement can be marked by competition, judgment, adversarialism, and distrust.

Coming, as we are, from centuries of land theft, enslavement, genocide, and systemic inequities that threaten our daily ability to survive, let alone thrive, it is understandable that we are angry—righteously so. And yet, the world we are seeking to create together requires that we move beyond anger to harness the transformative power of love.

In Ojibwe, one word for love is *zhawenim*: to show loving kindness. It is a transitive animate verb, which means it is an action done by one to/ with another. It is relational. Love is not something that is hidden somewhere, waiting to be found. It is something we create together—something that must be cultivated and practiced.

Medicine to Harvest

One of the many ways systemic injustice works is through the story it teaches us to tell ourselves: A story that locates responsibility within individuals for the effects of settler colonialism, enslavement, extractive capitalism, and US global domination. This is how we, as BIPOC people, can become defined by the trauma that we, our families, and our ancestors have experienced.

As James Baldwin reminds us, "History is not the past, it is present. We carry our history with us. We are our history."[2] So the question becomes: what do we carry and how do we carry it? Our histories are filled with music, dance, ceremony. And, too, our histories are filled with violence, starvation, captivity. But we are not our trauma. We *experience* trauma, yet we are

---

[1] Shiree Teng and Sammy Nuñez, *Measuring Love in the Journey for Justice: A Brown Paper* (San Francisco: Latino Community Foundation, July 2019), 5.

[2] James Baldwin, "Black English: A Dishonest Argument," 1980, in *The Cross of Redemption: Uncollected Writings*, ed. Randall Kenan (New York: Pantheon, 2010), as quoted in *I Am Not Your Negro*, 2016. See Rachel Herzing and Isaac Ontiveros, "Looking the World in the Face: History and Raoul Peck's *I Am Not Your Negro*," Center for Political Education, accessed February 7, 2022, politicaleducation.org/resources/looking-the-world-in-the-face-history-and-raoul-pecks-i-am-not-your-negro/.

infinitely more powerful than the harm done to us. And the just and liberatory world we want to create will not be birthed from our unhealed wounds.

In *My Grandmother's Hands*, Resmaa Menakem describes how whitebody supremacy "doesn't live in our thinking brains. It lives and breathes in our bodies."[3] This is why any effort to advance racial equity–based systems change that addresses other intersectional forms of oppression must be an act of community care, one that centers our collective well-being— the well-being of our bodies, our hearts, our spirits. What is needed is to acknowledge trauma, honoring its impact while striving to relinquish its stronghold. It is through this effort that we claim our strength, our purpose, our aggregate power to transform the world.

There are many different somatic and energetic practices that can support us in healing trauma—both on our own and together. So, we have a great deal of medicine to harvest. What is necessary is that we all tend to this important work for the sake of ourselves, our communities, our vision of a just and liberated world. It is also critical that our social change work centers healing and inner work as a fundamental aspect of all our efforts collectively. (For an in-depth discussion of why this matters and what can be made possible as a result, please read "Toward Love, Healing, Resilience & Alignment: The Inner Work of Social Transformation & Justice" by Sheryl Petty, Kristen Zimmerman, and Mark Leach.)[4]

Without careful attention to how we want to be together, what we do together will be nothing more than the replication of centuries on centuries of harm.

Cancel Culture

Cancel culture is a phrase that is relatively new to our shared lexicon.[5] It is a term that describes a phenomenon many of us can loosely identify in shape and form, but struggle to explicitly name what it is and isn't. "Canceling" someone was most prominently brought to our collective consciousness through online engagement in the 21st-century public squares of Twitter, Tumblr, and Facebook. It served as a way to bring attention to

---

[3] Resmaa Menakem, *My Grandmother's Hands: Racialized Trauma and the Pathway to Mending Our Hearts and Bodies* (Las Vegas: Central Recovery Press, 2017), 5.

[4] Sheryl Petty, Kristen Zimmerman, and Mark Leach, "Toward Love, Healing, Resilience & Alignment: The Inner Work of Social Transformation & Justice," *Nonprofit Quarterly*, May 12, 2017, nonprofitquarterly.org/toward-love-healing-resilience-alignment-inner-work-social-transformation-justice/.

[5] Aja Romano, "Why We Can't Stop Fighting About Cancel Culture," Vox, August 25, 2020, www.vox.com/culture/2019/12/30/20879720/what-is-cancel-culture-explained-history-debate.

behavior that could broadly be deemed reprehensible, abhorrent, or just generally disagreeable. Often, it has been used in jest. Over the past five years, however, the act of canceling someone has risen to such cultural significance that our last three sitting presidents have remarked on the role in which it is influencing how we engage with one another. For better, or for worse?

In July 2020, movement theorist and visionary adrienne maree brown wrote a blog post titled "unthinkable thoughts: call out culture in the age of covid-19," in which she interrogates the practice of publicly calling people out.[6] For some, there was immediate resonance in brown's words; for others, feelings of frustration, as they felt her blog didn't adequately highlight the seismic disadvantages survivors of harm, abuse, and oppression are often confronted with as barriers to their healing. This blog post later evolved into the book *We Will Not Cancel Us: And Other Dreams of Transformative Justice*, which brown wrote in order to add the much-needed nuance and context that critics of the original post had suggested were missing.[7] In the book, she writes, "I have felt a punitive tendency root and flourish within our movements."[8] And she worries about what she perceives to be an inability to draw distinctions, as well as a lack of knowledge regarding "how to handle conflict or how to move towards accountability in satisfying and collective ways."[9] It is a must-read for anyone attempting to make meaning of the promise of practices for embracing public accountability while also honoring the need for a humane disposition when seeking atonement, justice, and reconciliation.

In our nonprofit sector, we are often confronted with making sense of the widespread translatability of cultural moments and forces. We don't have to look far to see how cancel culture informs the way in which we experience everyday interactions on the internet and in real life. The emergence of cancel culture has given way to the mainstream media's ability to capitalize on its age-old motto, "If it bleeds, it leads." Our relationship to being entertained has transformed, with the very notion of what fandom requires of us having evolved over the last few years: "fans" and supporters of the curators of culture are now confronted with constantly revisiting

---

[6] adrienne maree brown, "unthinkable thoughts: call out culture in the age of covid-19," July 17, 2020, adriennemareebrown.net/2020/07/17/unthinkable-thoughts-call-out-culture-in-the-age-of-covid-19/.
[7] adrienne maree brown, *We Will Not Cancel Us: And Other Dreams of Transformative Justice* (Chico, CA: AK Press, 2020).
[8] Ibid., 1.
[9] Ibid., 21.

who deserves the gift (and, as many might say, curse) of celebrity, and who doesn't. More directly, it's flavoring the way we work through conflicts, tensions, and transitions within our organizations.

A part of what makes exploring cancel culture so fascinating is understanding how it's a byproduct of our larger culture, and how it has become a subculture in and of itself. A culture can most simply be broken down into the beliefs, values, norms, customs, and knowledge shared by a group of people. So, what happens when our values are shaped by a desire to cancel one another? What happens when our beliefs are directly or indirectly influenced by who we understand to be cancelable and who not? It leads us to a place that is not new at all but rather all too familiar.

A culture that positions us and requires of us the ability to cancel one another is a direct descendant of centuries of colonization. Imperialism and colonization have thrived on "us versus them" categorizations for several hundreds of years.[10] To be canceled or not to be doesn't leave us with much room for understanding the nuance and complexity of human morality and interactions. It is a cultural force that assigns us clear roles: prosecutor and defender. The prosecutors hope to find affinity in justifying the need for cancellation, and defenders find refuge in staunchly denying that any wrongdoing or harm has occurred. Pick a side: the issue is black or white; you're either right or wrong, good or bad. And there is often no charted path forward suggesting that perhaps multiple truths can be present at once.

It is a phenomenon that can swiftly be weaponized by those with power and influence; and, conversely, it may leave many of us wanting more when it is positioned as a liberatory tactic. Why? Because it all too often fails to leave us with direction or some guided sense of what to do about the more systemic challenge at the root of the behavior, beliefs, or actions we wish to disrupt. What is the lesson to be learned for those who are canceled? The term *canceling*—through linguistic origin alone—may invoke feelings of abandonment, disposability, and an abrupt "ending" of sorts that doesn't provide a path toward redemption and atonement. For those seeking healing or accountability, has cancel culture permanently transformed the motivations that enter our hearts and minds, or is it primarily reactive in nature? If it is reactive, where do we turn for the visionary motivation we so desperately need when we are constantly overwhelmed by all there is to react to?

---

[10]Thomas B. Edsall, "The Political Magic of Us vs. Them," *New York Times*, February 13, 2019, www.nytimes.com/2019/02/13/opinion/trump-2020-us-them.html.

Cancel culture has not received mainstream legitimacy because it is innately transformational; it has become commonplace because it pairs neatly with a vast tool kit of oppressive strategies but can be practiced while masquerading as a liberatory tactic.

The unintended consequence of cancel culture being such a directive phenomenon is how it largely pushes us to anchor ourselves in uninspiring notions of what accountability and responsibility should and could look like. If we truly hope to commit ourselves to tearing down the dominant culture that prevents us from arriving at a liberated world, we would be well served to unpack how the legitimization of a cancel culture requires us to pull from ways of interacting encoded through centuries of designed divisiveness and a retributive thirst for blood sport.

Building a Bridge Together—One Ancestor, One Bone, One Ligament at a Time

After so many centuries of oppression, it is easy to see how seductive the power of canceling another might be. But reparation does not repair if all we are doing is disposing of one another.

In their recently published article "Into the Fire: Lessons from Movement Conflicts," Ingrid Benedict, Weyam Ghadbian, and Jovida Ross outline the ways in which we "enact subtle and gross forms of anti-Blackness, white supremacy, sexism, homophobia, transphobia, ableism, classism, and other structural oppression [to which we would add *settler colonialism* and *Native erasure*]. This overlays with our unprocessed trauma and habitual coping strategies, and they ricochet off of each other to create interpersonal tangles that can blow up organizing teams and organizations."[11]

These toxic ways of being with one another reflect and reinforce the larger toxicity in our society. But we cannot create a better world by reproducing the poisons of the current one. We must recognize, disrupt, heal their effects, and transform them in order for us to bridge from our current

---

[11] Ingrid Benedict, Weyam Ghadbian, and Jovida Ross, "Into the Fire: Lessons from Movement Conflicts," *Nonprofit Quarterly*, January 25, 2022, nonprofitquarterly.org/into-the-fire-lessons-from-movement-conflicts/.

state to a just, loving, and liberated world. In order to do so, we need to draw on inner work and healing practices to both replenish ourselves and cultivate our individual and collective resilience. For example:

- **Tapping into an awareness of our divine connection.** Individualism has wreaked havoc on ourselves and our relationship to the divine, to source, to the wellspring of spiritual connection. Whether we find resonance with the teaching from physics that we are not separate or even solid, or from spiritual traditions that help us to develop a relationship with god, having an awareness of our divine connection is core to replenishment and resourcefulness.

- **Honoring the sacred.** Honoring the sacred looks very different depending on our cultural backgrounds and learned practices. Essentially, we are recognizing and celebrating the profound gift of everything and everyone, expressing gratitude, and honoring our interdependence.

- **Cultivating compassion for all beings.** We all suffer, and we all make mistakes. While power and privilege have huge implications for the consequences of mistakes, we can still witness human error—our own and that of others—from a place of compassion. Compassion doesn't mean a lack of accountability or that there aren't consequences when we cause one another harm. Compassion means recognizing that we are all doing the best we can in the moment, even if our best is sometimes awful.

- **Centering presence and awareness.** The only change that is possible is change that happens in the present. And in order to be agents of positive change, we must be present and aware. We must be breathing. We must have both feet touching the earth. We must be able to hear the murmurings of the wind.

- **Re-yoking our bodies and spirits.** We are spirits having a human experience. Both our bodies and our spirits must be in cooperative connection in order to participate in the change we came here to create. This means knowing we are more than our mortality; we are working generations backward and forward.

- **Oxygenating, moving, and nourishing our human forms.** Without attending to the nourishment, breath, and health of our bodies, nothing but distress, disease, dissimulation are possible. Liberation requires our vitality, whatever that looks like in our different human forms.

It is only when we have strengthened ourselves and our collectives that we can really engage in the essential work of transforming our world.

As Tarana Burke reminds us, "Our humanity, our individual and collective vulnerability, needs and deserves some breathing room."[12]

Loving Accountability—an Antidote

The healing and inner work lays the foundation for us to be and act from our fully resourced selves—to be rooted in what bell hooks defines as a *love ethic*. "Domination cannot exist," hooks writes, "in any social situation where a love ethic prevails."[13]

Coming from love, being rooted in a love ethic, does not mean we, as BIPOC social justice leaders and activists, are accepting systemic oppression. Rather, it means we are not continuing to "reshape the same tools that we use to dismantle the ever changing systems."[14] We cannot rely on strategies of resistance to chart a path to liberation. Coming, as so many of us do, from movement work, there is a tendency to show up in a fighting stance, to focus only on what is wrong, to distrust everything and everyone. But liberation does not come from adversarialism; it comes from connection and loving accountability.

In *Braiding Sweetgrass: Indigenous Wisdom, Scientific Knowledge, and the Teachings of Plants*, Robin Wall Kimmerer explores the wisdom of lichens. She writes, "Some of earth's oldest beings, lichens are born from reciprocity. . . . These ancients carry teachings in the ways that they live. They remind us of the enduring power that arises from mutualism, from the sharing of the gifts carried by each species. Balanced reciprocity has enabled them to flourish under the most stressful of conditions."[15] Our conditions are indeed stressful; attention to our connections, to our mutualism and interdependence, is essential not only for our survival but also for our ability as BIPOC people to thrive.

The sacred nature of our connection does not preclude conflict, disagreements, misunderstandings, hurt feelings. We affect one another. It is important that we understand the impacts we are having: what we are

---

12 Tarana Burke, in Brené Brown, "Introduction to *You Are Your Best Thing*: A Conversation," January 25, 2021, brenebrown.com/articles/2021/01/25/introduction-to-you-are-your-best-thing-a-conversation/.

13 bell hooks, *All About Love: New Visions* (New York: William Morrow, 1999), 98.

14 "Introduction," in *You Are Your Best Thing: Vulnerability, Shame Resilience, and the Black Experience*, Tarana Burke and Brené Brown, eds. (New York: Random House, 2021).

15 Robin Wall Kimmerer, *Braiding Sweetgrass: Indigenous Wisdom, Scientific Knowledge, and the Teachings of Plants* (Minneapolis: Milkweed Editions, 2013), 275.

doing and how we are being and what effect it is having on our collective change efforts. At the most basic level, it is about giving and receiving feedback, about holding one another to our best possible selves. We deserve that. It is why we are trying to change the world. *We know a better one is possible.*

Our mutuality flourishes when our love ethic is strong. And our love ethic is nourished by the practice of loving accountability. Loving accountability means we are learning together, and that we are risking vulnerability in service of creating authentic connection and a better future. If we refuse to take risks, and if we attack others to protect ourselves, we are avoiding being held accountable to the collective. And without collective accountability, we cannot work together to create a meaningful, equitable, just society.

The practice of loving accountability consists of honest and authentic communication, vulnerability, and the willingness to hold each other accountable for our impacts—beyond just words. If a collective value or guiding principle is repeatedly violated by someone, and no amount of communication and support can interrupt it, then loving accountability instructs us in employing meaningful consequences—not as punishment but rather as ensuring the health of the collective through meaningful boundaries. Not rigid structures, but something firm and porous as skin. Without attention to healthy boundaries, our espousal of values and group agreements are just words—and what holds us together ceases to exist.

Mia Birdsong describes accountability as being "about ourselves in the context of the collective":

> *It's seeing the ways we cause hurt or harm as actions that indicate we are not living in alignment with values that recognize our own humanity or the humanity of others. It's about recognizing when our behavior is out of alignment with our best selves. . . . . Accountability is also about recognizing and accepting that we are necessary and wanted. It's understanding that when we neglect ourselves, don't care for ourselves, or are not working to live as our best selves, we are devaluing the time, energy, and care that our loved ones offer us.*[16]

Loving accountability supports our ability to make meaningful and transformative change *together*. This means tending to our genuine

---

[16]Mia Birdsong, "We Long for Freedom and Accountability," in *How We Show Up: Reclaiming Family, Friendship, and Community* (New York: Hachette, 2020). See www.creationsmagazine. com/2021/01/31/ we-long-for-freedom-and-accountablity-by-mia-birdsong-oakland-ca/.

connection, coming from a place of deep curiosity, and being and acting from a wellspring of love.

> *Our breathing is sacred because energy that connects us is older than the structures we are unlearning and will persist beyond the imagination of this species.*
> *The energy moving through us, as air and so much more, is eternal.*
> *I call it love. Thank you for the love moving through you.*
> *With every breath.*
>
> —**adrienne maree brown,** *Holding Change:*
> *The Way of Emergent Strategy*
> *Facilitation and Mediation*

Dimensions of Thriving

Learning from Black LGBTQ+/SGL Moments, Spaces, and Practices

Dr. Kia Darling-Hammond

In order for me to thrive as a person I need to be doing something that I love and be surrounded by people that I love and have a community that I can call my own.

—Lara[1]

Thriving means having your identity supported, your identity affirmed . . . being in a situation where you can learn, fail, make mistakes, and still understand yourself as someone who will be capable of greatness and is worth greatness.

—Dante[2]

Humans have imagined thriving across our entire history, from *Iwa* (living virtuously) to *eudaemonia* (good spirit) to contemporary theories

---

This article is from the Winter 2021 issue of *Nonprofit Quarterly,* "We Thrive: Health for Justice, Justice for Health."

[1] In Kia Darling-Hammond, "To Simply Be: Thriving as a Black Queer/Same-Gender-Loving Young Adult" (PhD, Stanford University, 2018).
[2] Ibid.

of flourishing.[3] Models abound. They often reflect the voices of those empowered to articulate and record such ideas (scholars, philosophers, politicians), who, in turn, reflect the power structures of the societies in which they reside.

There is no single accepted model of thriving. Some people approach it with a physiological focus, or a psychological one. Sometimes, people use *resilience* and *thriving* interchangeably; some call it *flourishing*.[4] My research focuses on intersections of race, ethnicity, gender, sexual orientation, age, and ability. And in doing so, I have been able to advance an inclusive, intersectional, and developmentally grounded model. However, within the minuscule pool of scholarship that centers Black LGBTQ+/SGL youth and young adults, for example, there is almost none attending to their lives beyond surviving oppression. Select another intersectional suite of identities and you'll find the same. Disabled trans women? Native girls? Nonbinary Latiné adults? If anything has been written, it is most likely hardship centered. This is understandable (we want to end suffering), but insufficient.

Rejecting the Deficit Approach, the Medical Model, the Status Quo

We need to suspend "'damage-centered' research . . . that intends to document peoples' pain and brokenness to hold those in power accountable for their oppression" but "simultaneously reinforces and reinscribes a

----

[3] *The Nicomachean Ethics of Aristotle*, translated and with an introduction by David Ross; revised by L. Ackrill and J. O. Urmson (Oxford: Oxford University Press, 1980); and Omedi Ochieng, "What African Philosophy Can Teach You About the Good Life," *IAI News* 68, September 10, 2018, iai.tv/articles/what-african-philosophy-can-teach-you-about-the-good-life-auid-1147.
[4] Kim M. Blankenship, "A Race, Class, and Gender Analysis of Thriving," *Journal of Social Issues* 54, no. 2 (Summer 1998): 393–404; Charles S. Carver, "Resilience and Thriving: Issues, Models, and Linkages," *Journal of Social Issues* 54, no. 2 (Summer 1998): 245–66; Corey L. M. Keyes and Jonathan Haidt, eds., *Flourishing: Positive Psychology and the Life Well-Lived* (Washington, DC: American Psychological Association, 2002); Laura M. Padilla-Walker and Larry J. Nelson, *Flourishing in Emerging Adulthood: Positive Development During the Third Decade of Life* (New York: Oxford University Press, 2017); Sarah Reed and Robin Lin Miller, "Thriving and Adapting: Resilience, Sense of Community, and Syndemics among Young Black Gay and Bisexual Men," *American Journal of Community Psychology* 57, no. 1–2 (March 2016): 129–43; Carol D. Ryff and Burton H. Singer, "Know Thyself and Become What You Are: A Eudaimonic Approach to Psychological Well-Being," *Journal of Happiness Studies* 9, no. 1 (January 2008): 13–39; and Martin E. P. Seligman and Mihaly Csikszentmihalyi, "Positive Psychology: An Introduction," *The American Psychologist* 55, no. 1 (2000): 5–14.

one-dimensional notion of . . . people as depleted, ruined, and hopeless."[5] Under our dominant medical model, people under duress whose coping or survival behavior is pathologized must be "fixed" so they can fit in. Psychologist Martin Seligman calls for the "[curtailment of this] promiscuous victimology," elaborating that "in the disease model the underlying picture of the human being is pathology and passivity . . . The gospel of victimology is both misleading and, paradoxically, victimizing."[6] Focusing too narrowly on problems and what writer and professor Edward Brockenbrough calls "victimization narratives" gets in the way of building something visionary and liberatory, something that needs to be, and is already being, shaped by marginalized people themselves.[7]

I feel whole when I really . . . nurture my sense of spirit, which is in my creative outlets, which is in nature, which is in cultivating just the little things, cultivating gratitude and positivity.

—Sailor[8]

We're putting most of our energy into making people "fit" into systems and institutions that are fundamentally flawed—violent, even—and, in the process, reinforcing the belief that these sociopolitical structures are natural. They are not. It's not a flex to participate for the sake of participating in a society that's designed to destroy us. Assimilation, compliance, compromising personal needs, and becoming smaller than we authentically are all require rejection of one's true self. We activate our precious energy for survival instead of passion, pleasure, fulfillment, and innovation. We also find ourselves increasingly disconnected from one another. Laurence J. Kirmayer and colleagues note that "Aboriginal values and perspectives emphasizing interconnectedness, integration, and wholeness can provide an important counterbalance to the ways of thinking about resilience . . . that tend to dominate current scientific writing."[9] By considering "the whole state of the person," as well as the communities

[5] Eve Tuck, "Suspending Damage: A Letter to Communities," *Harvard Educational Review* 79, 3 (Fall 2009): 409–28.
[6] Keyes and Haidt, *Flourishing*. And see Martin P. Seligman, "Foreword: The Past and Future of Positive Psychology," in *Flourishing*, xi–xx.
[7] Edward Brockenbrough, personal communication with the author, April 23.
[8] Darling-Hammond, "To simply be."
[9] Laurence Kirmayer et al., "Community Resilience: Models, Metaphors and Measures," *Journal of Aboriginal Health* 5, no. 1 (2009): 62–117.

and systems within which they exist, an "Aboriginal perspective [moves] resilience away from a simple, linear view of risk exposure, resilience, and outcome, toward a more complex, interactional and holistic view [that] . . . includes the role of traditional activities, such as spirituality, healing practices, and language in dealing with change, loss and trauma."[10]

Beyond resilience, we need to create the space and the conditions to design a much better now and a much better future. Here, I highlight what Black LGBTQ+/SGL communities have taught us about the dimensions of thriving, offering a way to move forward. Hardship is not the only story.

So, when I go out with a bunch of queer folks of color and we're all together in that space, but also then . . . being able to see all these other queer folks of color who I don't know, but I feel this connection with, and see them joyfully losing their inhibitions and finding joy, in ways that I see queer folks of color not really being able to completely find joy in their daily interactions . . . there's a beauty and a joy that I find there.

—Dante[11]

Black LGBTQ+/SGL people have crafted moments, spaces, and practices of activism, belonging, wellness, beauty, and possibility, even as they have revealed and pushed back against heavy challenges. L. H. Stallings talks about the "imaginative, agentive, creative, performative, uplifting transitional space[s] established and occupied by queer youth of color"[12]—while Bettina Love celebrates identity formation and expression grounded in "performance of the failure to be respectable" and the freedom granted by "contradictory, fluid, precarious, agentive, and oftentimes intentionally inappropriate" *ratchetness*.[13] The act of claiming joy or pleasure, especially when in defiance of norms of respectability, is healing work. The tendency to focus on adversity and pathology leaves little space for a concept like pleasure. It then fails to recognize the immense power that Black LGBTQ+/SGL people have called on for generations in the face of oppression. *More than simply being self-accepting, insisting upon*

---

[10] Ibid., 78–79.
[11] Darling-Hammond, "To Simply Be."
[12] L. H. Stallings, "Hip Hop and the Black Ratchet Imagination," *Palimpsest: A Journal on Women, Gender, and the Black International* 2, no. 2 (2013): 135–39.
[13] Bettina Love, "A Ratchet Lens: Black Queer Youth, Agency, Hip Hop, and the Black Ratchet Imagination," *Educational Researcher* 46, no. 9 (December 2017): 539–47.

self-expressing (often ratchetly) is a crucial, adaptive facet of thriving—really, for any oppressed community. It is holistic stress relief.

Consider James Baldwin's 1956 novel *Giovanni's Room*, which he was initially told to burn due to its "homosexual" content.[14] Consider Street Transvestite Action Revolutionaries (STAR), founded by Marsha P. Johnson and Sylvia Rivera in 1970.[15] Consider the Ballroom culture so lovingly portrayed in the films *Vogue Knights: A Short Documentary on Ballroom Culture in Hell's Kitchen* (2014) and *Kiki* (2016), as well as the scholarship of Marlon M. Bailey[16] and activist scholarship of Michael Roberson (and his Ballroom Freedom School).[17] Consider the work of Alexis Pauline Gumbs, like her chapter "Something Else to Be: Generations of Black Queer Brilliance and the Mobile Homecoming Experiential Archive," written with Julia Roxanne Wallace in 2016;[18] the dynamic catalogs of Janelle Monáe and Meshell Ndegeocello and Lil Nas X;[19] and the visionary Afrofuturism nurtured by adrienne maree brown with Walidah Imarisha and a slate of activist-writers in the collection *Octavia's Brood* (2015).[20] These imaginative products and others like them must be taken up as dynamic blueprints for a different kind of future—one in which the grand metric for success is thriving among people currently faced with disproportionate struggle.

Bringing these innovations to light is part of how we locate hope. It's as important as understanding how large social forces make things difficult. More so. A critical perspective that resists the hypnotizing pull of the

[14] W. J. Weatherby, *James Baldwin: Artist on Fire, A Portrait* (New York: D.I. Fine, 1989).

[15] Ehn Nothing, Marsha Johnson, and Sylvia Rivera, *Street Transvestite Action Revolutionaries: Survival, Revolt, and Queer Antagonistic Struggle* (Bloomington, IN: Untorelli Press, 2013).

[16] Marlon Bailey, "Performance as Intravention: Ballroom Culture and the Politics of HIV/AIDS in Detroit," *Souls* 11, no. 3 (July–September 2009): 253–74; and Marlon M. Bailey, "Engendering Space: Ballroom Culture and the Spatial Practice of Possibility in Detroit," *Gender, Place & Culture* 21, no. 4 (2014): 489–507.

[17] "Michael Roberson on the Ballroom Freedom School, interview," ArtsEverywhere, September 10, 2016, video, 13:00, at 06:30, com/216007645.

[18] Alexis Pauline Gumbs and Julia Roxanne Wallace, "Something Else to Be: Generations of Black Queer Brilliance and the Mobile Homecoming Experiential Archive," in *No Tea, No Shade: New Writings in Black Queer Studies*, ed. E. Patrick Johnson (Durham, NC: Duke University Press, 2016): 380–94.

[19] Jon Dolan, "Lil Nas X Makes Us Like Him Even More on 'Montero,'" *Rolling Stone*, September 17, 2021, com/music/music-album-reviews/lil-nas-x-montero-1226841/; Larry Nichols, "Running for Covers: Meshell Ndegeocello talks Inspiration for New Album," *Philadelphia Gay News*, March 22, 2018, epgn.com/2018/03/22/running-for-covers-meshell-ndegeocello-talks-inspiration-for-new-album/; and Brittany Spanos, "Janelle Monáe Frees Herself," *Rolling Stone*, April 26, 2018, rollingstone.com/music/music-features/janelle-monae-frees-herself-629204/.

[20] Walidah Imarisha and adrienne maree brown, *Octavia's Brood: Science Fiction Stories from Social Justice Movements* (Oakland, CA: AK Press, 2015).

status quo lets us attend to strength, desire, and love; our pasts, presents, and futures; wisdom, hope, and joy. Especially, the ways they are complex.

Pursuing a Bridge to Thriving

The Bridge to Thriving Framework© (BtTF©), which was born out of conversations with Black LGBTQ+/SGL youth and young adults, explores three big ideas: (1) surviving encounters with oppression, (2) what thriving can be, and (3) what's on the bridge to thriving (i.e., healing, chosen family, etc.).[21]

Although thriving is not a permanent state of being—and people can thrive in some aspects of their lives more strongly than in others—it is possible to increase one's capacity for and duration of thriving, and return to it over time. Some of this is on an individual level, but ultimately it is a community- and society-wide project.

Surviving Encounters with Oppression

Violent, oppressive systems shape our lives. The United States imprisons more adults than any other country. In fact, we have numerous states that "lock up more people at higher rates than nearly every other country on earth."[22] Politicians choose cost savings over human safety, as we heard and saw loud and clear in Flint, Michigan. Quieter is that the EPA estimates there are 7.3 million lead pipelines nationwide servicing as many as 10 million homes. According to the CDC, roughly 24 million homes in the nation contain deteriorating lead paint and 4 million of them house small children.[23]

Almost half of the children in the United States are affected by adverse childhood experiences (ACEs), which can be linked to systems of

---

[21] DrKiaDH (Kia Darling-Hammond), "Bridge to Thriving Framework," Wise Chipmunk, February 25, 2021, com/2021/02/25/the-bridge-to-thriving-framework/.

[22] Emily Widra and Tiana Herring, "States of Incarceration: The Global Context, 2021," Prison Policy Initiative, September 2021, org/global/2021.html.

[23] "Childhood Lead Poisoning Prevention," Centers for Disease Control and Prevention, accessed December 23, 2021, cdc.gov/nceh/lead/prevention/sources/paint.htm; and Alison Young, "Got Lead in Your Water? It's Not Easy to Find Out," *USA Today*, March 16, 2016, www.usatoday .com/story/news/2016/03/16/testing-assessing-safety-of-drinking-water-lead-testing-assessing-safety-of-drinking-water-lead-contamination/80504058/.

economic exploitation, patriarchy and the misogyny that shores it up, anti-Blackness, racism, xenophobia, and so on. "One in ten children . . . has experienced three or more ACEs" and are, in many cases, being raised by adults who have themselves experienced adverse childhoods.[24] The Centers for Disease Control and Prevention (CDC) ACEs resource page lists such potential long-term effects as autoimmune disease, cancer, pulmonary disease, liver disease, memory disturbances, depression, and more.[25] The more ACEs a child experiences, the higher the risk that they will develop a chronic condition later in life. These issues disproportionately affect disabled communities, Native, Black, and immigrant communities, and LGBTQ+/SGL communities.

Lives are cut short from mental and physical anguish, through accumulated toxic stress resulting in illness, through acute violence at the hands of police and other state and institutional actors, and so on. We are ranked and sorted during our earliest, most impressionable years, internalizing ideas about intelligence, worthiness, rightness, and goodness. We are taught to ignore our needs, including our joy.

Creating the conditions for thriving requires attending to threats to survival—emotional, spiritual, and physical. This can include teaching children how to communicate with adults and authority figures in a way that reduces risk to the young person. It includes learning how to demonstrate "knowledge" in order to have one's work "taken seriously" or counted. It includes helping people remain attuned to their authentic self and needs, despite the powerful forces encouraging them not to. It requires social justice activism, from marches to lawsuits to boycotts to unionizing.

Researchers[26] recommend such individual-level interventions as improving one's amount and quality of sleep,[27] avoiding psychological distress,[28] increasing optimism,[29] improving self-esteem,[30] eating a nutrient-dense

[24]Vanessa Sacks and David Murphey, "The Prevalence of Adverse Childhood Experiences, Nationally, by State, and by Race or Ethnicity," *Child Trends*, February 12, 2018, org/publications/prevalence-adverse-childhood-experiences-nationally-state-race-ethnicity.

[25]"Adverse Childhood Experiences Resources," Centers for Disease Control and Prevention, accessed December 3, 2021, gov/violenceprevention/acestudy/journal.html.

[26]See for example Irene Christodoulou, "Reversing the Allostatic Load," *International Journal of Health Science* 3, 3 (July–September 2010): 331–32.

[27]Ilia Karatsoreos and Bruce S. McEwen, "Psychobiological Allostasis: Resistance, Resilience and Vulnerability," *Trends in Cognitive Sciences* 15, no. 12 (December 2011): 576–84.

[28]Bruce McEwen and Peter J. Gianaros, "Stress- and Allostasis-Induced Brain Plasticity," *Annual Review of Medicine* 62 (2011): 431–45.

[29]Bruce McEwen, "Protective and Damaging Effects of Stress Mediators: Central Role of the Brain," *Dialogues in Clinical Neuroscience* 8, no. 4 (December 2006): 367–81.

[30]Ibid.

diet,[31] finding social support,[32] and engaging in regular physical activity.[33] In fact, high levels of social-emotional support and excellent sleep are particularly powerful. They can protect against and even repair damage caused by toxic stress. Research suggests that when people belong to a community in which their stigmatized identities are celebrated[34]—where they can find pride in their community's history, legacies, stories, and triumphs[35]—they experience a kind of protection from psychological threat, which has physiological implications.

The urgent focus of so many efforts on resilience and survival makes sense. Too many of us don't survive our encounters with oppression, particularly where complex marginalization is at play. Still, there is more to life; and, as Michael Roberson points out, we have to claim our "divine right to exist."[36]

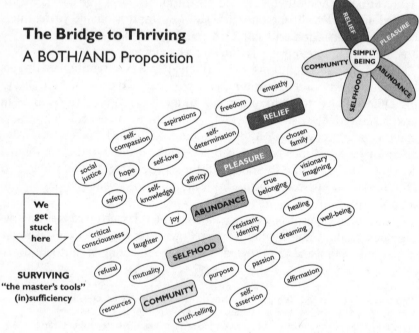

Graphic © 2021 Kia Darling-Hammond.

....

[31] Ibid.

[32] McEwen and Gianaros, "Stress- and Allostasis-Induced Brain Plasticity."

[33] Ibid.

[34] Kathleen Bogart, Emily M. Lund, and Adena Rottenstein, "Disability Pride Protects Self-Esteem Through the Rejection-Identification Model," *Rehabilitation Psychology* 63, no. 1 (February 2018): 155–59.

[35] William Bannon et al., "Cultural Pride Reinforcement as a Dimension of Racial Socialization Protective of Urban African American Child Anxiety," *Families in Society: The Journal of Contemporary Human Services* 90, no. 1 (January 2009): 79–86.

[36] ArtsEverywhere, *Michael Roberson on the Ballroom Freedom School.*

What Is Thriving?

A framework for thriving that centers marginalized communities goes beyond resilience or integration. People experience thriving when they:

- Have supportive, affirming communities (particularly affinity community focused on applying critical consciousness to advancing social justice)
- Can come to know their true selves, love themselves, and self-assert in a self-determined and empowered way
- Have not just economic stability but also abundant resources for thriving, including time, space, funds, and—crucially—hope, aspirations, and dreams
- Can engage in pleasurable activities (with or without others), pursue their passions, and be joyful
- Can heal and experience relief from stressors like unsafety, erasure, economic hardship, and social isolation, among others

In particular, people describe an optimal state of thriving—one in which all five "petals" of the thriving model are activated—as "simply being," or being able to exist fully and wholly. This requires an ability to know and value oneself, which calls for activation of a resistant identity—one that positions us as central and treasured, not marginal; one that refuses the ways in which the world conspires to make us feel small. *Simply being* typically happens in the company of a close kinship network, like chosen family; in spaces that feel shielded from unsafety; with the resources of space and time (and sometimes money) available; where the outer world's stigma and stress are impotent; and where there is joy, pleasure, or even a sense of purpose.

I was getting rid of . . . things that were bringing me down, for sure . . . I would say, yeah, [it was] a time when I was really focused on myself; making concrete steps towards my future . . . I had mental and physical confidence. I had a swagger . . . . . not like, "I'm the shit!" but just, "I am me, and I'm comfortable with my skin." Some India Arie song or something. It was definitely a swagger: "Pssh. I'm ready to be me. I am me. Boom."

—Marcus[37]

---

[37] Darling-Hammond, "To Simply Be."

Possibilities for thriving grow when people are invited to (1) recognize themselves as someone who is entitled to thrive, (2) imagine what their thriving can look like, and (3) receive affirmation and resources to support their vibrant, present *and* future dreaming and designing. It is immensely helpful to be able to do that with people who believe in one's thriving possibilities and who honor that each of us, regardless of age, stage, or position, is entitled to exert authority over our lives, needs, and futures.

As people center thriving, they begin to notice the parts of their lives that don't quite measure up, and make plans to change them. People also begin to name strategies and practices they can (and do) use to advance their thriving—from prioritizing their musicianship, to activism, to changing jobs, to changing partners, and so on.

Sometimes it's gonna take that courage to be okay with not being the same and not conforming or trying to change yourself.

—Sonja[38]

Finally, people being asked to consider the question of their thriving is powerful. Time and again, people say that they've never been invited to really think about it. What make this exercise successful are conditions that allow for deep reflection. Moving through the BtTF© reshapes people's ideas about themselves, their present, and their future. It is an invitation to consider what constitutes life success—particularly as it is defined and understood by people who are asked to "not be" when offered access to the dominant frameworks for becoming in this world.

Pursuing the Bridge to Thriving is a both/and proposition (see Figure 1). It acknowledges the need to pay attention to survival and healing, but urges us to balance that with dreaming in order to advance a visionary remaking of our relationships with one another and our world. Because the systems that confound thriving are so strong, this work begins with a demand. We must believe that thriving is what we deserve, and we have to unapologetically imagine it into existence. The world we need doesn't yet exist.

The Bridge to Thriving is the space between survival/insufficiency and a state of vibrant wholeness. The pathway is not linear and it's not a one-time journey. Think of the Bridge to Thriving as portable—it can be applied to a variety of projects (building a school, building an office

---

[38] Ibid.

community, building oneself, etc.). It is, essentially, a way to remember what people need in order to flourish.

It is also important to remember that individuals or communities may construct their "bridges" differently. One person may require the time, resources, and space to play music regularly, while another may need to be truly understood by a caring friend. One community may need clean drinking water, while another may need a police oversight commission. Demands may be shared in some contexts and not in others. Ultimately, the bridge invites an analysis of what is needed for access, wholeness, and a life well lived. Whatever the case, we can be sure that communities are experts regarding what they need to survive, and deserve to exist under conditions that allow them to pause, breathe, dream, and design toward what they need to thrive.

Honestly, I associate thriving a lot with . . . like un-structuring the structure that is society, and government, and all of these things. And thriving, creating abundance around me and for me and for other people. Abundance in that things are taken care of. And that you could be at peace. There is abundance. There's love and . . . loving connection.

—*Kat*[39]

As you undertake the work of designing toward thriving, you can ask questions like these:

- What healing do I need to do in order to be a trustworthy partner in thriving?
- How do my efforts continuously seek, understand, honor, and amplify the deep wisdom of marginalized communities?
- How do my efforts provide opportunities for relief and pleasure? How do they create conditions that empower others to build lives rich with relief and pleasure?
- What kinds of "selves" are made available to me and the people I coexist with?
- What future possibilities can be imagined?
- How do I hold space for people (including myself) to simply be?

....

[39] Ibid.

- What practices will make it possible for others to tell me what they truly need?
- How will I intervene against the reproduction of precarity and oppression? How am I complicit or active in its reproduction?

Thriving for me is being able to build up my family, my friends, myself, and our futures, and make sure there is a future to have.

—Marcus[40]

For the sake of ourselves and the seven generations to come, it's time we work to exceed survival[41]—to design a visionary, liberated, harmonious future and join together in starting its construction today. *The world we need lives in the imaginations and practices of the people our world fails to celebrate.* They are worldmakers and waymakers. They weave futures in zines and memes, songs and graffiti. They plot at kitchen tables. They march, they write, they sign, they refuse, they demand. *Let's catch up.*

[40] Ibid.

[41] "Values," Haudenosaunee Confederacy, accessed December 3, 2021, haudenosauneeconfederacy .com/values/.

Pro-Blackness Is Aspirational

A Conversation with Cyndi Suarez and Shanelle Matthews

In this interview, Cyndi Suarez, *Nonprofit Quarterly*'s president and editor in chief, and Shanelle Matthews, communications director of the Movement for Black Lives and the 2022 Nonprofit Quarterly fellow, talk about what it means to be committed to pro-Blackness in a world where "everybody's experience of Blackness is on a spectrum."[1]

CYNDI SUAREZ: In conversation with you recently about how the spring 2022 edition of the magazine is centering on building pro-Black organizations, a comment you made piqued my interest. You said something like, "Supporting BLM is not the same as being pro-Black." I have questions beyond that, but I wanted to start by following up on that statement. What did you mean by it?

SHANELLE MATTHEWS: Several things came up for me when you first talked about this. First, I've spent the last six years—on and off—communicating on behalf of the Movement for Black Lives, and I have received, on the other end of that, a lot of public commitments and declarations from people about how they support the Black Lives Matter movement—and from some of them, how they're pro-Black. And I was asking myself—when

[1] NPQ Magazine, Spring 2022, https://nonprofitquarterly.org/copyright-policy/, last accessed March 09, 2023.

you initially said it, and when I would get these declarations—How do they understand Blackness? What does it mean to them to be pro-Black?

During my time with Movement for Black Lives and BLM, I have watched a lot of people's commitment—to the Black Lives Matter movement in particular—ebb and flow. And if we look at the summer of 2020 as one very recent and salient example of the increase in support for the Movement for Black Lives—and not just for our particular movement, but for Black people in general, for whom we're organizing every day to defend and support and celebrate—there were a lot of public commitments made in support of the movement.

This was a time when a lot of people used the phrase *racial reckoning*—when America was coming to terms with our racism, with the oppression against Black people and also other people of color. And—in particular because of Trump's presidency—also coming to terms with sexism and the interlocking oppressions that a lot of people face.

And during that time, we saw corporations of all shapes and sizes declaring that Black Lives Matter. I had emails in my inbox and text messages claiming that Black Lives Matter. There were 26 million people in the streets demanding justice for George Floyd and Breonna Taylor. And those are clear examples of extreme Black suffering, one of which was a visceral example that people could watch and see, and feel fear or anger or shame or guilt, and be motivated to go out into the streets, to buy a book from a Black author, to read about what it means to be antiracist, to sign a petition or give recurring donations to Black organizations—namely, large legacy organizations like the NAACP and the Urban League, but also organizations like the ACLU—and maybe to talk to their friends about going to a protest, too, and making a sign.

And I believe some data were showing that ultimately more than $50 billion had been committed to the racial justice movement, whatever that means to people—there is a wealth of different places that get determined as representative of the racial justice movement—but almost none of this was delivered to any organizations. And that's one example. But for all the people who bought the books, who had one-off conversations, who marched in the streets, who maybe replaced one white board member with a Black board member—well, I don't want to diminish people's commitments and their capacity to the movement in defense of Black Lives and for racial justice, but those actions are insufficient.

In many ways, the question we have to ask ourselves is, What are we willing to give up in order to be pro-Black? When we look at 2020, we come to understand or are reminded that when there are heightened moments of crisis in the United States—when something like the murder of George Floyd happens, and it's filmed, and you can watch it and see for yourself, and you say, "Hey, this is really bad"—there's an increase in uprisings on behalf of oppressed people, allies show up to support us, and then that support wanes. There's a long history of this, particularly regarding white people supporting justice and liberation for Black people.

And also—yes, of course it's bad! But why did it take this for you to say that you will be pro-Black or to stand up for Blackness? And going out into the streets is certainly worthwhile, but much more is needed. There are many ways to raise the bar for people to take deeper, more meaningful action. Because in these protest cycles, we see the support ebb. Today, for instance, in February of 2022, support for the Black Lives Matter movement is lower than it was before George Floyd's death.

I have grace toward and empathy for people when it comes to the challenges of being pro-Black, supporting the Movement for Black Lives, and/or getting involved in eradicating anti-Blackness or racial oppression more broadly. There's a spectrum of ways in which we come to these issues that are all predicated on how we were raised, on the communities that we live in, on the values and the principles on which we were raised in terms of religious ideology, and so on.

And for some, it takes a lot of personal reflection to make those kinds of public commitments—to say, "I want to be pro-Black," or "I want to support Black movements." Because for a lot of those folks who brandish the signs and go to the protests, once they go back home, they're still feeling the pull of everything else in their lives. People want to be a part of the change, but they also have these allegiances to the systems that allow for racism to exist. Classism, for example. I have empathy because people are often torn between those allegiances—desiring to be part of this reckoning [about] racial justice and anti-Black racism while also belonging to a class or caste that behaves in ways that are incongruent with pro-Black values.

CS: When you say class, do you mean economic class across race? Or do you mean particularly with respect to white folks?

SM: Yes, economic class. Undoubtedly, there is a tiny group of Black people with significant wealth who experience the world differently. And while they still face racism like the rest of us, the political outcomes of their unique experiences determine how they feel about these uprisings. So, we saw many Black people in different places on the socioeconomic spectrum participate. Still, wealthy Black people also have the privilege of surrounding themselves with people and experiences that might shrink their exposure to racial bias. And it's different for Black people with wealth than it is for white people with wealth.

CS: And when you say support for the movement is less today than it was before the death of George Floyd, what do you mean by that? How do you calculate that?

SM: Well, there's polling, for example. Pew Research and others do polls to look at how support for the

Movement for Black Lives and for racial justice more broadly exists within the demographics of white people in America, and of all people living here. And part of the argument is that people often support a particular type of Blackness. So, folks are comfortable with people going out and protesting, but if things get what they feel is unwieldy, or people start to uprise in a way that is uncomfortable to them—so, folks bashing in police cars, because police have killed their family and they don't particularly care about that piece of property over the dead bodies of Black people, or the movement's demand shifting from accountability to defunding the police—then we often see people's allegiances to the movement fade.

And I think this is one example in the context of movement building and demands [for] Black liberation—but generally, support for Black people is often on a spectrum. People value our culture, but if we laugh too loud, they want us to get kicked off of the bus—like that story a couple of years ago, in which some Black women on a wine tour train were laughing loudly and were asked to leave.

I mean, if we behave in the "right" way, if our demands are palatable enough, if it's a comfortable enough situation, then there's plenty of support for our activities and our commitments and demands and movements. But if white people become less comfortable, or if they start feeling a little out of place as white people, and they're being pulled in different directions, the support doesn't last.

CS: Yeah. And we're already seeing the backlash. I was reading an article about Florida a few weeks ago. They've passed a law that makes it illegal to make white folks uncomfortable.

SM: Yeah. And I think that's a critical point to bring up, Cyndi, because right now we're having a profound debate about the history of this country—and critical race theory is central to it. And many people have never been exposed to authentic Black culture—only to caricatures of it through media and television. And what this debate is doing by eliminating true American history from the history books in schools—eliminating Black history, cross-cultural, multiracial history—is not allowing our students to engage in what is accurate and true about this country.

And I think that also makes people's public commitments [for] social movements far less meaningful—because how can you be authentically pro-Black or support movements in defense of Black Lives if you don't really understand what the Black experience is about?

CS: What does it mean to you to be pro-Black beyond organizations or our sector?

SM: For me, the root of this conversation is power. So, that's being able to exist as a Black person in this country without the gaze of whiteness or having to pretend to be somebody that one is not, in terms of one's self, one's identity, and one's self-determination in one's everyday life. At the root of what I think pro-Blackness is about is advancing policies, practices, and cultural norms that allow Black communities to be self-determined and for us to govern ourselves. To have enough economic, social, and political power to decide how, when, and where to have families. To determine where to live. To have the choices and the options to be able to make the decisions, just like everybody else—about schools, about education, about jobs, and quality of life.

There's also an element [about] governance. What does it mean to be able to determine how our cities exist? We are often cornered into particular places inside cities that don't give us very many options in terms of grocery stores, hospitals, schools, and other essential needs.

The other thing that is important for me to say about this is that for Black people, Blackness exists on a spectrum. There is no one "right" way to be Black—or no one way to be Black. It's a way of knowing and being that each of us lives every day determined by cultural institutions, our faiths, how we're raised, the schools we attend, and sometimes the legislative bodies that govern us. And so what I think is pro-Black and how I would like to experience the world is going to be different from you or another Black person.

CS: And what would a pro-Black organization look like?

SM: I do not know that pro-Blackness is commensurate with the traditional nonprofit infrastructure. These organizations began as proxies of power for the rich. So, we're trying to fit a square peg into a round hole. That might sound a little nihilistic. But the charity model ultimately ends up being ineffective in many ways because the people who fund us often get to determine what our agendas look like. So, how could my agenda at my organization be meaningfully pro-Black if the people who are giving us the money are deciding what the agenda is?

I would say that an organization cannot inherently be pro or anti anything. It is an entity that is meant to receive resources. So, if we talk about the process for the individuals inside of that organization to start the profoundly transformative and hard work of becoming pro-Black, then I think it starts with the self. There is no way to enter movement and genuinely advocate for radical ideas without interrogating your allegiances to oppressive systems. So, if we're not offering political education to our staff and board to understand the complexities and history of anti-Blackness, not only in the United States but also globally—so that they can have enough context to be able to authentically make some of the political decisions and commitments that they want—then we're missing the mark.

The debate [about] critical race theory illustrates just how hard it is for us to educate people in America about the history of atrocities that this country has perpetrated against Black people. So, we have to make that commitment in our organizations—and not just [about] anti-Blackness but [about] all kinds of issues. For example, at Movement for Black Lives, we do political education—weekly lunch-and-learns. We learn from people inside of movements and who often but not always overlap with oppressed communities. So, there's this process of edification and also of unlearning. Unlearning what we thought we knew.

Organizations are made up of people—and in order to build a more inclusive world, those people have to identify why it's so hard for them to have a lasting commitment to advancing an agenda in defense of Black lives beyond moments of uprising. Having that honest conversation with the people closest to you is a start—and then individuals leaning into making the long transformative commitment process that ultimately leads to an organization coming to more precise terms about how to support their Black staff and defend Black lives.

But it's insufficient to say that you're pro-Black, to swap out board members, to put a Black person in an executive director position without the proper support or infrastructure to help them learn what it means to grow an organization. Organizations also have to reckon with the hard truth that the non-profit model is rooted in sympathy. And you cannot truly be pro-Black if you are sympathetic toward me instead of wanting to, in some instances, give away your power to me, in other instances, help me to be better without making me feel like I'm less-than.

CS: Something you've said that was really interesting to me was about how in movement spaces people use the tools to dismantle oppression against each other. My mind went to, Oh, so maybe movement spaces aren't always pro-Black either. Is that true?

SM: No, they're definitely not.

CS: That's really interesting. So it's not just organizations, it's also movements?

SM: Oh, yes. I mean, organizations are part of movements. We must come together and identify the shared problem within the frame of social justice that is rooted in the margins, identify the solution, identify our targets—and that's how we build power. Collectively, through these organizations. We don't build power as individuals for oppressed people. And because the organizations are made up of people, and the movements are made up of organizations and coalitions, and everybody's experience with Blackness is on a spectrum, it's just a lot. Everybody has to come to the table and be willing to do the self-work, the organizational work, the coalitional work, and the broader movement work.

Movements are, simply put, groups of oppressed people who have realized that they have a shared problem and want to make change. And Blackness is not a monolith. So, our ideological differences come together in a big pot, and we spend a lot of time thinking and pontificating about how to come to shared ideals [about] advancing our goals.

I've been a part of several movements. Some movements are better with discomfort and disagreement than others. Some organizations are better prepared to have complicated conversations and for individuals to leave not feeling personally attacked but instead challenged to think through their beliefs and where they came from—to consider that maybe they have allegiances to oppressive systems because that's what they were born into and taught when they were young, and that now those things have to be challenged and changed. But some movements and organizations are very conflict averse, internally. They do not want to engage in the hard work of dealing with shame and fear and guilt and transformation. I mean, change is not easy.

When you interrogate the self, there can end up being a lot of shame. I have heard white people articulate shame over their whiteness; people with wealth have shame about having money. I have seen people sink into guilt-ridden places and just not know how to move from there. And our movements can be inhospitable to people who are growing, who are trying to evolve. And yes, there has been a tendency to weaponize the tools that we use to dismantle the state against each other. What's often important, I think, is not people's individual public commitments or their individual actions so much as our collective actions to eradicate these terrible systems. That's how change happens—it is through all of our collective commitments that we can hold powerful people accountable and make some of these changes that, being pro-Black, we proclaim we want to make.

Being a committed member of a social movement doing the deep work over time is not easy. It requires you to transform over and over again—which means shedding layers and dealing with the shame of your old self. When I look at my old writing from college, I'm so embarrassed. It's so respectable, because my parents taught me to: "Pay attention." "Keep your head down." "Keep your legs closed." "You're a Black woman and you have two strikes against you, and you need to keep yourself out of trouble." And so that's what I would say: "Well, if we—Black people—just do this, and if we just do that " And I really believed in my early 20s that if we "acted right" we'd experience less harm. And so I have empathy for people when they come into movement and are still shedding layers of their old shape. People do ultimately need to reckon with themselves and do the work. But in some of these movement spaces, because of how we are raised, because of who we are in the world, the shame and the guilt and the fear and the conflict aversion keep us from engaging in the hard conversations. And so, no, movements are not necessarily pro-Black. There are many movements that I think would proclaim to be pro-Black, but if you dig beneath the surface, they really don't measure up.

CS: Do you have an example of that?

SM: Here's what I would say. . . . Pro-Black is an aspiration. If you look at the trajectory of the Black liberation movement throughout the 20th and 21st centuries, there are some clear indications that the movement is becoming more pro-Black. One distinction between the civil rights movement and the Black Power movement of the 60s and 70s and this current iteration of the Black liberation movement is that our leadership is decentralized and queer- and women- and nonbinary-led. Some people might ask, "What does that have to do with being pro-Black?" Well, if Black people who are nonbinary, transgender, and/or women do not have power in your movements, then you cannot proclaim to be pro-Black, because you are only pro-Black for some. Even now, there are important critiques about this iteration of the Black liberation movement—and our job is to listen, repair harm, discuss, and course-correct

There are still concerns [about] there not being enough Black trans leadership within our movement spaces. And it's a fair critique. We have had and will continue to have conversations [about] representation. And not just trans folks but also people with disabilities, and people who are undocumented, and people who are living more marginal lives and experiencing incredible suffering and oppression that we maybe don't see every day but that we know exists.

There is no pinnacle of pro-Blackness at which one will arrive. The practice is to know and remember, as Grace Lee Boggs teaches, that the political conditions around us are always changing. We are changing, and our material conditions are changing, all the time. And we have to evolve with those changes. Every single day, there are new ideas we have to contend with—and that means constantly evolving our strategies, our thinking, and our behaviors to be commensurate with those new ideas.

CS: As you talk, it reminds me of when I was in Cleveland some years ago, evaluating the Movement for Black Lives convening, and the trans issue was a really big one then. Were you there?

SM: Yeah, I was working at the press table.

CS: It was very interesting. I remember, toward the end, during one of the close-out sessions, a man came in—a Black man wearing a cowboy hat and cowboy boots. And he wouldn't let our group talk about trans issues. He just wouldn't. And I remember feeling the tension, and people having a hard time saying to him, "No, you can't stop us from talking about that." There were maybe 10 of us. But he did. And I finally got up and walked over to a different group.

I also felt tension from the older folks there who were upset that they hadn't been brought in as leaders or mentors. I just felt the tension everywhere. And I thought, Wow—we're so used to having to unite against white oppression that when we have just ourselves. . . . it's almost like we haven't had decades of having those conversations, right? I feel like those are newer conversations. I'm also talking to consultants who do racial justice work, who tell me that doing the work within their communities—whether they're Southeast Asian, whether they're Latinx, whatever—is unfunded and informal. It's not what gets paid. Most people are paid to do the work vis-à-vis white folks, right? So, we all get to our marginalization in different ways—we're not all in the same space. So, I'm really intrigued by that, and by those conversations within groups and across groups of color.

And this leads me to another question: what would a pro-Black sector sound, look, taste, feel like? I'm just trying to get to the imagining that you're talking about—as you say, it's aspirational. But in terms of the sector, where people are paying some attention to this, how can we flesh it out more for people? I'm in various racial justice portfolios, oftentimes led by Black people, where the dynamic of the funder stays the same—it doesn't matter that it's all Black people in the room. So, I've been trying to dig into this question of how do we make that change people are saying we need to make, regardless of who's there?

SM: I think what's helpful about having sectors, broadly, is that this gives us a group of people—ostensibly, people who we can be challenged by and learn from—with whom we can negotiate the terms of our political and public and personal commitments [for] social justice. But I feel that thinking about the sector as a whole might be too broad, because even within fields there are all these different formations. The divergence among organizations' level of radicalism can be vast. For example, I worked as a narrative consultant for two groups working on food justice. One was helping people in Detroit and right outside of Detroit grow their own food and become part of a collective community of growers who can be self-sustainable. The other was a larger organization with a considerable budget preserving the charity model—where they're talking about eliminating hunger via top-down strategies. And they're having different conversations about race.

CS: Can you give me a slice of those conversations? How are they different?

SM: The conversation at the grassroots level is about the social determinants of health—such as how Black people's access or lack of access to food determines how long they live, or about how redlining eliminates Black people's access to healthy foods. There's new language for this now—"food apartheid"—reflecting how we're evolving our understanding of these massive systems that impact our lives. The other, larger organization is only just beginning to have conversations about race in relationship to hunger and food insecurity, only just starting to make the connection that your racial or ethnic background may determine how much food you have access to.

So, social justice is on a spectrum, and also people's commitment to Blackness is on a spectrum, because we enter the conversation from vastly different places. And that has a lot to do with how we grew up. If I was food insecure when I was younger, I may be much more empathetic and committed to the idea of eradicating food insecurity as an adult. But we did some polling, and there are people who just don't believe that you can go hungry in a place like the United States, even when there are tens of millions of people—especially children—who are food insecure in this country. And by food insecure, I mean they're not just hungry for one day—they have ongoing issues with access to food. And a lot of those children are Black.

CS: What keeps you going as you do all this work—and as you move through different movements and learn and keep up with the evolution of understanding and language, which is so important? What keeps you going?

SM: Sometimes I think, What else would I be doing? We play this game, where we're like, "Okay, if you weren't working in movement, what would you be doing?" I feel like maybe I'd be an acupuncturist. Acupuncture is so helpful to me. But these issues are personal to me, Cyndi. I'm a great-great-granddaughter of sharecroppers. My Big Mama Odessa migrated from Louisiana to California, looking for more opportunities for her children. My family lived through the war on drugs, the war on poverty. I've lost family members because we don't have a national healthcare system. The mass incarceration system kept people that I love in cages. So, what keeps me going is my own personal commitment to the people I love—my accountability to my family and to my friends and to my tight community.

I keep going. I'm here. I'm committed to this for the rest of my life—one way or another. My life's work is rhetoric and narrative power building for social movements broadly and in the Black radical tradition specifically. And I love it. I love the puzzle of determining what we need to mobilize people and what will create a desire within them to be part of a broader movement for significant change that centers people experiencing the most suffering.

CS: Thank you—for all your work, for working with us at *NPQ*, for taking time today to speak with me, for everything. And I hope you have a great rest of your day.

SM: Thanks, Cyndi. I appreciate it.

About the Authors

Cyndi Suarez is the *Nonprofit Quarterly*'s president and editor-in-chief. She is author of *The Power Manual: How to Master Complex Power Dynamics*, in which she outlines a new theory and practice of power. Suarez has worked as a strategy and innovation consultant with a focus on networks and platforms for social movements. Her studies were in feminist theory and organizational development for social change.

Dax-Devlon Ross's award-winning writing has been featured in *Time*, *The Guardian*, *the New York Times*, *Virginia Quarterly Review*, *The Washington Post Magazine*, and other national publications. He is a Puffin Foundation Fellow at Type Media Center and a principal at the social-impact consultancies Dax-Dev and Third Settlements, where he designs disruptive tools and strategies to generate equity in workplaces and education spaces. Ross is the author of six books, including his latest, *Letters to My White Male Friends* (St. Martin's Press, 2021). You can find him at **dax-dev.com**.

Sequoia Owen is the founder of The Brilliant Lead, a coaching and consulting business that assists nonprofit professionals in building leadership skills and creating a positive work culture. She is passionate about teaching leaders how to unlearn toxic habits and use their power of influence for good. She holds a master's degree in mental health counseling and has served in the nonprofit sector for nearly a decade in various roles including trauma-informed work with victims of violence, program management, thought leadership, executive coaching, and governance. You can find out more at **thebrilliantlead.com**.

Liz Derias is coexecutive director at CompassPoint (CP). Derias's work focuses on ensuring that CompassPoint is values driven, sustainable, and ultimately impactful in supporting leaders, organizations, and movements committed to social justice to realize their full power. Derias has more than 20 years of national and international social justice, youth, and community organizing, popular education training, and policy and advocacy experience.

Kad Smith is the founder of Twelve26 Solutions, LLC. Smith is also a member of CompassPoint's teacher team, and a lead designer and cofacilitator of CompassPoint's B.L.A.C.K. Team Intensive. He is most passionate about changing the material conditions of BIPOC folks across the country.

Smith spends a significant amount of his time focusing on civic engagement, political education, climate justice, and imagining the bridging of worldviews across the globe. He currently serves on the board of directors for Berkeley's Ecology Center and GreenPeace Fund USA.

Shanelle Matthews partners with social justice activists, organizations, and campaigns to inspire action and to build narrative power. From Sierra Club and ACLU to Black Lives Matter Global Network and Aspen Institute, she has collaborated with influencers and changemakers to transform complex ideas into persuasive political messaging. Today, she is the communications director for the Movement for Black Lives, an ecosystem of 150 organizations creating a broad political home for Black people to learn, organize, and take action. In 2016, Shanelle founded the Radical Communicators Network (RadComms) to strengthen the field of strategic communications, as well as Channel Black, a program that prepares progressive spokespeople to make critical, real-time interventions through the media. In 2017, Shanelle joined The New School as its inaugural Activist-in-Residence. She is currently on faculty, teaching critical theory and social justice with an emphasis on Black resistance. She holds a degree in journalism and new and online media from the Manship School of Mass Communications at Louisiana State University and is coauthoring *Framing New Worlds: Resistance Narratives from 21st-Century Social Movements*, a forthcoming anthology.

Kitana Ananda is a former racial justice editor at *Nonprofit Quarterly*. She has worked on program outreach and communications for nonprofits ranging from community-based organizations to higher education. Prior to joining *NPQ*, Kitana was an associate editor for two educational learning and assessment programs, a nonprofit consultant, and a postdoctoral scholar at The Graduate Center of the City University of New York, where she led communications and public engagement for the CUNY Humanities Alliance, a Mellon-funded initiative for equitable teaching and learning. Kitana earned a PhD in sociocultural anthropology from Columbia University, where she researched war, migration, and diasporic political communities. Her writing has appeared in *Prism, CNN Opinion, the New York Times*, and elsewhere.

Isabelle Moses is Faith in Action's chief of staff. Previously, Moses partnered with numerous nonprofits and foundations as a consultant and coach through roles with Community Wealth Partners and the Management Center. She holds undergraduate and MBA degrees, as well as a certificate in leadership coaching, from Georgetown University.

Aria Florant is cofounder of Liberation Ventures, a field catalyst and philanthropic organization fueling the US Black-led movement for racial repair. Previously, she served public and social sector clients at McKinsey & Company and helped develop the McKinsey Institute for Black Economic Mobility.

Venneikia Williams (she/her) is a person whose pursuit of justice is informed by the radical Black tradition. She is the campaign manager for Media 2070, a media reparations project.

Savi Horne is executive director of the North Carolina Association of Black Lawyers Land Loss Prevention Project. She is also a member of the leadership team of the National Black Food and Justice Alliance/Black Land and Power.

Dr. Jasmine Ratliff, based in New Orleans, is co-executive director of the National Black Food and Justice Alliance, a coalition of Black-led groups that build Black leadership and institutions for food sovereignty and liberation.

Dr. Aisha Rios is the founder and learning and change strategist at Coactive Change. In her role, she partners with change agents working to dismantle systems of oppression and create more just, liberatory futures. She brings Black intersectional feminism and abolitionist principles and practices to her ethnographically grounded evaluation practice. She relies on approaches and methodologies that center collective knowledge and collaboration—rather than solely relying on her knowledge and experience—because she believes that learning does not happen in isolation but in partnership with those working in the field to advance social justice change. What this looks like in practice is slower paced, reflective, and contextually grounded learning and evaluation projects where she provides thought partnership, creative facilitation, and strategic guidance.

Esther A. Armah is an international award–winning journalist, playwright, radio host, and writer. She is CEO and founder of the Armah Institute of Emotional Justice, a global institute implementing the Emotional Justice framework she created. The institute focuses on projects, training, and thought leadership.

Nineequa Blanding is former *NPQ*'s senior editor of health justice. Blanding has dedicated the entirety of her career toward working at the intersection of health and social justice. Prior to joining *NPQ*, Blanding was vice president of Health Resources in Action, where she led the direction and growth of the organization's grantmaking services. Blanding was the former director of health and wellness at the Boston Foundation (TBF), where she applied her vision, leadership, and racial equity lens to develop, implement, and evaluate TBF's strategic priority to improve population health. Prior to her work at TBF, Blanding held senior leadership positions at the Boston Public Health Commission, where she led local and statewide strategies to advance health equity. She also held former roles with Mount Sinai School of Medicine and the New York City Department of Health and Mental Hygiene. She currently cochairs the Harvard T.H. Chan School of Public Health's Prevention Research Center Community Advisory Board. Blanding has a BA in psychology from Spelman College, and an MPH with honors from Long Island University, and she was previously funded by the National Institutes of Health to conduct postbaccalaureate research in trauma-related risk factors for post-traumatic stress disorder at Emory University and the Center for Cognitive Neuroscience at Duke University.

Amira Barger, MBA, CVA, CFRE, is an award-winning executive vice president at Edelman, the largest communications firm in the world, where she spends her days providing senior diversity, equity, and inclusion (DEI) and communications counsel to clients. She also serves as an adjunct professor in marketing and communications at California State University East Bay. In her spare time, Amira and her family collect stamps in the National Park Service Passport Cancellation Book. She lives in Benicia, California, with Jonathan, her life partner of 17+ years, and their daughter, Audrey.

Trevor Smith is a narrative and cultural strategist who writes and researches on topics such as racial inequality, the wealth gap, and reparations. He is currently the Director of Narrative Change at Liberation Ventures, where he is building the first narrative lab dedicated to building narrative power behind reparations. He has previously worked in program and communication roles at the Surdna Foundation, ACLU, and the Center on Budget and Policy Priorities.

Sonia Sarkar is former editor of health justice at NPQ, a public health practitioner, advisor, and storyteller passionate about partnering with and amplifying efforts to democratize health. As the founder of Healing Capital, as well as a Social Entrepreneur-in-Residence at Common Future, she works with BIPOC-led grassroots organizations and national networks who are envisioning liberatory models of health that reclaim community power and decision-making.

William A. ("Sandy") Darity Jr. is the Samuel DuBois Cook Professor of Public Policy, African and African American Studies, and Economics and the director of the Samuel DuBois Cook Center on Social Equity at Duke University.

A. Kirsten Mullen is a writer, folklorist, museum consultant, and lecturer whose work focuses on race, art, history, and politics.

Natasha Hicks is a senior associate with the Insight Center. She applies her housing, policy, and design expertise to Insight's racial and gender wealth inequality and economic security initiatives. Natasha spent several years in the public sector designing a program for coordinated housing stability services with the City of Detroit, authoring the City of Charleston's first strategic plan for affordable housing, and devising a strategic plan for public art for the Municipality of Tirana. She received her master's degree in urban planning and design studies from Harvard University's Graduate School of Design, and her bachelor's degree in architecture from Stanford University.

Anne Price is former president of the Insight Center, a nonprofit focused on advancing racial and gender economic equity.

Rakeen Mabud is the chief economist and managing director of policy and research at the Groundwork Collaborative. A nationally respected policy expert, Rakeen is a leading thinker on the economy with a unique ability to communicate complex economic concepts in an accessible way. She played a key role in Groundwork's pioneering effort to expose the role of corporate profiteering in inflation and serves as a leading policy expert and spokesperson on how economic trends affect people's everyday lives, with a particular attention to structural disparities by race and gender. Rakeen holds a PhD in government from Harvard University, and a BA in economics and political science from Wellesley College.

Aisha Nyandoro is CEO of Springboard to Opportunities, a nonprofit serving subsidized housing residents in Jackson, Mississippi, which runs the Magnolia Mother's Trust guaranteed-income program for Black mothers living in extreme poverty.

Steve Dubb is senior editor of economic justice at *NPQ*, where he writes articles (including *NPQ*'s *Economy Remix* column), moderates *Remaking the Economy* webinars, and works to cultivate voices from the field and help them reach a broader audience. Prior to coming to *NPQ* in 2017,

Steve worked with cooperatives and nonprofits for more than two decades, including 12 years at The Democracy Collaborative and 3 years as executive director of NASCO (North American Students of Cooperation). In his work, Steve has authored, coauthored, and edited numerous reports; participated in and facilitated learning cohorts; designed community building strategies; and helped build the field of community wealth building. Steve is the lead author of *Building Wealth: The Asset-Based Approach to Solving Social and Economic Problems* (Aspen, 2005) and coauthor (with Rita Hodges) of *The Road Half Traveled: University Engagement at a Crossroads*, published by MSU Press in 2012. In 2016, Steve curated and authored *Conversations on Community Wealth Building*, a collection of interviews of community builders that Steve had conducted over the previous decade.

Darnell Adams, co-owner of Firebrand Cooperative, is a dynamic, Boston-based leadership coach and business strategist with more than two decades of experience in nonprofit, for-profit, and cooperative businesses. Adams develops and facilitates strategic plans, special projects, and workshops, providing expertise and training on an array of topics including implicit bias, power, and equity.

Francisco Pérez is the director of the Center for Popular Economics, a nonprofit collective of political economists whose programs and publications demystify the economy and put useful economic tools in the hands of people fighting for social and economic justice.

Alicia Garza is founder and principal of Black Futures Lab and Black to the Future Action Fund, and a cofounder of the Black Lives Matter Global Network.

Carmel Pryor is the senior director of communications at the Alliance for Youth Action, the premier youth organizing and power-building network growing progressive people power across America by supporting local young people's organizations to strengthen our democracy, fix our economy, and correct injustices through on-the-ground organizing.

Aja Couchois Duncan is a San Francisco, Bay Area–based leadership coach, organizational capacity builder, and learning and strategy consultant of Ojibwe, French, and Scottish descent. A senior consultant with Change Elemental, Duncan has worked for many years in the areas of leadership, learning, and equity. Her debut collection, *Restless Continent* (Litmus Press, 2016), was selected by *Entropy* magazine as one of the best poetry collections of 2016, and awarded the California Book Award for Poetry in 2017. Her newest book, *Vestigial*, is just out from Litmus Press. When not writing or working, Duncan can be found running in the west Marin hills with her Australian cattle dog, Dublin, training with horses, or weaving small pine needle baskets. She holds an MFA in creative writing from San Francisco State University and a variety of other degrees and credentials to certify her as human. Great Spirit knew it all along.

Dr. Kia Darling-Hammond is a leader in the worlds of youth development, education, thriving and well-being, and social justice research, with decades of work across communities, nonprofits, universities, K–12 schools, think tanks, and foundations. Dr. Darling-Hammond's mission is to increase possibilities for thriving among those who experience complex marginalization. Her particular focus at the intersections of age × sexual orientation × gender × race × ability is grounded in the knowledge that design driven by those furthest from power improves all of our lives. Through her scholarship, Dr. Darling-Hammond has developed an intersectional Bridge to Thriving Framework© (BtTF©), which she uses with educators, students, scholars, activists, youth, and others to advance the shared project of building universal thriving.

Index